Candlemas
Bay

RUTH MOORE

Candlemas Bay

Originally published by William Morrow & Co.
1950

©1994, Estate of Ruth Moore

ISBN 0-942396-70-7

Cover photography by Elizabeth Leonard

Blackberry Books
RR1 Box 228
Nobleboro, Maine 04555
Gulf of Maine Bioregion

For Sarah Driscoll Capen

Who recalls with affection,
as I do, the old times.

CONTENTS

PART ONE
The Chart

JEB ELLIS sprawled in his wet bathing trunks on the platform of his father's boat. It was early September and cool, though still warm enough in the sun to dry a hot crust of salt across his back. Guy, his father, had told him to keep off the boat and Jen, his mother, had promised to skin him if he swam out in the dirty harbor. But Jeb had wanted to have one more good look at Great-Grandfather Malcolm's old chart; next week, after school started, he wouldn't have any time. His father's mooring was a hundred yards from the beach. If he rowed off in the punt, Pa would spot him. Besides he was sixteen and practically amphibious. He figured he ought to know a little about what he could do.

"You keep to hell off of that boat," Guy would say. "I catch you hanging around her, I'll kick your pants off over your head, Jeb, and that's that."

Guy had gone to navigation school and he had learned fishing from his father, Grampie Jebron, but so far as he himself was concerned, a kid was a nuisance aboard a boat, fooling around with the machinery.

Not that Jeb had ever touched any of the boat's gear. He told himself with cold resentment that he'd die before he ever laid so much as a finger on her switch key. He could learn about dragging on his own, going out with Russ Allen. Russ had a boat exactly like Guy's—built from the same model. She was not so new, but she was faster, and Russ took great pride in his gear. Like most men who start in working by hand and add to their power-machinery piece by piece, as they earn it, Russ never stopped marveling at what it could do.

"Look at that damn little winch," he would say, in wonder. "You wouldn't think a little thing like that could snake up that big drag so fast, would you, now?" Or, "Look at that depth recorder, by gorry. There's ten fathoms of water right here, and darn' if I ever knew that before."

He never seemed to mind showing Jeb how to handle the gear. Whenever Jeb had gone fishing with him, this summer, Russ had paid good wages, too.

It was tough to have to feel so stinking about Guy's new boat. She was less than three months off the ways, with all modern equipment. Just glancing around him made Jeb itch. But to heck with it.

"You want to learn fishing, God knows why," Guy said. "Well, I ain't got the time to waste. Go talk to your grandfather. Buckle to and learn what's on Gramp Malcolm's old chart. Don't expect someone else to pour it into you."

Time to waste, Jeb thought. That's funny, coming from him. And how does he expect me to learn that chart, when he carries it aboard the boat, wrapped up, in the locker?

Guy never used the chart. He had a new U. S. Coast and Geodetic Survey chart of the same area, in case he ever needed one, which he didn't often, for, like most of the Candlemas Bay fishermen, he carried his information in his head. What he liked to keep Gramp Malcolm's for, was to show to the summer people, when he had a sailing party aboard, as he had, sometimes, in the season.

"Now, here's something might interest you," Guy would say, sliding it out of its oilskin case. "My grandfather's chart, dated 1871, with all his navigation notes on it. He was quite an outspoken old party, so maybe you'd better not show it to the ladies."

Guy would grin, tossing back the crest of curly hair that he kept cut long, so it would fall over his forehead. Oh, he could really lay himself out for the summer people. No one could deny that Guy was something, when he really wanted to lay himself out. Sometimes, when he felt like it—not often now—he would let go and be decent to Jeb, or to Jen and the kids around home; and when he did that, Jeb would find himself getting choked up in the back of his throat, because you caught a kind of dim picture of the fellow Guy started out to be. But, always, the summer people thought he was wonderful—the big, redheaded, romantic-looking fisherman, so capable and so respectful.

"Oo," they would go, and "Ah," and "How dreadful!" over Great-Grandfather Malcolm's chart.

"I don't doubt," Grampie Jebron said once, "that some of them cusswords your great-grandfather wrote down when he was good and roaring mad, like anyone would. But a lot of them, if you knew the time and the place and what happened there, you'd know they wasn't meant for swearing, Jebby."

Jeb smoothed out the chart, spread on the warm, scrubbed boards of the platform. Under his hands, the linen-backed parchment felt soft, the cracked and torn places as cottony as an old cocoon.

Capt. Malcolm Ellis was written in the upper left-hand corner, and then, in the old-fashioned, script-like print: *CANDLEMAS BAY* and the date, *1871*.

"*Fifhing grounds,*" Great-Grandfather had added, in his crabbed writing, with the middle "s's" that looked like "f's." "*From Iron Ifland on the weft to Gimbal Ifland on the south and eaft to Sheepfkin Rock.*"

There was no eastern boundary to the Candlemas Bay fishing grounds except the drop-off of the continental

3

shelf, or wherever water was too deep to use an otter drag.

Jeb looked at the clutter of Candlemas Bay—islands, islets, reefs and shoals, bars and isolated ledges—the ragtag and bobtail of a drowned coast which, in some geologic era, had once been a range of mountains. Outside the channels, the fathom marks showed depths of anything from a hundred to zero, the water shoaling crazily from ten fathoms to one in less than a boat's length, or dropping bold from some headland deep enough to sink a battleship. From Sheepskin Rock, a lonely blot on the chart twenty miles at sea, to Seal Island, the Bay was open, fifteen to a hundred fathoms deep. But inside Seal Island, no man would wish to navigate unless he knew his way.

"*Nathan's Reach, Phil's Ifland,*" Jeb read, his eye traveling the familiar, crinkled contours. "*Abner Shoal, Cow Ledge, Dory Head,*" and each had its handwritten notation.

"*Hell in a Notheaft Snowftorm,*" Great-Grandfather had written in one place, and "*Muddy Bottom, God Blaft!*" in another. Little Nubble Shoals had "*an old baftard of a tiderip;*" and there were other epithets elsewhere, explicit and unprintable, in green ink now faded to a pale bile.

Chandler's Ledge. The Weaver. Red Rock. Grindstone. "*Crofs currents. Ebb tide sets here southeaft by southe. Eben killed, Dec. 24, 1880.*

John loft, Jan. 12, 1888."

Eben, Gramp Malcolm's brother. Died of cold and exhaustion trying to row home against the tide and a northwest gale. They found him frozen to his skiff on Christmas Eve.

Great-Uncle John, Malcolm's youngest son. He had been setting a load of lobster traps off Little Nubble Shoals in a dory. They never found anything of him.

No, Great-Grandfather's notes weren't anything to hold up as a curiosity to strangers, unless you showed them

4

with pride and told what was behind them. The way Guy made it out, Malcolm had been an eccentric old character, who wrote down cusswords on his chart just for the heck of it. But Capt. Malcolm Ellis, in his day, had gone from a rowboat to a pinky to a mackerel schooner, and finally to a fleet of mackerel schooners, all earned with his own hands. And there was a lot more on his chart besides cusswords.

This was a man's work-sheet, and not only one man's. There were navigation notes here that had been handed down from times before the coast was mapped. Ellises had been Candlemas Bay fishermen when the U. S. Coast and Geodetic Survey was a gleam in its founder's eye. And if you planned to be like them, this was your work-sheet, too, from a record that went a long way back into time.

It was funny about time. If Jeb shut his eyes, he could see the years stretching back like a funnel, himself at the big end, and at the small end some little pictures, far away and dim. Sometimes they got clearer, sometimes not. It depended on how much he could find out about them.

Grampie Jebron could tell you almost anything you wanted to know. He was a great reader, mostly of history and books about the sea. Old stories, old ballads, old songs, he knew them all by heart. Out in his room in the L, he had dog-eared books and town reports from way back, salvaged from people's attics; he knew the town records by heart. He could sit down on an old foundation and say who had lived there, and who before that; or who wheeled the stones for the cellar and built the house; and when it was torn down or burned, which might be as long ago as 1812. He and Jeb even had a collection of Indian axes and arrowheads, dug out of the Otter Cove shellheap. Jeb remembered he was five years old when he first went down to the shellheap with Grampie.

People were always after Grampie to tell stories about the historic times and to sing his songs, some of which

5

dated back before the Revolution, like "Lizbeth and Ring-gold the Pirate," which the kids loved so much. Some-times Grampie wouldn't sing, because his ballads often had two versions, one for men and one for women and children. Grampie told Jeb privately that, in his opinion, a song that there were two versions of never ought to be sung in front of women. They always knew what the changed words were, and knew that you knew. Grampie was modest with women. He would sit singing, his cheeks turning red above his whiskers; but his voice always came out deep and steady, like the sound of long ago, if long ago could make a sound instead of being forever lost and silent.

In the old days, according to Grampie, the menfolks had been quite a bit over life-size. Great-Grandfather Malcolm had been, and his father, James; and Daniel—Old Smack-over—who had been such a terrible fighter with his fists.

"Once he hit a feller and the feller ducked," Grampie would say, "and Old Smackover's fist went right through a hardwood hogsid." He glanced around to see how Jeb was taking it. "I can see you're a-whittling that one down to size," he went on. "But wouldn't he have got a bonny blow, if he'd have hit him?"

Old Smackover Ellis had been Grampie's great-great-grandfather, who built the big old house the Ellises lived in now, the son of Nathan Ellis; and Nate Ellis was the first white man ever to settle at Candlemas Bay and start a town there. But of them all, Jeb's hero was Great-Grand-father Malcolm. He seemed not so far away, not so small at the end of the funnel of time.

"Like to have you had a ride in one of your great-grandfather's mack'rel schooners," Grampie would say. "Them vessels could travel. They could carry sail."

Jeb and Grampie might be coming in from tending Grampie's lobster traps in a northwest breeze, and about that time a big slop of salt water would slash in past the

6

canvas sprayhood and take the old man in the face. The little boat would be jumping like a flea, and Grampie standing there in his rubber boots and oilskin barvel, steering her as easy as if he were sitting at home in the parlor. He would not pay any attention to the dollop of water, just let it run down and stream off his whiskers.

"Them mack'rel boats," he would say, recalling the white, taut canvas of a bygone day. "I remember one time we was coming home loaded, racing the fleet to the Boston market. Blowing down the devil's foghorn, no'theast; and right outside Boston Harbor, we overhauled the New York Yacht Club, reefed down to bare poles and lady's handkerchiefs. We had up every rag we could find on the ship, including our washing and the cook's mop, because first vessel in got top price for fish. We went by six-seven them big yachts, and when we overhauled the eighth, Pa he couldn't stand it no longer. He leaned out over the taffr'l and hollered to her skipper.

" 'Christ!' he says. 'You'll never git home!' "

No, there was nothing unreal about Great-Grandfather Malcolm, Jeb thought, his hands on the limp texture of the chart. That might be his gray, blurred fingerprint alongside the compass-rose. Those brown stains, there, you might take for extra islands, if you didn't know that was where his thumb had bled, once when he stuck it with a mackerel-jig. Grampie Jebron said that quite a while after the old man jabbed that jig into him, you couldn't get your breath aboard the pinky. Grampie Jebron was a living link with him; he was somebody Grampie had known and touched, his father, who had taken him with him on his boats; not said, "A boat's no place for a kid, Jeb. Get to hell ashore and stay there."

Well, in the days when a man did his work with oars and sails instead of engines, he probably had some use for his kid. It must have been quite a job, rowing a dory out to Little Nubble with a load of lobster traps on.

7

Wonder what Gramp Malcolm would think of some of the equipment we've got today? This boat, Jeb thought, glancing up at the new dragger's sleek machinery.

Or automobiles, for that matter. Or the three jet planes that buzzed the town the other day.

He grinned, remembering the planes.

Drrt, drrt, drrt, they had canvas-ripped over the roof-tops, so low you could look right down their black gullets; the pilots just feeling good, that was all, hustling back to the base after maneuvers.

"Jeb, did you see those *planes?*" Aunt Evelyn said, as if the word "planes" had been "saber-toothed tigers."

Jeb said, before he thought, "Gee, yes, Aunt Evelyn, weren't they swell?" because his heart had jumped right out of him and flown after them; and she had looked at him as if she thought he'd gone crazy. "What if they'd been going to drop bombs?" she said.

Of course, Aunt Evelyn had been in a state of mind about planes all through the war. But there were a lot of other people who couldn't take the jets. "Them cussid things," they would say, whenever one went over the town—and there'd been plenty over since the Air Force had put its big peacetime training base on the flatlands a hundred miles inland.

Nobody ever thought about the amount of brains it took to invent and put together a turbo-jet engine. If they'd soaked up everything they could get their hands on about it, in books and magazines, they wouldn't just gripe and quack about the noise and scaring the hens. Or if they'd built even the wings and fuselage of a few model planes, they'd know there was more to it than noise.

I'll bet jets would have been right down old Gramp Malcolm's alley.

Jeb flopped over, lazily, to dry his underside.

Gramp Malcolm would've liked anything that's as good a job as a jet. Taken it right in his stride. Look at what

8

he took in his lifetime. Look at the guys before him, sailing to hell-an-gone along the coast in Chebacco boats, settling the country. Look at old Nathan Ellis.

It was hard to think of a man who lived so long ago as anything but old. But Nathan Ellis, on the morning when he first saw Candlemas Bay, had been nineteen.

In a plane, you could come down from Gloucester in an hour or so. This dragger could make it overnight. Alone, in nothing but a kind of little open sloop, when you didn't know the coast—how long?

The picture down at the end of the funnel now was Candlemas Harbor, without the houses, the shacks, the canning factory, the wharves. No black and white can buoy to mark the channel; no nun buoys by Butler's Ledge. No moorings in the harbor—no sardine boats, draggers, lobster boats, scows, storage cars, old skiffs full of tubs. The tidal inlet, running for miles up into the land toward Winter Mountain, was the same. But on the shores the forest came down to the water's edge—big trees, virgin growth never yet touched by an ax. Nothing moved except a few gulls, and the small, open sloop stealing in past Lantern Point, over waters silent and deserted and clean.

Nathan Ellis, sailing from Massachusetts, alone, to find himself a place to live. Going ashore carefully, pulling up his boat, tying it to a tree. Looking around for a good place to build a cabin. Watchful, as a man would have to be, in a new land, where no one of his kind had ever lived before.

The sound of oars in rowlocks startled Jeb, and he peered warily to see if it could be Guy, coming off aboard in his punt. But it was only Russ Allen, rowing past to his own dragger, whose mooring lay next to Guy's.

Russ jerked his head as he went by. "Cussid little seal," he said. "I'll be going ashore pretty soon. You better go with me. You don't want to paddle next-to-nekkid through all that sludge."

9

"Okay," Jeb said. "Your new cable come, Russ?"

"Hell, no," Russ said, disgustedly. "Got to go after it, I guess."

He rowed leisurely alongside his boat and climbed aboard.

Jeb settled back on to the platform. He tried to remember Nate Ellis again, but the picture was gone.

Well, anyway, Nate Ellis could have gone swimming in the harbor without having to take a bath, afterwards. Jeb glanced down at his own smeared ankles. He couldn't dream of a time in which a man, after a three-hundred-mile sail in a boat, wouldn't go swimming the first thing.

The water in the harbor then must have looked the way it did now on the offshore islands—green and sparkling, so you could see bottom in it a long way down.

Now, the sewers of the town came down below low-water mark, where the fish wharves dumped their waste. The harbor was shiny with old oil and gray with scum. Seagulls cleaned up a lot of the fish guts; but on a hot day you walked into the stink around the wharves like walking into an old rotten blanket. Last year, the flats had had to be closed to clamming because of the poison waste. In summer, even the flounders you caught were soft with it. Their flesh peeled off with the skin, as if the fish had rotted while still alive.

Jeb didn't swim, often, in the harbor—only when it was flood tide, and he had a good reason to, like today. But swimming was almost as necessary to him as breathing. It wasn't always possible to get the seven miles inland to the lake, and out around Lantern Point, on the ocean side away from the harbor, if the sea was rough, no one could go in off the ledges. He had gone in there, though, on some days when the breakers and undertow had scared even him; and he thanked the Lord Jen or Guy or Grampie didn't know about that. The harbor was all right, if it happened to be a time when wind and tide worked together and took most of the filth up the inlet.

The inlet itself would have been a fine place to swim—just about deep enough and the water warmed by the sun; but it was silted up with muck and trash. In Grampie's day, it had been a place for sea-going salmon, but none had been caught there for years. There were a few trout left, up at the head where some fresh-water brooks flowed in; but of the salt-water fish, not even smelts went up the inlet now.

Grampie sometimes got pretty mad about that. It was one of the things Guy liked to touch him off about.

"I seen the time you couldn't see bottom up that inlet for Atlantic salmon," Grampie would say. "Time Joel Walls had his net, one night he caught seven hogsids—more'n the whole town could use. Had to salt some down. And in that deep pool by Lemminses', I've caught fifty trout an hour."

Guy would wink at whoever was around, Jeb or Neal or Andy.

"Sure," he would say. "If you hadn't caught so many, there might be more there now."

A faint red would start coming up from under Grampie's whiskers.

"The Injuns done the same thing for generations," he pointed out. "A trout lays upwards of two hundred thousand eggs to a clip. No. It's that rotten trash they heave off the wharves poisons everything."

"What would *you* do with it?"

"Haul it a ways off shore and dump it. Wouldn't cost much. Or use it for manure. We used to."

"Bury a couple thousand pounds of trash fish every week in Jen's flower bed? That it?"

By that time, Grampie's face would be good and red. He never could argue with Guy. He and Jeb could thrash out something for hours, and Grampie might get mad, but never the way he did at Guy.

11

"Trash fish!" he would growl. "I wouldn't kill two thousand pounds of baby cod and haddock, in the first place. I'd have my dragnet with a mesh big enough so's it'd only catch market-size, not gut out the fishing grounds, the way you fellers do."

Guy would grin. "There'll be fish when I'm dead. If there ain't, Christ, I won't know it."

"How about Jebby, here? His kids live on sculpins, will they? I wouldn't argue with one of you grabby boys, but there used to be some haddock inshore. They ain't now. And in my own time, I've seen the salmon go."

"Oh, hell, Pa. What'd you want? Stop the whole works of the town? Go back to the good old one-hoss days? We got a nice little fish-packing business here in Candlemas Harbor, making work for people, and, by God, the more it stinks, the better I like it. A good stink means a lot of fish coming in. I'd rather smell it than flowers. Who cares for a few salmon? Taste better out of a can."

Grampie would look Guy up and down, his mouth puckering as if it tasted bad.

"I paid for a good education for you, Guy. God knows what you learnt. To hear you talk, a man would think you never saw the inside of a schoolhouse."

Then Guy would begin to get mad.

"Yes, and I wish to Christ I never had seen the inside of one. You want to know what I learnt, I learnt that there's people in the world got money enough to live decent, not drag their days out trying to lug a wife and six kids around hungry corner. Go to hell, will ya, Pa? I don't earn my money burying fish guts."

"All right," Grampie said. "But they's no need to leave a mess of stink and disease laying around. Somebody'll have to clean it up someday. You will, or your kids will."

"Let the damn kids do it. It's all they're fit for. That and to eat a man's life out."

Grampie would stump away, and as he went, Guy's ill

humor would slacken. "Which you rather have, Pa? A hundred hosspower engine or an ash breeze?"

That last crack was at Grampie's old boat, Jeb knew, because an "ash breeze" was a pair of oars.

Guy was always taking jabs at what he called Grampie's one-hoss ideas, and so was Aunt Candace. Not Aunt Evelyn—she never made fun of anybody—and Aunt Marilyn, of course, she was younger, and full of the deuce, she could plague you and you didn't mind. But to hear Pa and Aunt Candy, you'd think Grampie's brains had died before the Flood. It made Jeb sore. Because, actually, the old man was as up-to-date in his thinking as anyone.

He was as proud of the new dragger as Guy was, and as excited as Jeb over her machinery, the hundred and twenty horsepower Chris-Craft engine, the winch, the fathometer, the ship-to-shore radio telephone. When local fishing boats first started putting in fathometers and depth recorders, Grampie had said he'd bet you could spot a school of fish with one; and not long afterward, a magazine article had come out saying that the unexplained marks recorded on fathometers were turning out to be schools of fish, and that fishermen could use the information.

Guy liked to make out that the reason Grampie never went near the new dragger was because he liked his own old-fashioned gear, but Jeb knew better. Grampie's boat was a little double-ender, a model not built nowadays. She was narrow, so that she pitched and rolled something wicked in almost any sea. He could handle her, but he said she was probably the boat Christ got out of and walked away from on the water. If Grampie stayed off the dragger, it was for the same reason Jeb himself did, because Guy didn't want him aboard. And if he didn't have a new boat of his own, it was because he had laid out so much money on Guy's.

Grampie had lent Guy the cash to build the dragger,

and while she was building and Guy was broke, the whole family had gone to live with Grampie in his big old house on the hill. Aunt Candy and Aunt Evelyn and Aunt Marilyn lived there too, and he supported them, even though Aunt Marilyn had a job in the library, and Aunt Candy had money laid away. .

Jeb wouldn't have known about Aunt Candy's money, but he'd overheard her and Pa fighting about it. He'd been lying in bed one morning, in his room over the kitchen; their voices had come through the open hot-air register.

"It wouldn't hurt you a mite," he heard his father say. "I only need five hundred. A man with a wife and six kids—"

Aunt Candy said, "No," in an icy-cold voice. "No, Guy."

"Three hundred, then."

Aunt Candy said, "No."

"You must have thousands stashed away, for christsake! You ain't touched a cent since Gram Ellis left it, and that was seventeen years ago."

There was a short silence. Jeb judged Aunt Candy was winning the argument by keeping her mouth shut, which was a way she had.

"It ain't all yours anyway," Guy said. "It's part Lyn's and Evelyn's. I'll borrow some from them."

Aunt Candy said, "Gram left me the say of it, Guy."

"And don't I know it," Guy said. "I wish to Christ she'd left me something."

"She never liked you. Or Chris. And don't swear in here, please."

"Well, we neither of us liked her, so we're even."

"I rather think," Aunt Candy said, "that Gram came out a little ahead of you, Guy."

Jeb heard the angry scrape of his father's chair as he pushed away from the breakfast table, and his heavy steps crossing the kitchen.

Chris—that was Uncle Chris, Pa's older brother, who

1 4

had got killed in a car smash-up, years ago, before Jeb was born.

"Well, at least shell out enough to help Pa with the bills till I can get back on my feet," Guy yelled suddenly.

"I'm not going to pay your bills, Guy."

"You might pay your own board and the girls'. Not let Pa."

"A father's supposed to look out for his children," Aunt Candy said calmly.

"Children? Oh, my God! How old are you? Forty-five!"

"And you are thirty-five."

There was another silence, punctuated by the slam Guy gave the door.

Jeb remembered how he lay for a long time, feeling hot and ashamed for Guy, not wanting to go downstairs.

Guy was making money, now that he had the new boat. But they were all still living with Grampie, and Grampie still had his rattletrap old gear.

The dragger yawed a little and swung slowly at her mooring, beginning to head north instead of south. The ebb tide was making.

Golly, he hadn't realized he'd been out here so long. He'd better snap out of here, if he didn't want Guy to come down and catch him. It wouldn't be good sense to let that happen. Not today.

Jeb folded up the chart and tucked it into its stained, waterproof case. He'd had a lot of fun this summer, going fishing with Grampie or with Russ, studying this old chart at odd times until he knew it almost by heart. Now that he'd learned it, though, he couldn't go fishing. Next week, school again.

Two more years of school, always starting in the best part of the year, so that you sat with your feet under a dusty desk and looked out through windows at the blue September weather. *Caesar's Gallic Wars*, and the boats

1 5

out on Grindstone, with the sun shining and the wind tearing the top off of the tide rip.

He unhooked the hatch to the cabin, reached his long arm in around the coaming and put the chart carefully back into the locker.

Wonder if Pa'd ever give it to me, he thought. Gee, it would be wonderful to own that chart.

Probably Guy wouldn't, unless you happened to catch him at just the right time. If you did that, he'd be likely to give you his shirt. You never could tell what he'd do.

Jeb climbed up on the stern of the boat.

As he poised to dive, Russ called across, "I'll be going right ashore, Jeb."

Jeb said, "Okay."

Thinking about Guy, he hardly noticed what Russ had said.

The time, when Jeb was five, that Guy had jumped overboard to pull him out of the water and nearly drowned. Guy couldn't swim. Even at five, Jeb could swim better than Guy could. But the splash of his falling in, off the stern of the boat, had scared Guy. To him, if a kid fell into water over his head, it meant simply that the kid was drowning. He had gone, feet first, into the harbor, mackinaw, hat, rubber boots and all, and had sunk like a stone. If Johnny Allen hadn't come along in his punt and gaffed him out, Guy would have died there.

The times, when Jeb was a kid, that he'd stood on the wharf watching for Guy's boat to come in, the old, stubby, square-ender, bulling it up the harbor, spanking all the water out of the bay, but a beautiful boat, because it was Guy's.

His shrill, excited yell, as Guy went by, "Hi, Pa, how many'd you get?" and Guy's cheerful bawl, "Ninety"—or ten, or nineteen, whatever it was—"pounds, Jebby, old socks."

Oh, what had happened to him—what ailed him? Jeb

thought, and the familiar choke came into his throat. He was such a heck of a decent fellow, then.

Not now. Not any more. He wasn't like that now.

Jeb took a long dive off the stern of the boat and went deep, feeling the cold water grab at him, washing the hot sting out of his eyelids. He came up blowing, headed for Russ's punt, tied up alongside his dragger. As he came abreast, Russ said amiably, "Don't upset the punt, you crazy nut."

Jeb grinned at him. He braced his arms on the punt's stern, half lifted his body out of the water, swung first one leg and then the other in over the gunnel. He was pleased to see that beyond settling with his weight, the punt had hardly moved in the water.

Russ watched him admiringly. "I could've rowed over and got you," he said. "You didn't need to swim it. How to hell am I going to keep telling your ma I'll keep my eye on you, if you don't co-operate? You'll freeze your tossle off, one of these days, going into that water."

"Isn't very cold," Jeb said. He untied the punt, steadying her while Russ got in. "What's with your cable, Russ?"

"Them dukes and lords up to the supply house can't seem to take the time to wrap it up and put it on the express truck," Russ said. "Thought I'd take a run up to town this afternoon, see if I could holler loud enough to make them hear me. Want to go?"

"Yeah," Jeb said. "What time?"

"Around two, if Ma's ready. She wants to go buy a hat."

The cable on Russ's otter drag, through hard usage, had started to fray, and he was replacing it. He had his gear all unrigged, expecting the new cable would arrive on the morning's express.

"Holding me up like the devil," he complained. "I sure hate to lose this good weather too. Everybody else is out—"

He stopped, embarrassed, for it was evident to anyone that everybody else was out, except Guy.

"Guess his alarm didn't go off this morning," Jeb said stiffly.

Russ nodded. "Oh, hell, boy," he said.

When Guy didn't go out, anyone knew why, and Russ better than most. He and Guy and Johnny, Russ's twin brother, had grown up together, gone to the same school. For a while, the three had owned a fish-packing business as partners. When the business broke up in a quarrel, Johnny stayed sore, but Russ was still Guy's friend. He was probably the only close friend Guy had, now.

Jeb liked Russ. He was a wide-shouldered young man of thirty-five or so, with mild blue eyes and a round, pleasant face. His thick corn-colored hair had an almost perfect wave in it, which people were always kidding him about—not that Russ minded the kidding. He could generally give back as good as was sent.

"What the heck?" Russ would say. "What's wrong with my wave? Pretty, ain't it? I like it, myself, and the girls love it. You'd have to go to the beauty parlor to get one like it in that wad of oakum you wear, boy."

Russ liked to talk, and he generally had something to say. His boat, which was one of the best in the harbor, was also the fastest, and he had done well with her since he had come back from the war. He had fought for three years in the South Pacific, the only part of his life he never would talk about. Only once had he been known to mention it, and that was to George Otis, in answer to a point-blank question, after George had been retailing his own ferocious experiences in France.

"Well," Russ said laconically. "Once I spent about two months with a rifle, guarding the general's backhouse."

Now that he was home again, he had gone into business with Johnny, who was the local lobster buyer, dealing as well in fishermen's gear and supplies. Russ was something of a silent partner, preferring to go fishing while Johnny ran the store; but the sign over the Allen wharf read

"Allen Bros."; and it was the consensus that however silent a partner Russ might be, he was two-thirds of the brains of the business.

He had, in recent months, been coming up to the Ellises' to see Jeb's Aunt Marilyn; at least, he had taken her out to some dances; enough so that Aunt Candy was agog about it. As for coming up to the Ellises', he had been doing that for years, sitting around on the screen porch, yarning with Guy and Grampie, or listening to the radio with the kids. Both he and Aunt Marilyn seemed pretty casual. Jeb felt it wasn't the way he'd go courting, himself, say he was interested in any one girl; but it was Russ's business.

As they got out of the punt in front of the fishhouses, Russ said, "Want a ride up the hill?"

He always rode down to the shore in his Chevvy, though the house where he lived with his mother and Johnny was only a few hundred yards up the road. He wouldn't walk if he could help it; he said if the Lord intended a man to walk, He wouldn't have seen to it that someone invented the wheel; which was funny, when you knew that Russ could move like a streak if he had to.

Jeb shook his head. "Got to get my clothes on. They're in the fishhouse. Don't bother to wait, Russ."

"No bother," Russ said. "I'll wait." He dropped the punt's anchor on the beach and went on up to his car.

Jeb loped up the short path to the weather-beaten building where Guy kept his extra gear. He closed the batten door behind him, reached for his pants and shirt, which he had left on the workbench, and saw they weren't there.

"I got 'em right here," Guy said hoarsely.

He was sitting on a tub behind the door. He had Jeb's clothes rolled in a tight ball under one arm. His eyes were bloodshot with rage, and in the small, close room, Jeb could smell the whiskey on his breath.

Jeb said, "Take it easy, Pa," backing away from him.

1 9

and Guy got up from the tub, moving forward with a stumbling monkey-shuffle. His crooked arms and rounded shoulders made Jeb think, for a sickening moment, of a big ape.

"I might's well hoot in a bunghole as talk to you," Guy said. "So now I'm going to do something besides talk."

"Look," Jeb said. "I don't blame you. But you said to study the chart. That's all I've been doing off there."

"Look nothing, you damn little—" The loose curses poured out of Guy's mouth. "I told ya all summer, keep off that boat. You been off there, underrunning that machinery like a blasted little weasel. Now, go on. Git home."

"Okay. I've got to get dressed first."

"You can damn well go the way you are. You're lucky I don't tear them jeasly trunks off you and make you go in your hide."

"Okay."

Jeb made to go past his father. Guy made a grab for the trunks and yanked, but the tough wool stretched and did not tear. He dropped Jeb's clothes and lashed out with the leather belt he had hidden in his other hand. It was the buckle end of the belt and it cut off some skin. Jeb let out a yelp.

"You'll walk up through town in front of me," Guy yelled. "By God, I'm right behind you with this belt. Blast ya, maybe you'll learn, time we get home."

Damn him, nobody but him could think of anything like that, Jeb thought furiously. He can lick me here or after we get home, but he won't lick me half-naked through town.

Jeb made a grab for the belt and yanked it out of Guy's hand. He backed into a corner and put up his fists.

"You fight back at me, will ya?" Guy snatched up a can half full of paint and hauled back to throw it. "I'll—"

Somebody shoved against the fishhouse door. It was Russ, standing there with his pleasant grin. He reached over and picked the paint can out of Guy's hand.

"Hi. I heard you talking in here, Guy, thought you might like a ride up the hill. I said to myself, There's Guy, and I've got a whole empty car."

"Hell with it," Guy said. "I'm going to beat the living pickle out of this goddam sprout of mine. Put up his fists to his father, by God. I'll take it out of him."

"He did!" Russ said, admiringly. "Why, he's a chip off the old block, Guy. Spunky. Fight anybody, like you always would."

"By G'r, tha's truth. I would. Fight the devil from hell. Tha's Guy Ellis for you."

His speech was thickening, and he shook his head, as if to clear a blur from his eyes.

If Russ can only keep him talking long enough, Jeb thought. He'll pass out in a minute.

Russ grinned with his mouth, but his eyes were bleak and watchful. "That's the old fight," he said. He slapped Guy heartily on the shoulder, and Guy staggered.

"Say," Russ went on, "you hear about Joe Grady dragging up the dead whale today?"

Guy stiffened. "Joe Grady ain't even in yet," he stated, eying Russ shrewdly.

Jeb's heart sank. That was the trouble with Guy—he still had brains, even when he was drunk. You had to be smart to fool him.

"I don't doubt the Radio Commission is going to come down on Joe," Russ said. "I had my radio-phone turned on, when I was off aboard the boat just now. Joe was telling the airwaves, in Biblical terms, just how dead that whale was."

A wide, foolish grin spread on Guy's face, as he began to realize the implications of a dead whale in connection with an otter drag.

"No!" he said. "He never, did he?"

"Tell you going up the hill in the car," Russ said. "Got to get home, Guy. Ma wants to go to town this afternoon. Come on, boy. Got to get home."

He held back the door and Guy started out. Russ glanced back at Jeb, jerking his head toward the back window, as he tried to close the door on Guy's reluctant back.

Jeb scooped up his trampled clothes from the floor. The window hadn't been opened in a long time. He felt the rotten old sash give a little as he yanked at it with the full force of his arms. Then he wriggled himself through, landing on the ground in a heap. He ducked into the woods behind the fishhouse and ran along the path that came out into Grampie's back pasture, by the pond.

In the tepid, sun-warmed water of the pond, he washed the blood off the cut on his thigh. It wasn't a bad cut, but it had bled quite a lot, and the bruise around it was coming up blue and puffy. His leg already felt a little stiff, but it was nothing that a day's healing wouldn't cure.

Maybe I had a licking coming all right, he told himself soberly. But not that kind.

He'd thought he was going to be okay until he started to put on his clothes. They were a mess, all covered with tar and stuff off the fishhouse floor. The dungarees had been clean, the shirt sweet-smelling from Jen's flatiron; and all at once it came over him that they were a symbol of what had happened—a filth and a humiliation that no one could stand. He stretched out, face down, and for a while the hot tears trickled down over his folded forearms and out of sight into the secret moss.

"Maybe if Guy gets his new boat," Grampie had said once, "he'll straighten out, Jen. A man gets discouraged, he ain't himself."

That was when Jeb's mother had tried to persuade Grampie not to put so much money into the new dragger.

He hadn't straightened out. It didn't look as if he was ever going to. He was worse now than he'd ever been.

For a while Jeb lay, then he got up and put on the soiled clothes.

Ma'll have to know, he thought, thinking with affection of Jen. I wouldn't put it past her to lick me herself, when she finds out I've been in the harbor.

But she'd show him how to get the tar off his pants and shirt, afterwards, and she'd probably insist on doing the job herself, if he'd let her.

He went slowly along the woods path toward home. If it had been in his mind to ask Guy to give him Great-Grandfather Malcolm's chart, the uproar had driven it out. He didn't think of the chart again until later, the night he and Grampie heard the call come in on the short-wave radio.

THE radio was Guy's. He had come rolling home with it, wheeling it up from the shore on the wheelbarrow, one afternoon after he had sold a good catch of fish in town.

Quite often, Guy sold his fish at Bellport, eighteen miles across the Bay, instead of at one of the Candlemas Harbor wharves. Bellport was the nearest good-sized town, with a Coast Guard station and boatyards; offshore draggers made it their supply base or put in there in foul weather. There was always company there and a good deal going on—movie places and dance halls, restaurants and beer parlors, and Bellport had a state liquor store.

Guy was feeling pleasant over his good day's work and some beers he'd had, and over having bought the radio. The kids gathered around, Neal and Andy, Mertis and Maggie, and even Clay, the two-year-old, crazy wild with excitement. Jeb had been excited himself, though Jen had just glanced around once at the radio and at Guy, and had gone on getting supper. Guy's fingers were all thumbs, but Jeb had known how to hook up the radio, and it was a dandy.

It had FM and standard broadcast, and two short-wave bands. The FM wasn't much good—you had to have a special aerial for that, which Guy had forgotten to buy; but the short-wave bands worked fine. Down at the end of one of them, you could get the Coast Guard, and the Marine Operator talking to ships at sea; and, best of all, you could pick up the offshore draggers talking to each other on their radiotelephones. Guy turned them on, first thing.

"There, Jen," he yelled gleefully. "Now, when I'm on the way in from fishing, out there, I can let you know."

Jen didn't even turn around.

"Or don't you care?" Guy said.

"That's good," Jen said, still without turning around.

Guy stopped short and looked at her straight, unyielding back. He grinned and winked at all the kids. He pulled a big roll of bills out of his pocket and waved it in the air before their popping eyes.

"Sh-sh!" he whispered, so comically that the kids giggled and crammed their fingers over their mouths.

Oh, when Guy felt like this, all he had to do was wink or beckon, and the kids would do whatever he said.

Then Guy wadded the bills into a ball and heaved it at the back of Jen's head. The ball split and bills went all over the floor and the cupboard in front of her. Two of them even fell into the batter of the fritters she was stirring up for supper.

She said, "For heaven's sake, Guy!" But not as if she were pleased; only as if she were mad, clear through.

She picked the bills out of the batter, took the batch over under the faucet and washed it down the sink. Then she began to mix up a new batch.

Guy hadn't noticed.

"Two hundred and ten dollars, that's what I grossed on this trip out," he crowed. "I loaded her down so deep she had an inch of freeboard, and most of the time not that. Have it, Jen. It's all yours."

The kids scrabbled up the money off the floor and cupboard, and Neal, the twelve-year-old, counted it. A lot of the bills were ones. There was only sixty dollars in the big wad.

Jen said, "You lost some, somewhere, I guess, Guy," and her tone said that she didn't believe he'd ever had any two hundred and ten dollars.

She went on getting supper, her long strong hand skillfully flipping over, with the spatula, the fritters in the frying-pan. Her cheeks were pink and her thick, light hair was fluffed up in a cloud, curling from the heat and the moisture of the cooking.

"What to hell?" Guy said. "The radio cost a hundred bucks. It's a good radio. About time we had a few things around here, quit living below-decks, for a change. Turn her up, Jebby. Your mother can't hear her."

Jeb turned her up, and a dragger skipper, thirty miles at sea, spoke into the room, in the gargly voice of the short-wave radio.

"*Nothing doing around the Whiskers, Amos. Might's well drag the kitchen floor. We're going to try fifty-two-seventy-five, and if there ain't nothing there, we heading down east to Scatteree. Over.*"

"Fifty-two-seventy-five, he's on loran, see?" Guy said. "That's Amos Coughlin in the *Wanderer* he's talking to."

"*Okay, Jerry,*" another voice said. "*See ya. Wanderer signing off from the Mary Belle.*"

"The *Mary Belle*," Guy said. "Jerry Canneri. Or Canoodle. Some such damn spik name. He's from the west'ard."

"What's loran, Pa?" Andy asked.

Andy was the ten-year-old. He was a smaller, second edition of Guy, in looks, with the curly, red-auburn hair and the same dark brown eyes.

Guy explained loran, as he always could explain such things if he chose, simply and easily.

"Radio towers ashore broadcast signals into an area, say it's Candlemas Bay," he said. "Area's marked off into

2 5

squares by lines, see, on your receiving gear. Each line has a different-sounding signal. Say you're outside in a snowstorm or a fogmull, and you want to go into Boston Harbor. You tune in on the beep-beep or the toot or the squawk that you know is on the line to Boston, and follow the sound on in. Take you right to the Customs House Tower. Up Atlantic Avenue, if you want to go that far."

Gee, Jeb thought. He knows so much. If you could only get him to tell you some of it. If he'd only feel like this oftener.

Guy was looking over at Jen, to see if she wasn't, at last, smiling at his nonsense. But she still didn't turn around. He flushed a little and gave the radio tuner a jerk.

Another voice came in, talking some kind of a foreign language.

"That's a Portygee," Guy said. "A lot of them fellers off there, draggers out of Provincetown and Boston. You want to get your mother to tell you what they say, kids. She understands all that dago lingo."

Jen wheeled around from the stove, her eyes hot.

"All right," she said. "We know there's only one language in the world, Guy, and that's yours. It don't always make sense either."

Guy winked at the kids.

It was an old squabble. Jen's grandfather had come from Holland, and she could speak some Dutch. Her father, Jones Keppel, had been head chef at one of the Bellport resort hotels, and Jen had been a cook under him, before she was married; she had been known for her cooking, too, though that was never one of the things Guy mentioned when he kidded her about foreigners.

Jen noticed the wink.

"Thick-headed ideas speak their own language," she said icily. "And we all know that one by heart."

Guy turned a darker red.

"You don't care for presents it would seem," he said.

2 6

"I like them fine, if we could afford some. It's a nice radio, and sixty dollars is a lot for a man to bring home all in one lump, Guy. I appreciate it, and don't think I don't. But it won't pay a trifle on the bills we owe, and you know it."

Aunt Candy, who had, apparently, been standing just inside the dining-room door, listening, stuck her sharp, thin face in through the doorway.

"Jen's absolutely right, Guy. You haven't any right to buy such stuff, when you owe Pa so much money."

"Oh, shut your trap," Guy said. The black look, well known to them all, came into his face. He went out into the shed, slamming the door, and in a minute he was back with the ax.

"You don't like the radio, I'll fix it for you," he said.

Jen stepped over in front of the radio.

"All right," she said. "Take the ax back into the shed, Guy."

For a moment, they stood staring at each other. Then he looked away.

"Well, show a little appreciation, then, when I buy you something," he mumbled.

He turned to go out and bumped into Aunt Marilyn, who had been out feeding the chickens. She had a panful of eggs. One of them joggled precariously, then rolled off and smashed on the floor.

Aunt Marilyn grinned at him.

"That'll cost you a nickel, Guy," she said. "What are you staving up now? Jen? Or one of the kids?"

"You, if you don't get out of my way," he growled.

He pulled a nickel out of his pocket and dropped it into the pan. Then he went out in the shed to put the ax away.

The kids, who knew by now that Guy wasn't drunk enough so that his bellowing was anything to be scared of, had hardly looked around from the radio.

"I'll pay them bills in no time, a few trips like this one," Guy said heartily, coming back into the kitchen. "Come on and listen to her, Jen. Ain't she great?"

It was a good radio.

In the weeks that followed, they all got so they knew how Guy's voice sounded over the short wave. They could hear his jovial bawl as he talked through the radio-telephone on his boat to other draggers, which he did a good deal; sometimes, when he was heading in from outside, he would say, "Hi, Jen, you listening? I'll be home for supper."

No one was supposed to send personal messages over the ship-to-shore telephone unless they were emergencies. But it was all the same to Guy. Let the Radio Commission catch up with Guy Ellis if they could. Guy Ellis would get *them* told.

He seldom did get home for supper. Sometimes he came at ten o'clock at night, or twelve, or one; sometimes not until the next day. He would get into Bellport and sell his fish; but he didn't often feel like coming home.

The dragger talk fascinated Jeb. He would listen to it evenings until his mother made him go to bed. Sometimes he would sneak downstairs, late, to see if he could pick up talk from a boat that was making a night trip. It tickled him, the second or third time he did it, to find Grampie sitting in front of the radio in the dark, with the short wave turned down low. After that, they listened together, night after night, though on weekdays they had to stop early. Saturday, when they could sleep the next morning, they sometimes stayed up until one or two o'clock.

It was fun, listening with Grampie. He didn't have Guy's modern, technical information; but he could say what a boat was and where she was from; he knew all the local draggers and could identify many of the strangers from up and down the coast. And he could translate the strange-sounding, excited talk of the Portuguese skippers from New Bedford and Boston. Grampie had been a traveled man in his day.

It was on a Saturday night, late, that they picked up the message from Guy. Not much had been coming in.

A couple of disgusted skippers had just been speaking their plain opinions of the tremendous high-run tide which had set since dark, a vast flood whose swift currents made dragging tonight well-nigh impossible.

"*Jeezchrist, Joe, I'm hung up tight twenty-one miles outside Monhegan. This godalmighty high coast tide running's tore my gear all to pieces. It's calm's a dead hog's face, not a breath out here, water like glass. And I can't run gear if I go to hell. Come in, Joe.*"

"*Ayeh, ayeh, runs like a millrace, don't she? Come in.*"

"*Ayeh, bad's I ever saw, and the ebb tide'll be worse. Might's well lay over somewhere. I'm going to. Come in, Joe.*"

"*Ayeh, I will, I guess. Well, I'll see ya, Bill. Sea Otter signing off from the Kestrel.*"

"*So long, Joe. Kestrel out.*"

Grampie chuckled. "I'd hate to say how many times Bill Wilson's been in trouble for cussing like that over the radio. The Commission'll catch up with him for good one of these days. Don't blame him, though. She's a big tide, tonight."

After that, there was nothing, and Jeb had been jiggling the tuner. He caught the message on the Coast Guard wave length, in the middle of a sentence, but he knew the voice the minute he heard it. It was distorted by the short wave, it was gaspy and thin, but it was Guy's.

"*. . . aground on the Weaver Ledge. Send help quick. S O S. Calling the Coast Guard. Calling the Coast Guard. I'm aground on the Weaver Ledge. S O S. Calling any boat anywheres near the Weaver Ledge. S O S. I'm aground—*"

Grampie shot out of his chair without a word, making for the telephone in the kitchen.

2 9

"Gi'me the Bellport Coast Guard Station, quick, sister," he said into the receiver, and Jeb heard him relaying the message.

"Good. You got it, too. Ayeh. This's his father. It's Guy Ellis, ayeh. You'll send out a picket boat? Good. I'll git someone and hustle out there, too."

He put down the phone.

"Jebby! Hustle down and rout out Russ Allen. Tell him to step on it. I'll be there, soon's I tell your mother."

It seemed to Jeb that he himself had sat there paralyzed, not able to think of anything but the breathless, squalling voice, now faded away to silence. But as he jumped for his cap and mackinaw, a picture flashed into his mind, the section around the Weaver Ledge as it was marked on Great-Grandfather Malcolm's chart.

The crinkled blot, circled in red. Nine miles out, half a mile from any island. Deep water; the marks ten to forty fathoms at the foot of the lonely ledges. Grandfather Malcolm's inscription in his crabbed writing, with the "s's" that looked like "f's": *"Jefus Chrift!"*

THE night Guy Ellis was drowned was as calm as anyone remembered, not a ripple on the water nor a breath of wind in the sky. The moon was as big as a bucket, bright enough to read by. A man on the water couldn't have failed to know where he was, provided he was in any shape to know. In most people's opinion, Guy must have been drunk.

Guy hadn't been drunk—not what *he'd* have called drunk. Maybe he'd had a few beers. What of it? The way Guy would have figured, the accident wasn't his fault.

If he had lived to come home that night, he would have spent hours telling Jen how a whole chain of events, each one harmless in itself, had added up to disaster. Why, looking back, you could see how the whole thing had been planned for—as if the Devil himself had stuck his head up over the edge, grinned, and said, "Come on, boys, let's fix it so's Guy Ellis'll lose his boat."

He would have lain in bed, cleaned up and dry, reaching for cigarette after cigarette, telling Jen, not liking her silence.

The trouble was, everyone was too ready, even a man's own wife, to blame him for circumstances out of his control. It was almost as if people *enjoyed* blaming, as if blaming helped matters.

Look at the way the papers went for some poor devil of a pilot or an engineer when there was a plane or a train wreck. "Well," they said. "Now we know so-and-so was to blame, we can shut up shop and go home."

When, nine times out of ten, fellow wasn't to blame, whole thing swung on pure chance, the way it had with Guy.

Listen, Jen. It's maddening to look back on. If just one time, I'd decided one single thing a different way, this wouldn't have happened.

I could have come home this afternoon after I sold the fish—almost did. But when a man's et salt water outside for two days, he's entitled to some kind of a little blow-out. Ain't he? Well, for God's sakes, ain't he?

I had seventy dollars, clear, in my pocket. It was Saturday night.

Besides, no man could appreciate his kids more than I do, you know that, Jen, but they make an ungodly racket around suppertime, and when I get home, I'm tired.

So he had eaten at the restaurant, by pure chance, with a fellow who happened to mention the show up at the Bijou and they had gone to the movies.

All little foolish decisions that didn't make any more difference to a man than whether he reached out, right now, and picked up that cigarette.

After the movies, it had been a toss-up whether to come

home or to have some beers at Joe's. And then the thing fell into place as neat as an algebra problem. If Guy had left town a few minutes earlier or later, it wouldn't have been high-water slack over the Weaver, in a dead calm, in one of the biggest tides in years. Water would have been moving over the ledge. He would have seen it.

A cold, deadly plan, trumped up by the Devil, aimed straight at Guy Ellis, by God. Just the same goddam way the Devil had aimed things at him all his life. Jen must see it.

And Jen would have listened, as she had many times, to his life's frustration welling out of him. But not in honesty—never in simple honesty, she would have thought.

Somehow, I don't believe the Devil would have bothered with it, Guy.

Now, that was a hell of a thing for her to say. At a time like this, a man would be justified in thinking his wife would be glad to see *him* afloat, not rolling around in the crabs under the Weaver.

But, by God, they couldn't kill Guy Ellis. They could claw bad luck up over him till he couldn't see out, like a christless beetle in a pile of sawdust, but, by God, they couldn't kill him.

Not that it seemed to make much difference to anyone around here whether they had or not. After all—

And there would have been a full minute of silence, while Guy said to himself, After all, when I got to thinking about that bank loot, the way it was in the movie, and wishing I had a few bundles of it, it was for her benefit as much as mine, wasn't it?

For, by pure chance, again, the movie had been about a bank robbery, with shots of tens and twenties lying around in fat bundles. A beautiful sight.

And Jen would have known that now he was thinking about what actually had happened, the part he would never mention. You couldn't have lived with Guy for seventeen years, seeing him come home all hyped up from having got out of another jam, and not recognize that minute of speculative silence.

And, truly, Guy would not have told, even if he had lived to tell—that when he plunked his boat, full-tilt, on the south spur of the Weaver, he hadn't been steering at all. He had been figuring out on a piece of paper how big a box you'd need to bury a million dollars in, say you had a million in ten-dollar bills.

After Guy left the movies, he couldn't get the thought of that currency out of his mind. It kept coming back all the time he was drinking beer at Joe's; all the way across Bellport Harbor and out into the Bay; underlining the way he had to shove his own nose down on the grindstone now.

Things weren't always the way they are now, those bundles of tens and twenties said to him; most of the Ellises poor as pot-water, and he, Guy, the poorest of the lot. Time was, he had traveled high, wide, and handsome, with plenty to spend and a future coming up. He and Chris at navigation school, hell, they could've started in where most men left off, they had the brains.

Well, maybe not Chris. Chris was pure damn fool about some things. To get drunk and wind yourself around a whole dairy barn in a car, that was damn foolishness. But you had to hand it to Chris for always being a little more than life-sized, for doing things in a big way. He didn't die alone. He took four cows and a flock of hens with him.

No, not Chris. But he, Guy, could have been a big man in Candlemas Bay; or even the state. Hell, he'd had the brains to be president of the country, and would've been something like that, if he'd only had the breaks. If the old man hadn't lost the money.

He wished he could have had some say about Pa's chucking away all Gramp Malcolm's money on those fool boatyards. If he, Guy, had been Pa, he'd have known how to handle it, even in 1932; he'd see the day he'd go through bankruptcy. There were plenty of ways out, if you bothered to learn them.

Guy shook his head to clear it a little. That beer seemed to have fuddled him some. Or maybe it was the lousy restaurant food. His stomach wasn't what it had been, anyway. Well, it was nothing that a night's sleep wouldn't fix. Better hustle along home and get to bed.

He pushed the throttle to full ahead as the boat came out of Bellport Harbor, and stood leaning easily, one hand on the wheel.

Now the Ellises were all scratching gravel, except, of course, Candy. She had Gram Ellis's money invested somewhere. The devil wouldn't find out where.

Gramp Malcolm had put away fifteen thousand dollars in Gram's name, to take care of her in case anything happened to him. Gram had hung on to it. When she had died, she had willed it to Guy's three sisters, Candy, Evelyn and Marilyn, in Candy's charge because Candy was her favorite. He and Chris had come out the little end of the horn. Not that it mattered long to Chris—poor devil.

She might as well have left it to Candy outright. Neither of the other girls had ever seen a cent and Guy doubted if they ever would. Candy had them buffaloed. They were scared of her. She was tougher than tripe and tighter than the bark on a tree. She wouldn't even help Pa out the time the boatyards failed. If anyone so much as mentioned money to her now, she went into the air like a kite. There were times when Guy got pretty sore at Candy.

If anything happens to Pa, and I'm the head of the family, there'll be some changes made. By God, she'll pay her board and the girls' board. *I* won't support her, the way Pa does.

Pa went on, year after year, supporting the girls, and Guy knew for a fact that, between them, they'd just about

3 4

run the old man into the ground. He did all right with his lobster traps—always seemed to have a little laid by; but the money he'd shelled out for this new dragger was the last savings he'd had.

Of course, the difference was, Guy intended to pay him back as soon as he could. The girls never would.

But a man with a wife and six kids, naturally, couldn't pay for dead horses very fast. It takes just about what I can make, Guy told himself, to keep Jen and the kids going.

It wasn't right to expect a man sixty-eight years old, though, to keep on forever supporting three able-bodied women. You had to hand it to Marilyn, she tried. But the minute she got a job, Candy'd start picking at her.

Guy was sure living to see the day when Candy had to dig down and come up with some of that hoard. And she sure would, when he was man of the house.

Unless he found a way to make some big money. He'd been on the way to it, just after the war; would have pulled it off, too, if it hadn't been for Johnny Allen. Be kind of fun to make a million or so, and shove Johnny right back where he belonged.

It was a tough proposition, getting rich nowadays, but it could be done. Of course, the shape business was in now, the way it was run, you couldn't get rich honestly; but what the hell? Who cared? So long as you didn't get found out. Everybody pulled fast ones. You couldn't compete in business, if you didn't. If that bastard of a Johnny had let him label the cans of fish they were packing "Olive Oil" instead of "Soybean Oil," which they were, the three of them, Guy, Russ and Johnny, would have cleared ten thousand dollars on that dicker. But no. Johnny was honest. Honest enough to knock a man down, because some of the cans had already gone out before he found out about it. All right. Guy hadn't forgotten it. In the old days, everything an Ellis touched turned to money, and when he had his, he'd put Johnny Allen out of business, the first thing he did.

Look at Grandfather Malcolm. He started from scratch. The old boy might not have had a million, but he had what amounted to it, in those days. All gone now, damn it all! But it could be done again.

The moon was high in the sky, the water so still that there was no moonpath, only a glassy reflection of the moon. The trip from town across the Bay home was eighteen miles—open water for the first nine, except for two ledges out toward the halfway mark, Garrity's Rock and the Weaver. Both were marked with iron spindles, at least Garrity's was, and the north spur of the Weaver. The south spur wasn't marked, but it was always awash, in plain view, at ordinary high tide. A spring tide would put it under. Even then, there was generally some movement of water over it to show where it was. Besides, everybody knew the Weaver.

Early settlers in Candlemas Bay had named it the Weaver because of the shuttle of breakers that combed it in all but the calmest weather. The old boys had been scared of it. Nowadays, with a fathometer and all the rest of the equipment a man had, he didn't have much to worry about. Guy himself had rounded the Weaver in snowstorms, fogmulls, any weather you might care to name.

If he had been looking at his fathometer at the moment, he would have seen its reading-flash take a dizzying leap; but he was glancing off over the water, spotting his mark, which was Garrity's Rock. He saw it, or thought he did, and sheered off on the course out around the Weaver.

Actually, Garrity's Rock was under water tonight almost up to the iron barrel on top of its spindle. It had passed a few feet under his boat's keel. If he had glanced to port instead of to starboard, he would have seen the barrel as he went by, so near he could have reached out and touched it.

He did catch a glimmer of the red flash out of the corner of his eye. It gave him a temporary start; but since the ledge dropped bold into deep water, the fathometer now showed fifteen fathoms. Astern, everything looked normal in the moonlight, except he'd shaved an old floating hogs-head quite close—or that's what it looked like. The boat's wake bent in a couple of wide curves, he observed with a grin.

Steering crooked and seeing things, he told himself. Must be the beer.

How many ten-dollar bills would there be in a million, he wondered, and figured it out in his head.

Whew-ew!

What he wouldn't do with that!

Stick it away somewhere, not let the government get its claws on any. Why, you only had about thirty thousand left out of a million, after the government got through. The thing to do, get a box and bury it so no one could grab a cent or know how much you had. It would have to be a waterproof box, of course. Big, too. Take quite some container to hold a million. You'd want the money in tens, so no one would think it was funny, *your* trying to change a big bill.

Let's see.

Guy fumbled his wallet out of his pocket and smoothed out the bills he had left. Five tens? He'd thought he had six. Hadn't spent all that, had he? He sure as God hadn't drunk ten dollars' worth of beer. Hell, must've lost one somewhere. Well, no skin gone. Money—to heck with it. It was a man's skin he wanted to look out for.

Five tens seemed hardly to have any thickness at all. He weighted them down on the hatch, peering at their edges. Say it was one thirty-second—no, one sixty-fourth of an inch, for five tens, two inches wide by about four long, how big a box would you need for a million dollars?

He tore a leaf out of his memo book, rummaged around

in his box for a stub of pencil. If five equaled one sixty-fourth, call it that, then ten would equal one thirty-second, and so on.

The slash of moonlight across the white paint of the hatch was so bright that he could see his figures, clear and black, as if under a lantern.

The boat struck with a smash that threw him up against the cabin, knocking his wind out and dropping him to the platform, his mind full of stars and blackness.

When he came to, he looked up, in complete astonishment, at the sky past the rim of the coop, over his head.

The wheel had caught him across the stomach, and he lay gasping, trying to get his wind back, his breath coming in a kind of grate. As it eased, he heard a brook running, serenely and steadily close by.

What in hell? he thought, and realized the quiet gurgle of water running into the boat. A trickle of it touched his hand, as cold and deadly as a snake.

Guy came to his feet in a horrified scramble, all anyhow, pulling himself up by the boat's cheeserind. She was heeled over, her bow high on the ledge, her stern so low that he slid aft a couple of feet on the slippery platform and into water halfway to his knees.

My God, he thought. How long was I out? She's hit a ledge, maybe she's holed bad. No knowing when she'll slide off backwards, with all that water in her stern. I've got to have help, quick, his befuddled wits told him as he scrambled forward, pulling himself along to the coop and the radiotelephone. Maybe there's another boat out here. Maybe the Coast Guard . . .

"*S O S. Calling the Coast Guard. I'm aground on—*"

What was he aground on? What to hell was a ledge doing here? He'd been on his course, he'd been well outside the ledges. He stared wildly at the moonlit water, and for a moment it seemed as if he had gone right out of the world into some place he had never seen before—a big expanse of white, flat ocean; some black islands, far away and low; a bright light, wink, wink, against the horizon . . .

That light was the gas buoy on Red Rock. The height of land far away to the west'ard was Lantern Point. There, a hundred feet to starboard, was the north spur of the Weaver, with the spindle low down, as if it had sunk. He had hit the south spur, drowned under by one old rauncher of a high-run tide.

He stood at the radio, telling over and over where he was and what had happened to him. Since he hadn't got his breath back, the sound he made was like a cat yowling.

My God, he thought crazily, even while the thin squall poured out of him into the hand receiver. I'm glad there ain't nobody around to hear that.

Draggers all over the fishing grounds heard it, the nearest one the *Mary Pietro*, a big Provincetown Portuguese, three miles east of Seal Island. Her skipper didn't understand English very well unless he had time to concentrate; he had been cruising with his receiver on, as was customary, thinking he might hear from Pete Skoura, down off Sheepskin Rock somewhere. He didn't know the inshore waters along here any too well, and he couldn't make out the name of the ledge the fellow said he was aground on.

"Manny," he called excitedly, in his native tongue. "All you boys, see if you can hear what he's saying."

The four or five big, brown men stood with their heads bent over the radio.

"Meader's Ledge," one of them said. "I know where that is."

And the *Mary Pietro* set off, full speed, for Meader's Ledge, nine miles north along the coast.

There was no other boat within twenty miles. But two, the *Randolph Jones* and the *Waterloo*, out by Sheepskin Rock, headed inshore for the Weaver.

Guy sent his call until his breath was gone. Then he switched over to receiving. He heard the skippers of the *Randolph Jones* and the *Waterloo* saying where they were and that they were on the way. Then the Bellport Coast Guard Station answered him. Relief washed over him. Someone was coming. They'd be here in —

My Christ, he thought suddenly. Even a picket boat can't possibly get here before the ebb-tide current starts running.

He remembered with a sick feeling the way the ebb tide set out of the long narrows and shoals to the west. The whole Bay drained down past these ledges. It was the reason the old-timers had been so scared of the Weaver. That current, sometimes, could pull a man in a rowboat right down onto the ledge. And a tide as high as this one would run out something wicked.

Why, right here, he'd seen combers go over fifteen feet high in a southeasterly; in calm weather, when the tide was running, great slow masses of water heaved up and down. He'd watched it a good many times, in the days when he'd been lobstering, and had hauled traps out here. Usually, this south spur was out of water; everything around it would be quiet, not a thing stirring. Then, all of a sudden, there would be a *schloop* and a slurring sound, and the whole surface would suck back and down for twenty-five feet, leaving black, rockweed-covered slabs bare and streaming. Slow and lazy, it looked; but there was a hell of an undertow. The boat wouldn't stay here five minutes, after the ebb tide made.

And slack tide can't last much longer. Maybe only a matter of minutes, he thought frantically.

Maybe he could get an anchor off the bow to take somewhere down on the ledge. It might hold her till someone could get him off. There was just a chance; he might try.

His anchor and rode were stowed down under the stern. He'd have to wade for it; the water was nearly up to the cheeserind down there. He went aft, gingerly, holding on with both hands. The water crawled icily down his boots and around his thighs as he knelt, fumbling under the stern-deck for his anchor. Thank the Lord, it was rove and ready. He'd been using it just the other day. He worried it out and stood up.

At that moment, the boat gave a shiver under him and started to slide backwards off the ledge.

My weight! he thought, as he lunged forward, scrambling and floundering. It's my heft down here's started her off.

She slid about six inches and stopped.

Guy clawed himself up onto the bow. His water-filled rubber boots hindered him, but he couldn't stop to take them off now. He threw the anchor over, heard it clink against rock a few feet down.

Hell, that wasn't any good. He'd have to haul it in, see if he couldn't heave it farther. Maybe it would take, in a crevice, somewhere on the ledge.

He bent over to pull, and it was then the boat went. As she went, she rolled upright. The jerk tilted him off the bow into the water.

Guy hit spread-eagled and went under. His clothes all of a sudden weighed a ton and his boots went down like rocks. He opened his mouth to yell and swallowed water and his hands filled full of icy strings of rockweed. Then he was standing on the ledge in water to his waist. The boat was afloat, about twenty feet away.

He thought, She's all right, she's floating. I've got to get back aboard of her.

Then he saw she was down by the stern, going deeper.

But I've got to get back aboard of her and get a lifebelt, he thought, in bewilderment. I ought to have a lifebelt on.

With a lifebelt, he could dog-paddle to the north spur of the ledge, which was out of water. He could hold on to the base of the iron spindle there till somebody came. But the spindle was across water, a hundred feet away. Guy had never swum that far in his life.

And there was nothing to hold on to here.

Where was that anchor? If he could get hold of that and wedge it, he might hang onto the rode, hold himself here on top of the ledge when the current started running. But the anchor was nowhere to be seen.

The lifebelts were neatly stacked in the boat's forepeak and she was sinking. No one could get down inside that cabin now. Must be two-three feet of water in her.

He stared, fascinated, at the water creeping up the boat's white planking. He could see the round dark patch on her side where he'd rubbed some paint off on a wharf piling, a while ago. He'd meant to fix that. Even as he watched, he saw it slide down and under, out of sight. She must have a good big hole in her to go that fast.

My God, he thought, the scupper holes.

The boat had a self-bailing cockpit and a watertight platform that drained through two two-inch scupper holes in the stern. The holes were normally above the water-line, but with the boat's bow high on the ledge, they must have been well under. All that water on the platform must have come in through them.

If only he'd thought, when he first came to, he might have got down there in the stern, driven those scupper plugs in.

She'd have sunk, in time, just the same—water must be running into her bilges from a leak in the hull; otherwise she'd have come up and drained her platform through the scuppers, as soon as she floated. But she wouldn't have sunk by the stern so fast—she might have stuck on the ledge. Till somebody got there.

If only I'd thought to put those plugs in. And got myself a lifebelt, first thing. But all I could think of was that christly radio.

Well, it was too late now.

4 2

And no boats in sight yet. No one coming.

He heard the sound like a growing waterfall, as water poured in over the boat's cheeserind. She went down all of a heap. The last he saw of her was the running light at the tip of the mast, sliding under in a spinning black whirlpool, a silvery underwater wink, quickly lost. She made a small wave that almost washed him off the rock. It rolled away behind him with a diminishing sound, and the water quieted.

Nothing moved around him, not a ripple, not a breath of air. The moon stood almost overhead in a cloudless sky. Through the clear water, he could see the granite slab he stood on, crisscrossed with scrawls of moonlight, round bright blobs with dark centers that quivered like jellyfish and grew still. Slashed out black, beside them, was his own shadow.

Beyond it, the Weaver went down into the moonlit water, dim terraces black with rockweed or mottled with sick browns and greens, like the hide of a big dead animal. It slid into a darkness vague with blocky shapes, and then nothing but an empty drop-off.

An icy fist squeezed shut in the middle of Guy's chest.

My God. That wasn't anything a man in his flesh and blood was ever supposed to see.

Even as he looked, the whole abyss stirred. The bright scrawls darted and vanished; and long ribbons of kelp, standing upright in the water, bent slowly sideways, streaming, in the direction of the open sea.

AS Russ Allen's big boat roared past the wooded bluffs of Lantern Point, Jeb could see the lights of the picket boat, standing out fast toward the middle of the Bay.

"There's the Coast Guard," Grampie said.

Russ said, "Ayeh."

He leaned down and tried to shove his throttle ahead another notch, but it was already open as far as it would go. Ordinarily, it would have goweled Russ that another boat, even a picket boat, could move any faster than his. Now he was only thinking of getting out there as fast as he could.

They watched the lights, the white and red ones show-ing for a long time. Then the green one brought to bear as the picket boat swung out around the Weaver, slowing and stopping. A searchlight came on. A horn let go with short blasts that echoed faintly across the water. Presently, the lights started moving again, slowly, the searchlight sweeping the water in short arcs.

Grampie drew a long breath. "They ain't found him on the ledge," he said.

Russ said, "Looks like they ain't."

He cleared his throat, watching the searchlight.

When they rounded the Weaver, the picket boat was a hundred yards outside of it, moving slowly to the eastward with the tide.

The moon was turning toward the west, beginning to drop down the sky, the Bay white and glassy, with not a ripple showing except around the ledges, where the ebb tide had started the water moving with a slow, sluggish heave, up and down.

The north spur of the Weaver was what Jeb had had in his mind. When you thought of the Weaver, it was of the blunt granite snout sticking out of the water, the spindle with the iron barrel painted white. But all at once, Russ swung the boat away from that, and headed her up into the tide, so that she had just way enough to stem the cur-rent. He and Grampie stood looking at the south spur, which was just beginning to uncover.

Russ said, "I guess that's that, Jebron," and Grampie answered him in a low voice, "Ayeh, I guess so, Russ."

Jeb stared at the ledge. He could feel his knees shaking

44

and he put both hands down on the cheeserind to steady himself. Grampie nudged him gently to look down.

"The oil slick, Jebby. The boat's sunk there."

And Jeb saw, overside, the vague, smooth whorls streaming greasily past on the water.

Russ said, "About ten fathoms there, Jebron?"

"There is some places. Nearer twenty, right there, I'd say. The way that slick lays, she may be hung up on the ledge, part way down. Can't really tell nothing till daylight."

Russ spun the wheel, letting the boat fall off with the tide. They slid down toward the picket boat, now moving in slow zigzags, her searchlight ribboning out ahead of her.

"He had lifebelts aboard," Jeb said, his stunned mind beginning to work on it. "He had time to put a call out. He must've had time to get a lifebelt on."

Grampie said, "Most like he did, Jebby."

He stood listening, looking off over the water, and Russ watched him, fiddling nervously with the throttle.

"He ain't within hollering distance, that's certain," Grampie said. "Or he'd have answered that horn. Le's slide over alongside them fellers, Russ, see what their idea of it is."

As they came abreast the picket boat, someone hailed and a petty officer leaned out with a flash-lantern.

"I thought that was you, Russ," he said.

He was Charley Josephs, who had been a Candlemas Bay boy, now on duty with the Bellport Coast Guard Station.

"Damnedest thing—you see anything in there?"

"Only the oil slick."

"Ayeh, we saw that, too. I thought he might've got over to the north spur, but he didn't. Could Guy swim any, you know?"

Grampie said, "No, not to amount to anything. Dog-paddle a little maybe. If he had a lifebelt on, he'd go with the tide."

"Cap'n Jebron." Charley's tone altered a little. "God, I'm sorry about this. Look, this current sets straight from here to Little Nubble, then the Shoal splits her, but I ain't sure about the Ridges."

"Nobody is," Grampie said. "The heft of her makes a big curve, sou'-sou'-east, but there's a lot of crosscurrents out on the Shoals."

"Guy might've got ashore on Little Nubble," Russ said. "We'll take a run out."

"Go ahead. I'll jig out slow, where I got the light. You got radio equipment—oh, sure. Okay, call me if you need anything. Got a flashlight? Here, take this one."

He tossed his lantern across to Jeb.

The men's voices were urgent, not wasting any words over the plan, or to say there was a hurry—that a man in a lifebelt would not be conscious long in the cold water, that he might have drifted anywhere, by now.

"I radioed for some more boats," Charley said. "I want some out around Seal Island. Anywhere from a quarter to a half-mile to the nor'ard of Seal, that right?"

Grampie said, "Just about," and Russ's big fingers closed on the throttle.

"Jebby, you up onto the bow. Keep a good watch out," Grampie said, as they slid away from the picket boat.

The boat moved eastward across the glassy water, faintly colored now, for as the moon dropped, a pale, transparent haze came drifting up from the mainland. It gave the moon a silver halo, made the light watery, hard to see by.

Jeb was glad to be alone up on the bow. He stared tensely at the vagueness ahead of the boat, trying to concentrate on it; but his mind kept shuttling over and over what had happened. It didn't register. It wasn't real. Only, in his stomach, a hard cold lump settled down, and he kept wanting to swallow.

Little Nubble had once been an islet, a hundred yards long and fifty wide, where grass and spruces grew. Now it was nibbled and gnawed away by the sea to a gravelly bar, with spines of granite showing through; and at low tide, on the southern end, you could see old tree stumps with their tough, seaworm-pitted roots clutching down into mud that once was earth and now was clamflats.

Russ nosed the boat in over the rapidly shoaling water, his eyes on the ledges overside. In the cove on the north end of the bar, he stopped the engine and let go with a blast on his horn. They listened, and Grampie shouted, a long-drawn, bass roar, "Guy, o-oh-h-h, Guy," but there was not a sound. Even the tide was draining away here silently.

"Better have a look ashore," Grampie said.

Here where the current set in close and curled around in a little swirling backwater, a man in a lifebelt might have drifted, to inch himself out on the rocks and lie unconscious there.

"Ayeh." Russ glanced over at the bar for a place to land. He hesitated, the scant fraction of a minute, thinking of the shallow water under the boat's keel, the tide running out fast now. "You handle her, Jebron, while I go ashore?"

Jeb said, "I'll go, Russ."

He had been standing on the washboard, holding to the rim of the coop, so as not to obstruct Russ's line of vision through the windscreen when they came in close to land.

Russ said, "Oh, Jesus, no, I'll go," thinking, What if the kid found his father up there dead?

But Grampie said, "He'll make out to go, Russ. All right, Jebby."

He put his hand briefly on the toe of Jeb's rubber boot, where it stuck in over the cheeserind, and Jeb knew he was saying to him, Go on, Jebby, you're enough of a man now, it's up to you to go.

And it was, of course, with Russ needed to handle the

4 7

boat and Grampie too stiff in the joints to do much climb-
ing around the slippery shore.

From the highest point on Little Nubble, even in moon-
light, you could see all over the tiny bar. The shores were
bare. The big tide had swept even the driftwood away. But
Jeb made sure. He walked around the bar, the beam from
Charley Josephs's big flash-lantern dancing on ahead of
him.

It was in the backwater of the cove, as he was getting
ready to climb back aboard, that he spotted the little pod
of Guy's things, spinning slowly, with some driftwood
pieces and a spidery mat of dead rockweed. He called out
and pointed with the white beam of the flashlight. Russ
slid the boat in, gingerly, for him to scramble aboard. Jeb
held the light, while they fished the things out of the
water.

Guy's hat was there, slimy with oil and soaked with sea
water; and his long-handled gaff with his initials "G.P.E."
cut into the wooden handle; and a limp, stained ten-dollar
bill.

Russ swore softly, under his breath.

But Grampie said, as if answering him, "He might be
outside of here, Russ."

If he's anywhere, they all three added silently.

Russ reversed the engine, backed away from the ledges.
He reached over, picked up the radiotelephone receiver.

"*Russ Allen, calling picket boat Ranger. Calling picket
boat Ranger. Over.*"

"*Coast Guard picket boat Ranger calling Russ Allen.
Come in, Russ.*"

"*You there, Charley?*" Russ said, and told swiftly what
they had found.

They'd come out, Charley said. Other boats were on the
way now. Russ had better go out to the Ridges and zigzag
in.

They ran out past Little Nubble Shoals, with the sprawl-

4 8

ing underwater Ridges less than four fathoms deep, where the tide checked in long, silent ripples and spread out like a fan. Then they circled, moving slowly back toward the distant, low-lying land.

The big tide was running out fast now, three miles an hour in the open Bay, four and five in the narrows. Lobster buoys tailed out seaward from taut warps, some of them towed a fathom under. On the placid shores of islands the water drained away, falling two feet an hour. Old driftwood piles that had lain undisturbed for years went with it, so that the Bay was full of indeterminate, dark objects hurrying seaward. A dozen times Russ swung the boat over to something floating, and it would be an orange crate, a rotten tree stump, a wharf piling, an old chunk of wood.

As time went on, other boats joined the search, so that the Bay was sparked all over with red and green lights. The *Randolph Jones,* a big dragger, went by, running full speed, and Russ hove her to. Her skipper told about getting Guy's call. She had come most of the way in from Sheepskin Rock, but her crew had noticed only drift stuff floating. They had not been looking for a man. Nor had the crew of the *Waterloo,* which came piling by fifteen minutes later. They went back toward the east and, like the others, moved in endless zigs and zags over the water.

The moon went down into a thickening haze bank, leaving a grayish twilight. The stars faded and sunrise came up with a streak of cold, clear green, like the green of ribbon candy. The west was woolly with clouds, but the sea stayed quiet. Not a breeze moved it, not a ripple, except over the shoals the crinkled tide rips.

"Jesus Christ!" Russ burst out. "You'd think it never blowed or stormed or anything could ever move it. Look at the christless old bitch!" he said, meaning the sea, and Grampie nodded.

4 9

"You'll see something move it before too long," he said. "The hazy way that moon went down."

He sounded absent-minded, as if, after so many years of watching on the weather, words about it came out of him without his thinking.

"We ought to start back if we're going to look around that ledge on the low-water slack, Jebron."

"I guess so, Russ. Jebby, you better come down from there, Russ's going to open her up. We're going in."

Jeb had been standing on the roof of the coop while the boat circled, so that he would be as high as possible above the water. He turned around with a little start, wondering if Grampie thought it was no use looking any longer.

Well, he told himself, if he thinks so, probably it isn't.

The lump in his chest tightened.

He looked down at the old man's face, seeing how tired he was and how grief-stricken, and yet able to think of all the things that needed to be done. The thought came to Jeb that this wasn't the first time, nor the second, that Grampie had helped look for somebody lost on the Shoals; and that one of the other times it had been Great-Uncle John, his brother.

He ought to go home and rest, he's all in, Jeb thought, and the big cold lump came up hot into his throat. He said, "Okay, Grampie," in a kind of choke, and jumped down into the cockpit.

"You could build a fire in the galley stove, Jeb," Russ said quickly. "We could all use some coffee."

Off across the water toward Seal Island, the picket boat circled patiently, and away east, as far as you could see, the water was spotted with boats. As Russ headed back inshore, they passed boats from all over Candlemas Bay—from Bellport, from Harborside, from Rocktown and the islands; and, as they went, men lifted a hand in the jerky salute that was the greeting of the country.

"Cap'n Jebron's going in," one called to another, in

passing. "He must think it ain't no use." And, "If he thinks so, likely it ain't. Jesus, what a thing to happen." But they went on, doggedly searching.

The Weaver lay drained bare in the morning sun. The ledges connecting the north and south spurs were uncovered now, in one long hackly spine. The south spur stood twelve feet out of water, kelp and rockweed lying limp on the stained granite bastions.

"God, I never see the tide so low in my life," Russ said.

He slowed, went into reverse and then neutral, letting the engine idle. His eyes were on the water at the side of the ledge, where the oil slick, lessened now, still slid to the surface in faint, many-colored coils.

"I have, once or twice," Grampie said. "But never any lower. Better not, yet, had ya?" he went on, as Russ thrust the gear lever forward and began to inch the boat slowly in toward the ledge. "It won't be long now till slack tide."

Russ said, "She'll take care of anything that goes on in there, now. I can circle once."

He watched overside, his eyes intent, his body thinned out and tense as a cat's; and Grampie saw that he was right, he knew what he was doing. It wasn't a rowboat, now, depending on the strength alone that was in a man's arms and back. Grampie smiled to himself, as if he were saying, I'm an old fool, sometimes.

They went quietly in over the Weaver's underwater ledges, beginning to show mottled through the softly lacing water, and as the boat swung a half-circle in the oil slick, they looked down and saw Guy's boat where she lay canted on a steep black slab, before the wash from the propeller, green froth and bubbles, creamed over her. Then they were away from the loom of the Weaver and in deep water again.

For a minute, Jeb couldn't move. He stood bent over, both hands on the gunnel, looking down into the green water and not seeing it, for the tears which hadn't come all night were fighting to come now, at the sight of the beautiful white boat lying sunk on the ledge.

Grampie's hand shut tight on his shoulder.

"We've got to write him off, Jebby," the old man said. "We tried, both of us, boy."

Russ said, "Oh, Jesus, Jebron," and stared at the place, his face white, so that the overnight's growth of whiskers stood out in individual small spines. He went on, after a moment, "There's only about twelve feet of water over her now."

"It might's well be twelve fathoms," Grampie said, steadily. "You see how she was laying?"

"Ayeh. Slanting."

"She's right on the edge of that drop-off. The first sea of any kind'll wash her off of there. I don't know why she didn't go with the ebb. There'll be wind come up with the tide."

"If I could get a cable on her," Russ said, his voice thickening with excitement. "Oh, Jesus God, I haven't even got a cable. I went clear to town after mine, and it hadn't come."

"You'd need two cables under her, likely more," Grampie said. "And two boats, hefty ones with powerful lifting gear. We can't do nothing alone, boy. We ain't got time."

But Russ, not listening, had grabbed for the radio-phone.

". . . Listen, Charley. We found his boat. Sunk, hung up on the side of the Weaver in about twelve-fifteen feet of water. She won't stay there when the flood tide makes, if there's any swell comes in with it. See if you can't get a couple of big draggers in here, quick, or any boats with heavy hoisting gear. Step on it, will ya, Charley? Over."

Charley's reply crackled in over the receiver.

"Ranger calling Russ Allen . . . calling Russ Allen.

Received your message. I'll get someone there as soon as I can, Russ. I don't think anyone's very near you. The Aberdeen's down around Gimbal Head, I'll see if I can contact her. She couldn't get in there very quick, especially if she's got gear over. Nothing out here could get there in less than an hour. Over."

Russ acknowledged. He said again, "Step on it, Charley."

The *Aberdeen* was the Coast Guard buoy-boat, whose job was maintaining navigation markers—putting down heavy granite moorings to hold spar and nun and can buoys, among other things. She would have heavy hoisting gear and cables.

But she can't get very close in there; she's too big, Russ told himself. And she won't have time.

Ordinary slack tide was about forty minutes; but it varied. In a spring or a neap tide, slack water was considerably less. Sometimes, on a big one like this, you could count on only fifteen or twenty.

And before long, he thought, with a quick glance at the softly feathering sky, it's going to blow. Probably from the east or southeast, the way it looks now.

East or west, though, what would be the difference? Off here by the Weaver, an east wind made a swell; but a west wind, on the flood, made a tide chop just as bad.

"Which way's it going to blow, Jebron?" he asked, easing the gearshift forward.

"East," Grampie said. "I should think."

"Right away?"

"Come up as the sun gets higher, likely."

"We're behind the eight-ball any way you look at it," Russ said, watching the boat creep in toward the ledges.

"That's about it. I wouldn't want you to smash up your boat, boy."

"No," Russ said. "Well, let's look it over, Jebron."

The water at the foot of the ledges was still now, in low-water slack. Russ laid the boat over the oil slick, and she hung there without moving. They waited while her propeller wash settled away.

"She don't look hurt much," Grampie said, staring down.

"Not that you can see."

They could see the bow and the forward part of the cabin clearly, and make out the steep angle at which the boat lay, tilted downward on a massive granite block and canted sideways on her keel. The cockpit door was open, swinging slowly. Aft, details were blurred where the water deepened; but they could make out the dark shadow that was Guy's otter drag, which he had had piled on the stern, and which had spilled over and now lay partly on the ledge.

"God, I could almost reach down and hook her with my gaff," Russ said.

He fumbled around in a tub and came up with a heavy handline, rigged with big hooks and a pound lead. He tossed the hooks and lead overside and lowered them to the ledge and after some maneuvering, managed to catch the hooks in the dragnet. They tore out the first time. The second time, he was able to haul a section of the big net to the surface of the water. They all three laid hold and pulled it in, but the doors of the drag were still in the water when the cable fetched up. It was a steel cable, wound, fathoms of it, around Guy's winch, and the brake of the winch was set, holding it there.

"Damn," Russ said. "Ought to be some way we could slack off that brake."

He ran the boat ahead a few feet. On the canted platform of Guy's boat, they could see the winch housing. Russ stood looking at it.

"If I only knew what to do, or how to do it. If I could lay hold of that cable, we might dope out some way to fasten it, hold her from sliding off till someone got here.

5 4

Lay it around the ledge to an anchor, or maybe my own hoisting gear'd hold her. I think maybe I could get down there myself, Jebron. Look—" He pointed to the mast, slanted out a few feet down in the water. "If I was to let my feet down on that mast, I could haul myself down to the winch, maybe."

"No, you ain't," Grampie said. "It ain't worth the chance. She might slide off any minute. There's been enough happen."

"Seems as if I could at least save his boat," Russ said.

"You've done an awful lot for him, in his lifetime, Russ. More'n most men would have. I won't let you do this. That water's like ice."

"Jesus, we can't let her go—"

The quick movement behind them made them glance around.

Russ, staring wildly, let out a stupefied, "Hey!"

Grampie yelled, "Jebby, don't you—" before Jeb went headfirst off the stern. His brown body shot down through the water, leaving a trail of bubbles.

He had known they wouldn't let him go. When Russ first said the brake had to be slacked off, he had slipped down and undressed in the cabin. He had come out on the run, his bare feet pounding on the platform. It wouldn't have been any use to try to convince them how easy it was. They wouldn't care if you had swum off the ledges at slack tide, a hundred times, in water deeper than twelve feet. And water that you were used to didn't seem cold, but like your second element. This was cold, though, this water out here.

He found the winch brake and drove the wooden block out from under it. He saw the cable begin to run free.

He saw the open, gently swaying cockpit door, which was what he'd been thinking about before Russ had mentioned the brake. He'd have breath enough if he hustled. It would only take a minute.

The hatchway to the cabin was murky green. Something blocked it and he yanked at the dark mass, with a cold clutch inside him, gripping the coaming with one hand. But only a tangle of floating lifebelts, with trailing straps, drifted past him, rising slowly through the water. He got his feet on the companionway steps, pulling himself down, groping for the wooden button of the locker.

For a minute, he thought the locker door was stuck.

Swelléd shut, he thought, prying at it desperately, his hoarded breath going.

Then it dragged open stickily, and his hand closed on the slippery oilskin roll, right where he had left it. No one had touched it since he'd put it there.

Jeb's head broke water a few feet from Russ's boat. With the first deep gulp of air, he realized how deadly cold he was. The water inshore was nothing like this. He was glad to grab the rope's end Russ tossed to him and to feel Russ's and Grampie's hands in his armpits. He dropped the chart in onto the platform, got his hands on the cheeserind. Then he was aboard, chattering and shivering. A chill morning breeze, like powdered ice, blew against his naked body.

"Good job, Jeb," Russ said. "Now we've got a cable on her, by the gods."

Grampie let out a bawl. The sweat was standing on his forehead, in spite of the cold wind, and Jeb could see he was pretty excited. "Git below, dammit, Jebby! Git dried off and warmed up. Go on, quick. Dammit, git!"

He wanted to say, I'm sorry, Grampie, but he couldn't make his jerking under-jaw stay still. He turned and dived down the hatchway.

Russ said, soberly, "Cussid little seal. What's that,-Jebron? That old chart?"

Grampie picked up the chart. "Ayeh," he said.

He held it a moment, turning it over in hands that shook a little. "I guess he figured he had some use for it."

It was warm in the cabin. Jeb rubbed himself dry with

an old sweater of Russ's, and he got dressed in his dunga-rees and wool shirt and mackinaw and rubber boots. There were some coals left in the stove. The coffee was still hot enough to do some good. He took a big swig of it, black, feeling it travel every inch of the way down his gullet that felt like a big, cold angleworm. Up to then, he hadn't been able to think of anything but how cold he was; but now that he was warmer, he suddenly realized that what he'd felt on his skin when he'd come out of the water was *wind*. It was beginning to breeze on. He dropped the tin cup and tore out on deck.

Away to the east, the water that had been pale glass was ruffled gray now; the sky was covered with clouds, behind which the sun shone with a brassy glow. Light ripples of the incoming tide were beginning to slap against the ledges, heaving the boat gently up and down. Wind was coming from the east in puffs; as Jeb came on deck, he felt it cold in his wet hair. Russ put the engine into reverse, backed away from the ledges.

He and Grampie had unshackled Guy's drag from his cable, and had shoved as much as they could of the big net down under the stern-deck to be out of the way. Be-hind them, Guy's cable payed out, unrolling from the drum on his winch, underwater. Russ backed thirty feet off, for a safe margin; then he swung the boat so that the cable lay off over her stern, and let the engine idle.

Grampie looked at him, and Russ looked back with a fleeting grin.

"I d'no, Jebron," he said. "I feel as if I had a goddam bear by the tail."

"I d'no b't you have," Grampie said. "Buoy the end and anchor it out here, Russ, that's all you can do. You can't fix it so she won't slide off, now. Even if you could hold her, she'd smash up there in no time, the way it's com-ing on to blow."

"Jebron," Russ said, "you remember the feller that tried

to lift himself in a bushel basket? You take the wheel and hold her about here, for me, will ya? Think I'll hook the end of that cable on to my hoisting gear."

"You'll only smash up your gear."

"I don't rightly know just how much one of these little winches'll stand, do you?"

"No. But it wouldn't raise a boat on a single drag-cable. That cable of Guy's is pretty old, too. And if it don't part, likely a winch'll tear out, yours or his."

"I know all that. And yet I don't know it. She ain't no ocean liner, Jebron, and she's a lot lighter, under water. I don't plan to try to raise her any. Only when she slides off, it might not take a hell of a pull to hold her from sinking deeper."

All the time he was speaking, he was working on Guy's cable, unscrewing the shackle from the end of it, reeving the end through the tackle on his davit. He carried it back through the drum on his winch, and bent a knot in it, which took all his strength, for the cable, made up of many small steel wires, was stiff. But he had to have the knot, to keep the cable from slipping out of the winch. He started the winch, wound up the cable on the drum until it grew taut against the pull of the sunken boat. Then he slacked it off quickly.

"Okay," he said, under his breath. "Now, where to hell is the *Aberdeen?*"

Off toward Little Nubble, a clutch of boats was headed in fast, draggers apparently, but of the *Aberdeen* there was no sign.

"Take her a while to get up here from Gimbal Head. Besides, she likely had gear overboard," Grampie said. He glanced around at the cable, and reversed the engine a little, making sure the cable stayed slack. "It's only been half an hour since you radioed."

"No!" Russ said.

It seemed as if they had been lying off the ledge for

hours. But even if the *Aberdeen* did get here now, what could she do? Russ, apparently, thought she could do something.

"Well," he said, "I guess I'm a damn fool, Jebron."

A long, low swell lifted the boat eight inches or so and slid past, and they all three spun to watch it. It washed up the ledges and sucked back down. That was all.

"There's the first one," Russ said. "Jebron, when I holler, you do what I tell you, quick, with the engine. Jeb, git down here in the coop, in case there's any cable ends flying."

The puffs of wind came steadily now. Off toward Little Nubble, pinpoints of whitecaps showed, growing bigger. The swells came rolling in, one out of every three or four a little higher, ten or twelve feet apart. It was hard to keep the cable slack. Russ, at the winch brake and Grampie at the wheel, tried not to let the boat fetch up too hard on it. They hadn't long to wait before Guy's boat stirred in her precarious cradle.

The cable sagged suddenly, tautened, cutting down through the water.

Russ yelled, "She's going! Full ahead, Jebron!"

The weight of the sunken boat began to pull them backwards toward the ledge. For a moment, they had the strange experience of seeing Russ's boat, with her throttle wide open at full ahead, shoot stern-first through the water. Then the cable, taut and humming, hung straight down from the davit.

The stern sagged deeper, until water swirled in over the washboard. From somewhere came a loud crack, and the davit began to buckle. And then, under water, Guy's cable parted. The stern bounced upward with a jerk, slatting them against their handholds. The boat shot ahead. Grampie slowed the engine to idle and looked over at Russ.

Russ yanked off the winch brake. The released drum

5 9

spun as he reversed it, winding the loose cable in over the stern. It ran in some ten fathoms, to its frayed and empty end.

Russ said, "She's gone, Jebron."

He stood, briefly, his hand on the winch brake.

"Well," he said. He fumbled in his pocket for a cigarette. "The feller said he'd have lifted himself in that bushel basket, if the handles hadn't come off."

He held the cigarette in his hand, unlighted, looking at the empty space of water under the Weaver, now creamed white with foam. Two tears brimmed over his lower eyelids and rolled down his cheeks; and Russ pulled out his handkerchief and, unashamedly, wiped them away.

"God damn it," he said. "God damn it to hell."

He reached over for the radiotelephone.

"Russ Allen, calling picket boat Ranger. Come in, Charley."

"Coast Guard boat Ranger, calling Russ Allen. Come in."

"She sunk in deep water, Charley. Call off the Aberdeen, will you, she can't do no good here now. We found four lifebelts. Guy's father says four was all he carried aboard his boat. Thanks, Charley, but that's all."

PART TWO

Jen

THE Ellis children, under the blossoming apple trees, were playing Great-Great-Gra'mother Lizbeth and Ringgold the Pirate. At least, they said "Great-Great," but nobody really knew how many "Greats" there should be. Grampie, when he sang the old song, said there was a string of them a yard long, for Lizbeth Ellis lived many years ago.

Maggie lay prostrate at the feet of Neal, her hair wispy against the grass, a smear of cranberry jelly, for blood, across one cheek. She was Lizbeth and Neal was Ringgold in a red bandanna and with a dagger of pine. Ten feet away, Andy stalked in circles and shook his fists, as Great-Great-Grampa Saul Ellis must have done, mourning his bride on the distant shore. Mertis and Clay sat apart under the red astrachan tree.

Andy wished Mertis would play, but she was mad because she couldn't be Ringgold. Clay didn't matter—he was too young to be anything. He had been coached to say, "Cuss you both, Saul Ellis and Ringgold the Pirate," like old Joel Wing, father of Lizbeth. But the ugly Rhode Island Red rooster had chased him again this morning.

The rooster was Clay's enemy. He never seemed to catch Clay; he stayed about three paces behind, walking with dignified but purposeful strides. Clay was never dignified. He would sense the rooster from afar; then, with horrified roars, he would run desperately for the house. Neal and Andy, this morning, had put the rooster to flight with rocks. The girls had comforted Clay, brought him down to the orchard and coached him to be old Joel Wing.

But apple blossoms distracted Clay, too, or a bird flying; now he had found a beetle snuggled into the tree's wrinkled root. He sat watching it, forgetting everything.

Ringgold wasn't much of a game without Mertis. After all, it was her game, made up out of the song; she had had all the good ideas about playing it. For one thing, the Pirate was from far away and long ago, and all Neal could think of was to wave his arms and talk tough, like some fellow off a Provincetown dragger. But he was bound to be boss pirate. You might as well let him, if you wanted to play the game at all.

"How you like that licking, hah?" he said now, swaggering.

Gra'mother Lizbeth lay like a maiden dreaming, hands folded, eyes closed. It could not be said of Maggie that she did not enter into the spirit of a game. No one, least of all Ringgold, could guess how, behind the frail eyelids, the shrewd strength was gathering. Let him, just once, come closer.

But not Neal. He straightened up and moved away. Maggie peered through her eyelashes and saw him well out of reach.

Mertis's cool stare said, "I told you so."

Neal was going to fix it so Ringgold came out on top; that was the trouble with Neal. Andy shrugged. When Mertis played it, you forgot she was Mertis, but you never could forget that Neal was Neal.

Ringgold snarled, "And, by gorry, you do as I say, or I'll mow ya down again."

Mertis snickered, a sound disagreeable and knowing.

"Oh, shut up," Neal said. "Stuff like that's what any tough guy would say."

But he went back and stood over the fallen fair one. "The next time you'll git the worst there is. You'll git the fate worse than death."

This was more like. On the distant shore, Grampa Saul Ellis gave a squawk of ultimate despair. He beat with his fists on the apple tree, and the tree let down a shower of petals thick as snow. They fell spinning and drifting through the dark old branches and the little light new green leaves. They speckled Clay's rompers and covered up his beetle, so that in his head a muzzy memory of duty unperformed found room to stir. He looked up and muttered anxiously, "Cuss. Cuss you."

Gra'mother Lizbeth stared balefully at Ringgold.

"I wun't do what you say, you dirty pirate," she stated. "You touch me, I'll claw the nose off'n your face."

That would fetch him. You might as well play the game Neal's way and get it over with.

Sure enough, he dropped to his knees beside her. With horrid deliberation, he drew the dagger of pine.

"All right. You ast for it."

The fate worse than death, according to Grampie, was to have your arms and legs cut off while you were alive and kicking. At least, he said, when they asked him, that was the worst fate *he* could think of, and he could think of se-vereal.

> "All beat and choked, her bones a-broke,
>   One bruise from toe to crown,
>   To take her life old Ringgold's knife
>   A-coming slowly down,"

Grampie sang.

> "No help was sent from any friend,
>   No succor from the skies,
>   Her thumbs upright with all her might
>   She stobbed into his eyes!
>   Ka-whango!"

6 3

He would jab his two thumbs upward, and the children, listening with eyes like gooseberries, would jump back as if snake-bit.

> *"The ships come down from Gloucestertown,*
> *All on the morning tide,*
> *And young Saul Ellis leaped ashore*
> *To find his stolen bride.*

> *"His blinded eyes turned to the skies,*
> *They hung old Ringgold well,*
> *His body went to feed the fish,*
> *His soul it went to—Massachusetts."*

The children would shriek and roll on the grass, laughing. Don't tell *them* that last word was "Massachusetts!"

"Oh, yes, 't is," Grampie said solemnly. "It's well known that the souls of all them old-time pirates went to Massachusetts. Else why would Massachusetts drivers act the way they do nowadays on the roads with their cars?"

But the children knew better. One of the best things about the game, when Mertis played Ringgold, was the way she made his soul come out of him and go away to hell. The very best thing, of course, was her making

> *"All day long the bloody heads*
> *Rolled down the bloody tide."*

But they all loved to watch Ringgold go away to hell, and sometimes even Neal would keep quiet until Mertis got it done. She would get up off of the ground after the hanging and creep slowly to the outside cellar door. She would look down, start back, as if at some sight too dreadful to see. Then, the last you saw of old Ringgold, he was going down, step by step, sucked right into the bowels of the earth.

Aunt Candace had caught her doing it once and had

6 4

made her stop; but when Aunt Evelyn saw it, she laughed and laughed.

"Well," she said, "I guess there's no doubt what happens to the wicked."

Neal never would go to hell, of course. He couldn't be bothered. Now he was prodding at Maggie with the pine dagger, saying, "There! That fixes you."

The wooden point was sharp, and Maggie was close to tears. She said, "Don't, Neal, that hurts."

She wiggled, but he could hold her with one hand, little old butterball Maggie. She wasn't even going to get a chance to make believe stob her thumbs upright into his eyes. Maybe, now, if she could have got her hands free, she'd have done it, truly, she was so mad. In a minute, she'd really start to cry.

Then Mertis got up, walked over and kicked Neal hard with her sneaker on the round of his bottom where the dungarees stretched tight.

"Let her go, you big bart-all," she said.

Neal scrambled to his feet, all anyhow, his mouth a big red "Ow!"

For a moment he stood rubbing his bottom, then he charged, head down, at Mertis. They rolled over and over on the grass.

Clay got up and walked carefully around the apple tree. With its sturdy trunk between him and the fight, he stood looking on with interest. Maggie scrabbled to her feet, crying in earnest, while Andy, with one delighted glance, legged it for the house, roaring, "Mama! Mama!"

There was nobody in the house but Aunt Evelyn. Aunt Candy was over calling on Claudie Allen, and Mama had gone down in the pasture violeting with Aunt Lynnie and Mrs. Floyd Clawson, one of the lady boarders. Andy knew she had gone. He disapproved of it. Mamas should never go away from the house unless they took their children with them. He had wanted to go, from the moment he heard Aunt Lynnie coaxing Mama in the nicey-nicey voice she used in front of the boarders.

"Mrs. Clawson wants to see that bank of blue and white violets down in the Alder Swamp, Jen. You'll have to come. I don't remember just where it is."

Aunt Lynnie didn't care any more about a violet than she did about a hoptoad, but she was always trying to suck up to the summer people.

"Oh, dear, Lyn, I don't possibly have time," Mama said, "and I don't remember, either, where those violets are," and then Ole-Crickety-Clawson piped up and said she was *so* disappointed. Aunt Lynnie said, "Jen, it's *such* a lovely day. We can hunt, and if we don't find them, we'll have had a nice walk. Evelyn, you'll start dinner, won't you?"

Aunt Evelyn was the one who could have shown them where the violets were. She knew all things like that, and a good many more besides that other people didn't. She had shown Mertis where a humming bird's nest was. Not that Mertis would tell.

Of the grown-ups, Aunt Evelyn should be the one to go; not that she would. You wouldn't catch her "sucking up" to anyone. Aunt Evelyn went out of her way to avoid people, even her own family. But it was children, really, who knew about banks of violets. Andy could have taken Mama right to five or six nice ones. And she wouldn't even let him go.

It was mean to plague Aunt Evelyn, he thought as he neared the house. She was your best friend, always ready to help you if you needed her, or to make up and play games. If you asked her to, she'd make lovely toys—boats or little animals—out of shore clay, just by squeezing it around in her fingers. Andy's heart smote him, but only briefly.

It was too much fun to come hollering trouble to Aunt Evelyn. She believed every word you said; and she always thought that what happened to you was as serious as things that happened to grown-ups. He put everything he had into his bawl of distress, as he burst into the kitchen and saw her slight back begin to stiffen at the sink.

Aunt Evelyn was peeling potatoes. She spun to meet him, her face full of concern. "Andy, what—what is it?"

"Come quick, they're murdering each other!"

"Who? Where?" Aunt Evelyn tossed a big wet potato and the paring knife, clanking, into the sink.

"Oh, come, come quick!" he wailed. "They've got each other by the necks and choking!"

Between his eyelashes, he watched with satisfaction. It would take a minute.

Then Aunt Evelyn breathed in, hard, through her nose. "R-r-r-run! Run for your grandfather!"

He tore headlong out the door. Better get out of sight now, for if she made him go get Grampie for nothing but the kids fighting, Grampie would skin him alive.

Evelyn stood in the middle of the kitchen floor. She was a small woman of thirty-three or so, with a great mass of curly dark-red hair, which she wore combed severely back from her serene white forehead and pinned in a knot at the back of her neck. Even so, odd curls strayed out, softening a hard line here and there. She wore heavy, horn-rimmed spectacles, vastly unbecoming. The eyes behind the glasses were grayish-green, quiet and, just now, more than a little amused.

The children were fighting, probably. Andy was working off this morning's temper and disappointment. She'd been expecting something of the sort ever since Jen had gone off and left them. The scamps, they ought to let their mother have a vacation from them once in a while, and it was so seldom Jen did. Well, it would make Andy feel better to have Aunt Evelyn come tearing out of the house, looking for a murder.

From its hook behind the kitchen door, she took down her sunbonnet and put it on, tying the strings under her

6 7

chin. It was an old-fashioned stovepipe bonnet, of the vintage ladies sometimes wore in 1910. Evelyn fluffed the strings into a bow. She stepped out on the back doorstep, looking this way and that.

The sun shone down on a scene of peace. A few hens scratched by the doorstep. The little cats, for once not chasing each other, curled on a wooden washtub turned bottom up to drain. Over the harbor, the gulls were flying, and a white boat going somewhere spun after itself a tranquil track. The orchard slept, its bloom a mystery on the golden air.

No murder, no sign of one. And God bless Andy for giving her an excuse to get out of that kitchen into this lovely June day.

Andy peered out from the lilac thicket that overlooked the apple trees. The two locked figures still rolled in combat. Aunt Evelyn was standing on the doorstep, looking which way to go. But the fight was as good as over. For up from the pasture, striding along, with Maggie running to keep up, came Mama. Maggie had gone after Mama.

Mama had a bunch of blue and white violets in one hand and her hair stood out like a gold bush in the sun. She .was almost six feet tall. She weighed a hundred and sixty pounds. She looked very fine as she came.

Oh, I wouldn't be them, Andy said, dancing in the lilac bush. I wouldn't be them for nothing!

Mama handed her violets to Maggie. She snaked Mertis and Neal apart, holding each one by the backs of their T-shirts.

"What do you kids think you're up to?" she said. "What kind of works is these?"

Neal's nose was bleeding. The front of his shirt was covered with grass stains. He had a scratch down one cheek and he was howling.

"She kicked me."

"Did you kick him?"

Mertis's eyes shone with battle. She had a lump in her eyebrow. One sleeve was ripped almost off her T-shirt.

"What'd you kick him for?"

" 'll, I never touched *her*," Neal said. "I was back *to* her. And she come over and let me have it right on the stern."

"He—" Maggie began something, but Neal caught her eye. She stopped, looking sorrowfully at Mertis.

"Mertis?"

"I can't *stand* him," Mertis stated loudly.

Mama turned Mertis over. She put on two spanks, only two, but good ones.

A pleased look came into Neal's face. He stopped crying and blew his bloody nose.

Mama reached for him.

"Twelve years old, going on thirteen, and having knock-down-drag-outs with the girls!"

"But I never done nothing, Mama—"

Out of the corner of his eye, Neal saw that Aunt Lynnie had come into the orchard, and oh, horror! Mrs. Clawson was just behind her, standing with a polite expression. Surely Mama wasn't going to lick him in front of the summer people. But she was.

When the Clawsons first came, Neal had overheard Mrs. Clawson say something about him to Miss Flora, her daughter.

"The next-to-oldest boy is good-looking, isn't he? Polite, too. So different from most of the scrubby children you see in these horrid little towns."

Neal was surprised. All he'd done was lug up some suitcases, the way Mama'd told him to, and he hadn't acted particularly polite. He was pretty sore about the boarders, anyway—he felt the way Aunt Candy did. If you took summer people, you lowered your whole family. Aunt Candy'd taken him into her room and told him all about the Ellises —how they'd always been the town's biggest, most important family. If you went back far enough, she said, you'd find they were descended from one of the English kings. It was criminal, she said, for any such family to lower itself so, and, "Neal," she said, "if there's any way you can make this riffraff that your mother's bringing into the house, uncomfortable, I wish you'd do it. Because that's all it is—it's riffraff."

She'd given him some salted almonds, too, which was more than any of the other kids ever got out of Aunt Candy.

He didn't see how he could make the Clawsons and Mr. Raymond uncomfortable without getting into awful trouble with his mother. He supposed he'd have to do something, sometime, if he was going to stay on Aunt Candy's good side. But, in the meantime, Mrs. Clawson had said that about him, and it seemed the least he could do was try to live up to it.

He began to wriggle away from Jen, and he saw, at once, that it was a mistake. If he had kept still, he would have got two licks, the way Mertis had, for Mama was always fair about such things. Now she gathered in his flailing arms and legs and put on some good ones, and it was enough to stop anyone fighting.

"There!" she said. "You both hop it into the house. Mertis, you take Neal's shirt, and, Neal, you take Mertis's. I don't want to see either one of you again until them clothes is cleaned up."

Jen turned around and her cheeks grew pink as she saw Mrs. Clawson. "I'm sorry about such a touse," she said. "You have to lick them, sometimes."

"Oh, do you think so?" Mrs. Clawson said. "Some people do, of course, but I brought up Flora without it, and I'm sure I've never been sorry."

Jen opened her mouth to say that if *she* had anyone like Miss Flora Clawson, she'd have put her in a bag and drowned her when she was small, but she thought and stopped in time. After all, these were the boarders. And just then, too, Lynnie let out a squeal.

"My soul, Jen, will you look at Evelyn? She's supposed to be getting dinner."

Evelyn was standing on the far side of the orchard, looking up into the Duchess tree at its cloud of blossoms.

"Oh, dear," Jen said.

She'd known from the beginning that she shouldn't have gone traipsing off, this morning. All that work to do, she should have done it, not gone paddling around in the swamp after violets. What on earth had she been thinking of, depending on Evelyn? But it had been such a lovely day!

Lynnie tossed back her curly bob, and the corners of her mouth quivered. She was the youngest of Guy's sisters, twenty-nine, and the prettiest. She liked to laugh, and there was no denying it, Evelyn did look funny, with the poke bonnet tilted upwards on top of her small shoulders and back.

"Well, never mind," Jen said. "I can snap up a dinner in no time at all, I expect."

"The boarders'll be ravening like buffaloes," Lynnie said, with a grin, sideways, at Mrs. Clawson.

Mrs. Clawson didn't smile back. She stared at Evelyn.

"What an, er, unusual hat!" she said.

Jen said, "My sister-in-law sunburns."

She couldn't keep the shortness out of her voice. Evelyn's bonnet might be queer, but doubtless she had her reasons for wearing it. Jen didn't think sunburn was one of them—lots of times she'd seen Evelyn, when she thought no one was around, out of doors with her sunbonnet off. Jen had an idea it had something to do with Evelyn's terrible shyness—she didn't want people to look at her face. Though, of course, it wasn't a bad face. There was no call for Mrs. Clawson to stare as if she were seeing something out of a zoo.

7 1

Mrs. Clawson said, "Oh, I see." She stared a moment longer, then she turned to Jen. "I hope lunch won't be too late, er, Jen," she said. "Mr. Clawson so easily gets past his appetite."

She moved off down the path toward the house. Nobody said anything until her neat back in its blue jumper had gone out of sight around the corner.

Then, from somewhere behind them, Aunt Candace snorted.

"Lunch!" she said. "La-de-da."

Jen jumped. She just never could get used to the way Candace came up behind people, not making a sound.

Candace had followed the path through the orchard, on the way home from Claudie Allen's. She looked after Mrs. Clawson, her lips held tight together.

"She's just used to having her dinner at suppertime," Lynnie said defensively.

"Yes, and she'll die of ulcers, going to bed on top of all that hot food. It wouldn't hurt her, nor that fat little man of hers, either, to miss a meal a day for a while. Evelyn! What are you making a holy show of yourself for in that blasted sunbonnet? If you're going to wear it, you'd better keep yourself out of sight in the woods."

"Yes, you were supposed to be getting dinner," Lynnie called.

Evelyn did not turn around. Her voice came muffled. "The potatoes are almost peeled."

"Potatoes not peeled, and it past eleven!" Lynnie began to flutter.

"No sense to get flustrated," Jen said calmly. "It won't hurt them to wait ten minutes. You could go put the potatoes on yourself, Lynnie, if you're worried. Evelyn and I'll tend to the rest of it."

Something in her voice said, Never mind, Evelyn.

Candace snorted again. She and Lynnie started for the house.

Evelyn turned around and came over to Jen. There were traces of tears on her cheeks. She said, "I'm so foolish, Jen. I get sidetracked so."

"Oh, shoot," Jen said. "There's no harm done."

Sometimes, she thought, she'd like to take Candy and Lyn and bat their heads together. She glanced around the orchard. "Where's the baby? Where's my good old boy?"

Clay came out from behind the tree. He leaned against Jen's leg, his chin wet with a bubble of love. She swung him up into her arms and started for the house.

"I'll look after him, Jen," Evelyn said. "That's the least I can do." She held out her arms for Clay.

Dear Jen, she thought. If I could only tell her it was just the apple blossoms brought the tears to my eyes.

"I'm such a fool, Jen."

Maggie burst out, "Andy went yelling and screaming to her that there was a murder, Mama!"

Maggie, too, was indignant over Aunt Evelyn's tears.

Aunt Evelyn said, too late, "Sh-h, Maggie!"

Jen came to a full stop. "I might have known it!"

That limb, plaguing his aunts again, disrupting the whole household, when she tried so hard to keep the kids from being a bother! Her wrathful glance swept the orchard, the lilac bushes, the white birch clump by the brook where the playhouse was.

"Andy! And-ee!"

No Andy in the orchard, the lilac bushes empty. The birch clump held nothing but a red-winged blackbird who flew up with a squall as Jen called.

From far down the shore road, Andy admired the sound of Mama's voice. It was always beautiful; but when she called like that, it was a trumpet to war, a gale at sea, a deep-chested bird flying over a mountain. His throat tightened with love and poetry. But you couldn't very well be two places at once, and Aunt Evelyn *had* told him to go find Grampie.

7 3

ON the March morning, three months ago, when Jen had announced at the kitchen breakfast table that she was planning to take some boarders this summer, she found she had started a war.

Candace laid down her spoon and stared across the table.

"Boarders!" she said. "In this house? Have you gone crazy?"

Jen said, "Why not boarders, Candy? This great big house, with two bathrooms, and all those upstairs front rooms not being used. Besides, there's money in boarders, and goodness knows, we need some."

Candace's mouth snapped shut. Her nose grew sharp and thin.

"Oh, dear," Jen said. "We can talk it over without getting mad, can't we?"

Grampie had warned her that Candace wasn't going to like the idea of boarders, but Jen hadn't been prepared for anything as mean as this. Candace had turned white; her hands were clenched around her coffee cup.

I suppose I could live a lifetime with Guy's sisters, Jen thought, and still not have any notion how one of them works inside.

When Guy had insisted on their moving into his father's house, Jen had fought against it. She loved Grampie, but she had never been able to feel at home with the rest of Guy's family, and she knew they didn't with her. Candace had made no bones of saying, through the years, that Guy had married beneath him. Old Grammie Ellis, Grampie Jebron's mother, who had run the house for years after his wife, Susan, died, had fought Guy's marriage tooth and nail. When she died, a few months after the wedding, she had left Guy out of her will. Guy said his marrying had nothing to do with that. Gram just didn't like boys—she had left Chris out, too. But Jen had her suspicions. She had always avoided the Ellises as much as possible.

7 4

She and Guy had had their family in a series of rented houses around the town; for Guy owned nothing except the small plot down on the shore on which his fishhouse stood. They could have moved in with Grampie long ago; but Jen knew how much Guy always depended on his father, running to him to borrow when he was low on cash; she was sure that if they were living in Grampie's house, the old man would be called on to foot the bills. After living with Guy so many years, you didn't need a compass to point the course he would run.

The war years were profitable for fishermen. Guy hadn't been drafted—fishing was an essential industry. Prices were high and he had done well, not saving much. Guy never saved. He had had some business projects which never came to anything, the last of them the partnership in Johnny Allen's fish-packing scheme. Johnny, one morning, had kicked him down the front steps of the office, in plain view of the whole town. Johnny hadn't said why, but Jen could guess. Ducks and drakes with the money.

Whatever it was, Johnny had paid a sizable fine to the government, and shortly afterward he had closed down the business, turning the wharf into a lobster-buying and marine-supply establishment, which he now operated with Russ.

From then on, Guy went from bad to worse. He came home one day, flung a dollar bill on the table and announced it was the last one he had. The engine in his old boat had sprung a leak that couldn't be repaired. He couldn't pay his back bills, let alone get credit for any new ones. So Jen gave up at last, and they moved the family in with Grampie.

She didn't plan to stay. She had made Guy promise that, as soon as his dragger was built, they'd look for another house. But now she didn't know what she could do.

It wasn't as if the old Ellis place didn't have room. It had been built in the early eighteen-hundreds, originally, so Grampie said, for a tavern, and remodeled two or three times through the years, but never made any smaller. In fact, James Ellis, Grandfather Malcolm's father, had added an L. James had had, in the course of his lifetime, three wives and nineteen children. The old house had accommodated his establishment with rooms to spare. Gram Ellis, the old lady, in the days of prosperity, had put in upstairs and downstairs bathrooms, a summer dining room, glassed-in front and back porches.

After her death, the family made no attempt to use the upstairs front rooms. Candace had them cleaned, spring and fall. She hired Myrabel Evans to come up from downtown, and Myrabel scrubbed and washed curtains and aired bedding. When she was done, that was all. There the rooms sat, clean and empty, never used. In winter, to save heat, the front stairs were closed off entirely by a fitted beaverboard partition, the water turned off in the upstairs bathroom. There was a long hall up there, and eight fine, furnished bedrooms, each with some kind of heating apparatus, either a fireplace or a stove; but to make them habitable in winter would have cost a fortune in fuel. And, of course, there was no need.

Candace and Evelyn and Lynnie slept in the downstairs bedrooms, which clustered snugly about the main house's four big chimneys, and Grampie's room was one of two in the L, where there was another chimney to heat the summer kitchen.

When Jen and Guy moved in, it had seemed sensible to use the backstairs rooms over the kitchen. The kitchen alone was tremendous, swallowing up stove, cupboards, sink and china closets, a table big enough to seat a dozen people, and still leaving plenty of space, so that Jen often wished for roller skates. Over it were five back rooms, including a big one with west windows. Two rooms were warmed by hot-air registers through the kitchen ceiling; in winter an airtight could be set up, which made the backstairs as comfortable as a big old New England house ever could be in cold weather. It was warmer for the children and more convenient and Jen would have chosen the backstairs, even if Candace hadn't made it clear that she'd rather not have the youngones in the front of the house.

After a while, Jeb had wanted to go out into the L bedroom next to Grampie. Jen had let him, first making sure Grampie wouldn't mind. From the beginning, she had been determined that Grampie's household shouldn't be disrupted. Children were always a nuisance, even in a house as big as this one, to four people who weren't used to them. Grampie and Evelyn loved having them around and showed it. Lynnie didn't care one way or the other. But Candace was edgy as could be. Jen kept a firm hand on her kids—a firmer one than she ever would have in her own house. To make up for everything, she duffed into the housework. As time went on, she took over the management of the house.

Not that Guy's sisters minded. They were delighted to have her do it. None of them was practical about running a house. Jen wondered what on earth they'd done before she'd come. She suspected that Grampie must have done most of the cooking. The girls didn't seem to be able to so much as fry an egg; and as for the house, she found slack tracks all over it—dried wugments of left-overs, months old, in the huge, old-fashioned icebox, venerable dust-kittens under rugs and furniture. But, of course, the girls had never had any training.

When their grandmother was living, she had kept hired help; Jossie Evans, Myrabel's mother, had worked for her for years, and Myrabel, too, off and on, while she was growing up. Grammie had never considered it suitable for the Ellis girls to work in the kitchen.

Grampie had wanted them all to go away to school. Candace had refused to leave home; Evelyn had gone somewhere for a while—to an art school in Boston, Jen had heard Guy say, though Evelyn never mentioned it. By the time Lynnie had got ready to go, her father's money was gone. Grammie Ellis hadn't approved of sending girls away to school, and Lynnie had gone to the local high school.

Of the three, Lynnie was the only one who had ever had a job. She helped in the library off and on, and each year at Christmas-time, she clerked in the dry goods store through the rush season. She had wanted desperately to go away to school; she was bitter, now, sometimes, because she hadn't. She seemed to be the most outgoing and capable of the three; but like the others, she didn't know the first principle about housework.

They had other occupations to take up their time. Candace read a great deal. She was surprisingly well-informed for a woman who hadn't had much schooling. If she felt like it, she could talk well on almost any subject that might come up. She sewed beautifully; and she belonged to every women's organization in town—the V.I.A., the Dorcas Society, the Literary Club, the Ladies' Aid, the lodges. Lynnie had a social life which kept her on the go; she had a good many friends and acquaintances among the summer people. Evelyn spent most of her time walking in the woods or sitting alone in her room. What she did, no one seemed to know. Except for the children, who seemed to be fascinated by everything Aunt Evelyn did, no one seemed to care.

There was no evidence in her room that she did any work, so far as Jen could see when she went in to clean and dust once a week. The room was as bare as a hotel room, and as impersonal, with Evelyn's cot-bed, almost like a child's bed, always tautly made under its white, tucked-in spread; a rocking chair by the window which looked out over the water; a big, bare deal table, with a straight chair placed so that whoever sat in it would be back to the door. A huge mahogany wardrobe occupied one wall, almost from floor to ceiling. Its doors and drawers were always discreetly closed. The bureau drawers were closed. The only possessions of Evelyn's in sight were a brush and comb, laid neatly on the bureau. There was one picture in the room—a framed, colored print of St. Cecelia at the Organ, with cherubs flying around her head. It had apparently hung in its place for years, for the wallpaper behind it, pink rose garlands on a white ground, was fresh and bright.

Jen had been in the room only once when Evelyn was there, and then almost by accident. She hadn't been able to make her hear a call to dinner; she had looked in the door to speak to her. Evelyn had jumped and scrabbled at something on the table in front of her, in an upset kind of way; Jen had never done it again. She was puzzled. She never snooped herself, and she agreed that if anyone wished to keep her own room private she surely had a right to; but in a good many ways, Evelyn was peculiar.

Those sunbonnets, for instance. She made them herself, wore them winter and summer, and looked like the wrath of God in them. People laughed at them on the streets. They drove Candace wild. But Evelyn wore them. She said, merely, that she sunburned and that she didn't feel at home in a hat.

When she took off her sunbonnet, you saw that her face was pleasant—oval-shaped and gentle, the cheeks a delicate pink which could change quickly, sometimes for no reason anyone could see, to a fierce, embarrassed red. Most of the time, you were hardly aware of her; you could come into a room where she was almost without realizing that she was there. Occasionally, Jen would notice, in the quiet gray eyes behind the glasses, a startling look, penetrating and aware. But you never did know what Evelyn was thinking. She was like a door closed in your face.

Candace had a good deal to do with Evelyn being the way she was, Jen knew. Candace had a tongue that would skin a burdock; sometimes when she started in on Evelyn, Jen had to bite her own tongue to keep from duffing in on it. If only Evelyn would fight back! But she never did. She would get a remote, folded-away look; occasionally, she would cry. Then she would vanish into her room or out of doors and be gone for hours.

Jen could understand that if you liked to keep your affairs to yourself, Candy's ways would be hard to put up with. Candy seemed to know everything that went on, no matter whether it was her business or not. She had a way of appearing behind people. Jen would be working, alone, somewhere in the house; she would happen to glance up, and there would be Candy. You couldn't tell how long she had been there; she would not be watching you. Candy never watched. Usually, what Jen saw was her lean back, in the neat, straight up-and-down sprigged housedress, and her smooth scroll of brown, gray-streaked back hair. But anyone would know that one flick of those quick black eyes had been enough to see what you were doing.

So far, relations on the surface had been smooth. But now, looking at Candy's face across the breakfast table, Jen realized she must have known all along that someday, about something, she and Candy had been bound to tangle.

"I'm sure we don't have to get mad," she said.

"I am *not* mad!" Candy said, and she bit into a piece of toast with a crack.

Andy giggled.

Jen said quietly, "Mertis, you and Neal take the kids out into the L kitchen. There's a fire in the stove out there, and you can have some doughnuts and make-believe coffee."

Lord, she thought, herding their reluctant bodies out of the kitchen. I *would* start this on a Saturday morning when the kids are all home.

Neal said, "Aw, Ma, I hate that darned cambric tea,"

and so all the others at once decided that the hot water and milk and sugar, sometimes considered a treat, was too horrible even to think of. It was too sweet, it hadn't any taste, it even made you sick. It *had* made Maggie sick once, only she never told anybody; and Andy gave forth a loud retching sound.

"Andy, stop that!" Jen said.

She looked at the graduated row of disgusted faces and couldn't help laughing. Drat 'em, they knew something would be going on in the kitchen.

"All right," she said. "You can have the picnic coffeepot and make yourselves some real coffee. There's a package of Kool-Ade in the cupboard, too. You can have that."

This laxity on her part took the wind right out of their sails. They were allowed coffee—a mild mixture of Jen's brewing—only on holidays; and the Kool-Ade was kept for picnics.

Jen left them boiling their own mixture over the L kitchen stove, and came in and shut the door. She had built a fire out there early, because after breakfast she intended to do the washing, and she thanked the Lord she had. If she and Candy were going to have the kind of argument that seemed to be banking up, then they'd better be by themselves.

Evelyn was up, somewhere around the house, but Lynnie was still in bed. Jeb and Grampie had left early to go out and haul Grampie's lobster traps, because it was a quiet day, and there were few enough days in March when the wind wasn't blowing a gale. So far, Grampie had been able to get only three hauls in as many weeks, which meant a big bill at the grocery store piling up. It was the grocery bill which had brought a good many things to a focus, and had made Jen mention the matter of taking boarders to Grampie last night and to Candace this morning.

Since Guy's death, six months ago, Jen had been worried out of her life about Grampie. It wasn't anything you could put your finger on. He might be a little thinner, but he always had been thin, and his appetite was as good as ever. The only thing Jen could liken it to was a clock with the mainspring slacked off.

Well, it was no wonder. Like her, he was worried to death over how to support such a tremendous family; and he probably felt the same way she, herself, did about Guy. Neither of them had been all wrapped up in Guy. They had spent too many years trying to get along with him, covering up his shady deals, paying his bills. For years, Jen hadn't loved him; but she had when she married him, and they had had six children together.

His dying didn't make you forget what he had become; but for a while you could think only of the pleasant times. The first night you were married. The first house you had, when you were eighteen and Guy was nineteen and Jeb was coming. Before he started to waste himself and everyone around him; for he had had it in him to make a good and decent man.

You wondered what had boiled up in him to make him go the way he had; how much he was to blame, or other people were, or the kind of a world he had to live and earn a living in, after the Ellises lost their money.

Was it the lost money, and his having to start scraping, with only an old, badly equipped boat, lobster-fishing, to keep his family going? But Guy had been the worst when he was making money, when he had had the finest boat that money could buy.

Maybe it was my fault, she thought. But I did the best I could with it. And I never wanted to stop loving him.

Now that he was gone, she felt a terrible sense of failure.

If we'd known what to do, how to put our finger on it, how to get at Guy. If we'd tried harder. But you get the habit of thinking people are permanent, and then, all at once, it's too late.

It had been like a woods fire starting—you see a little

wisp of smoke in the trees, and you think, "Somebody'll put it out, it'll go out itself," when what you should do was run, everybody, with brooms and buckets of water and wet crocus sacks, and mash it out before it got to be the monster nobody could touch.

And yet it was foolish to think like that. Remembering her life with Guy, she couldn't think of a thing anyone could do that she hadn't tried. Or had there been something?

And that must be the way Grampie's feeling now, too—wondering if it was his fault the way I wonder if it was mine.

Grampie's memories would be of a little boy. Like Andy. For everyone said that Andy, now, was the image of Guy, and, if so, then Guy must have been a beautiful little boy and dearly loved.

During the first few nights after Guy's death, Jen made herself freeze over. If you slacked off, you could let it grow on you. Sometimes she wondered whether it had been the right thing to take herself so in hand, for there were times when she felt as if all kinds of things were tumbling around inside, wanting out. But she had too much to do to sit down and worry over that. Guy wasn't all gone. He had left some legacies.

Bills kept coming in from Bellport stores for things that Jen had no idea he'd bought—mostly, fancy boat-accessories that now lay rusting in twenty fathoms of water under the Weaver. A brass-bound, built-in compass to replace the serviceable one he already owned. A flush toilet to be put into the boat's forepeak, which he had had on board but not yet installed. Part of the bill for the radio, which he had told her was paid for.

His assets had been the lone, wet ten-dollar bill, brought home in Jeb's pocket the morning after Guy's death, and the fishhouse down at the shore on its small plot of ground. There was some gear in the fishhouse; Jen didn't know how much. She figured it was very little, and she could leave it to Jeb to attend to. Russ Allen wanted to buy the fishhouse and Guy's shore privilege. Jen had more than half made up her mind to sell it. She hated to; it was part of the Ellis family's original shore privilege, and Jeb wanted fiercely to keep it for his.

"I need that fishhouse, Ma," he told her.

"But, Jeb, you've got your schooling to finish. It'll be years before you could make good use of a fishhouse, if ever. I want you to train for something."

He said soberly, "Please don't sell it, Ma."

She said brusquely, "I may have to," thinking of the terrible mountain of Guy's bills, and Jeb picked up his hat and left the house. At the door, he gave her a long look, and his jaw came out.

Lord, she thought, he's grown this year.

He was going to make a big man, like the Keppels—his shoulders were tremendous already, and he stood nearly six feet tall. Seventeen this spring, and wild to leave school and go to work. Jen realized that he might have to, but she wasn't going to let him until she'd tried everything else. She could be stubborn, too, she thought, and her own jaw came out, in exactly the same way Jeb's had.

She had racked her brains for some place to go where she could take care of the children and still work and earn. She could get a job cooking at one of the Bellport hotels; but there was no place to leave the kids. They needed her, too—the baby was only two and a half. It was no use even thinking of their aunts. Candace and Lynnie, of course, wouldn't want to take care of them; Evelyn would love it, until she got one of her vague spells and forgot all about them, when they would be left to shift for themselves.

The old Ellis house, of course, was a woman-killer; practical nowadays for only one thing—to board and room summer people. Jen had had long experience with summer people. Her father, Jones Keppel, head chef at the Answell House, hadn't had any scruples about his children leaving school and helping him. In a way, Jen was glad he hadn't. Herself, she didn't have the kind of brains that learned things out of high-school books. But she had learned a great deal from Jones Keppel.

At first, she hadn't seen how she could even mention bringing summer people into Grampie's house. He would hate it, she knew. He had definite ideas about a man's responsibility to his womenfolks; and he considered her and the children his responsibility now.

"I want you to stay here, now, Jen," he said. "I don't want you to have too much worry over the children."

But he's sixty-nine, she thought. He can't possibly take on any such job.

Boarders in the house would probably start some of the old-time Ellises to spinning in their graves—Gram Ellis, Jen thought grimly, would probably do some fancy flip-flopping. But Old Smackover, who built the house, might approve. It wouldn't be the first time it had been used as a tavern.

Jen meant to use only the rooms that were now closed off—the upstairs, the parlor, the big summer dining room. It wouldn't disturb any of the family sleeping arrangements, but the aunts would have to make some minor adjustments, and it was a good deal to ask of them.

I thought when I came here I'd do my best not to disrupt anybody, she told herself ruefully. And now look what I'm thinking of!

She cudgeled her brains, trying to think of some other way. But there wasn't any other way.

The grocery bill decided her, once and for all. Jerry Coleman, the storekeeper, handed it to her with an embarrassed, "No hurry, Jen, only I made it out twice, and I guess you folks overlooked it."

Since Jen did the buying, she usually checked over the

bills before Grampie paid them. When there hadn't been any for February and March, she supposed Jerry hadn't sent them. She hadn't seen this one at all.

She said, "Why, I don't believe we've had this before, have we, Jerry?"

"Well, I give it to Candace a couple of times she was in here," he said, avoiding her eyes. "Maybe she forgot it." Jen ran her eye down the long columns on the paper. The family marketing was familiar, but there were many items besides. Expensive ones, too. Salted nuts and candied ginger, imported Huntley and Palmer biscuits that Jerry stocked especially for Candace—all the stuff she liked to nibble on and kept in her room so she wouldn't have to pass it around among the children.

All except Neal, of course. Candy was partial to Neal. She quite often invited him into her room and treated him, but never any of the others. Jen wished she wouldn't. It wasn't doing Neal any good—he was cocky enough, anyway, without being anybody's favorite. And it was just one more thing for Jen to worry over.

On the way home, Jen did some thinking. It wasn't any of her business what Candy charged at the store. The girls had always charged things to Grampie, and they weren't making any changes now.

The Lord knows, I charge enough to him myself. If it weren't for me and the kids, he could handle his bills, the way he always has.

When she got to the top of the hill, she didn't stop at the Ellis gate, but went on past it and turned in at the Allens'. It was nearly dinnertime and Russ would be home, she knew, because it was too windy today for the draggers to be out.

Claudie Allen, Russ's mother, greeted her with pleasure.

"Jen, lamb, you're a sight for sore eyes. I was saying to the boys, a few days ago, that I hadn't seen you for so long

I'd forgot what you looked like. Set right down to the table. I'm dishing up in a minute or so."

Claudie was a little, hearty woman, talkative, as Russ was; and the more company she could get for dinner, the better she liked it. Her husband, Harvard Allen, had been dead for years; she had brought up her two strapping sons alone, at times scratching gravel to do it, until they were big enough to take over. Season after season, she had packed herring at the sardine factory, or cooked and cleaned cottages for the summer people, never letting on how tough the sledding was. No matter if she had two dollars in her pocketbook and no prospects, her establishment remained gay, her kitchen pleasant to come into. Hard times, of course, were over now for Claudie. *Allen Bros., Lobster Buyers and Dealers in Marine Supplies,* was the solidest business in town.

Jen was fond of Claudie. She had known her for a long time. The Allens and the Ellises had always been next-door neighbors, though the Ellis place was so big that the houses did not stand very near together. Russ and Johnny had gone to school with Guy. Russ had stood up with Guy at his wedding. In whatever house around the town Jen and Guy had lived, the three Allens had been constant visitors, up until the time Guy and Johnny had had the fight, when Johnny had stopped coming, though Russ and Claudie didn't let it make any difference. Claudie had done her best to patch things up between Guy and Johnny until they'd got completely out of hand and anyone could see that it was no use; and Russ had just gone on trying to get Guy back on his feet. No one but Jen knew how hard Russ had tried; how many times he had covered up for Guy, lent him money. She thought likely there were a good many unrecorded small sums—maybe large ones— still owing to Russ. If so, there would never be any way of finding out what they were. Jen smiled, now, at Claudie.

"Thanks just the same, Claudie, but I've got to get back

or the kids'll have their Aunt Candy in the nuthouse. I thought if I barged in around dinnertime, I might find Russ home."

Russ and Johnny, who were sitting in the bay window, males waiting for their dinner, both grinned amiably at her.

"You see how it is, John," Russ said. "The best-looking women in town come after me, right into my own home." But then he said, soberly, "What's on your mind, Jen?"

"Do you still want to buy Guy's fishhouse and shore privilege?" she asked him.

"Sure do. I wasn't going to press you about it, because I know Jeb wants it. But if you're going to sell it, someone else will grab it, and I do want it, Jen."

"I wish I could keep it for Jeb. But I can't, Russ."

Russ nodded. "How about five hundred dollars?" he asked.

"Oh . . . is it worth as much as that?"

Johnny suddenly let out a snort. "For Godsakes, Russ, it's worth double five hundred, what's the matter with you?" he said gruffly.

Russ shot a glance at him, which Jen didn't miss.

"Sure, it is," he said quickly.

Jen said, "What goes on here? Five hundred seems plenty, to me."

"John knows more about property values than I do, Jen," Russ said. "He went into a lot of stuff like that with lawyers, when we bought the wharf." He grinned at her. "I'm a good dragger, but a doggoned poor business man."

That wasn't so, and Jen knew it. Men didn't come any smarter than Russ.

What they were doing, they were trying to help her out by paying twice what the fishhouse was worth. The Lord knew, she could use the money, but she mustn't let them. She was already indebted to the Allens for what they'd done for Guy.

"I don't believe you boys really need that fishhouse," she said. "You've got that great wharf and all those buildings—"

Johnny said, his voice still gruff, "That's the best shore privilege there is."

"Sure," Russ said. "The Ellises got here first, so they got their pick, right on the beach. The wharf's unhandy for me, Jen."

"Only thing is," Johnny said, "you sure you want to sell for a thousand? What does Jebron say? That shore privilege's valuable. It's been in the Ellis family a long time."

"You're fast talkers, both of you," Jen said. "Well, I can't let you, Johnny. After all you did for Guy—"

Johnny got to his feet. "Ayeh," he said.

He went over to the desk between the windows, got out his fountain pen and checkbook and wrote a check.

"That better be only for five hundred, Johnny," Jen said.

"Okay. It's for five hundred." He waved the check in the air to dry it. "Ma, for Petesake, where's all the blotters? When Russ moves into the fishhouse and fixes up the deed or the bill of sale, he'll give you the other five hundred. Otherwise, there's no deal."

"You take it, now, Jen," Claudie said. "You poor blessed lamb, you're starting in right where I did, only you've got six and I only had two. I can't think what a little extra would've meant to me then, only I do know it would've been God's living blessing."

"All right," Jen said. "I can't thank you, Johnny." She would have said more, but she couldn't trust her voice. She'd have a word to say, though, she thought, folding the check and putting it into her pocketbook, when Russ came around bringing that other five hundred.

Russ followed her to the door. "Look, I won't need the fishhouse till June, Jen. If Jeb wants to keep his gear down there, he can."

8 9

"You don't need it at all, Russ," she said, shaking her head at him.

"Here, hold on. Of course I do. But my real season, dragging fish, don't start till June, you know that. I'm pretty busy helping Johnny in the store, right now. So Jeb can finish his projects down there. I won't even ask him for the key."

"What projects? Jeb's projects, right now, are his school work."

Russ waved his hand largely, to indicate that a kid's projects took in at least half the horizon. "Oh, he might have a dozen. You can't tell."

It occurred to her, as she went back down the hill, that she didn't know how on earth she was going to face Jeb. All at once, it seemed to her dreadful to have gone and sold his place behind his back without even telling him first. For it had been his place—he had carted most of his things down there. Grampie said he even had his great-grandfather's old chart pinned up on the wall.

Maybe she could make it up to him, somehow. Right now, she didn't know what else she could have done, she needed the money so.

Five hundred was all she was going to let Russ and Johnny pay. She might be in a spot, but she was going to get out of it herself. There had been too many years of taking, taking, taking from other people, so that now the thought of doing it any longer sickened her.

Whatever happens I and the kids are going to stand on our own two feet from now on out if we sink so deep there's nothing but a bubble to show where we went down.

She deposited part of the five hundred at the bank; the rest of it she took to Coleman's and paid the grocery bill.

When she came out of Coleman's, to her surprise, she saw Russ waiting at the curb in his Chevvy.

"Well, you swallowed your dinner some quick," she hailed him. "You must have had pea-soup-in-a-jug."

"Nope. Steak and potatoes," he said. "Hop in, I'll ride your groceries home. I wanted to talk to you, Jen."

She got in, gracefully depositing the big bags of groceries in the back seat. Russ drove all the way up the hill without saying a word, which was an astonishing performance from him, and stopped the car at the Ellis gate.

"Jen," he said, "I don't know how to say this. You think Guy owed me and Johnny something."

"Of course I do. I don't know how many times you've helped him. If I ever have any money, I'm going to try to pay you."

Russ ran his big hand thoughtfully around the circumference of the steering wheel.

"It's a funny thing," he said slowly, "about Guy. I did try to boost him, a good many times, Jen. I don't mean only with money." He took a long breath and let it out slowly. "Along toward the last, it was like yanking up a meal sack. You prop him in one place, he'd sag down in another."

"Yes. I know that, Russ."

"The devil of it is, the whole thing's left me with the feeling that there was something more I could have done. Why, Jen, I knew him all my life. He was all right to begin with. Not like Chris. You never knew Chris, did you?"

"No, not well. He died the year I was married."

"Chris was about the only real, honest-to-God stinker I ever saw. Most men, you can find a little something to recommend them, but you couldn't with Chris. There was a story going around, Ma says, years ago, that he was a throwback to some old-time pirate the early Ellises got mixed up with. Chris got a hell of a kick out of that— figured it was smart to live up to it. But I didn't mean to get off on him. I was thinking of the difference between him and Guy."

He was silent a moment, his fingers still slowly traveling the smooth contour of the steering wheel.

"I feel bad," he said at last. "Like I'd stood by watching a house burn down, and it could've been stopped if we'd moved a little faster."

"What could we have done?" Jen said.

"I don't know. I don't know just how far one man's responsible for another one, but I've got an idea it's farther than most folks think. Know what Johnny said to me after you went out this noon? He says, 'You let some poor devil get down and out, it's surprising how many'll stand around feeling righteous, because they can afford to be honest themselves, pay their own bills. Look at the poor so-and-so, they say, he ain't got any character. When what they really mean is, to hell with you, Jack, I've got mine.' That's what Johnny said."

"Russ," Jen said, looking at him, "what on earth more could any of us have done? Grampie hasn't got enough left to take care of him in his old age. I'm going to try to take boarders this summer, and the Lord knows, I ain't scared of work, I'd have expected to, anyway. But the money I earn now ought to go to feed and clothe and educate the kids, not to pay for Guy's gadgets. I—I guess I believe in character, Russ. I know what you mean about Guy. He was likable and generous when he was sober, and I was a fool about him when I married him. But I know this much. If I was to see that wild streak coming out in one of the kids, I *don't* know but I'd just about kill him."

Jen's voice started to tremble and she stopped.

Russ took his hand off the steering wheel and laid it over hers. "I wouldn't blame you. But it wouldn't be a wonder if there was some of Guy in the kids, Jen. No harm if there was—some of him. Is one of them worrying you? Not Jeb."

"No, not Jeb. Not really. I notice little things in Neal sometimes. He's not wild, of course. But his Aunt Candy— I guess I worry over that. She works on him. I think she promises him stuff, I'm not sure."

"Yeah," Russ said thoughtfully. "I would watch that, if I was you, Jen. Candy was always old lady Ellis's favorite, you know. Ma used to say the two of them made quite a combination."

"What was Guy's mother like?" Jen asked suddenly.

"Susan? I was talking about their grandmother, old Malcolm's wife, and she was a hellion. I don't remember Susan much, she died young. She never was very well, and old Gram Ellis ran her ragged. Always took the kids' parts against her, butted in on running the house. Things like that. Candy takes after her, you know it?"

Jen smiled grimly. "Yes. I know it."

"Why, the old lady even named all those kids—picked the names out of books she was reading. Not much like the old family names, are they?" Russ grinned. "I can just remember the touse that went up when Jebron wanted to call Marilyn Susan, after her mother. They even started calling her Sue. Gram Ellis called her Marilyn from the start. She cut up so over it that Susan and Jebron gave in for the sake of peace in the house."

"Why on earth did she care if it was only a name she picked out of a book?"

"No reason—she just wanted her own way. Boy, I'll never forget that old girl. To look at her, you'd think she was one of the nicest old ladies you ever saw in your life. I remember she used to have soft white hair and wear one of them little purple knit hug-me-tights. But, Jesus, if there was ever a steel trap in a velvet glove!"

His hand felt firm and comforting, and Jen turned hers over, so she could close her fingers around it.

"She didn't live very long after Jebron lost the boatyard in '32," Russ went on. "Ma says what time she did live, she made Jebron's life miserable, blaming him for throwing away the family dough."

"Poor old Grampie," Jen said.

"Ayeh, he's had it tough, in his lifetime." He went on

9 3

reflectively. "I was talking to Johnny, like I said. I kind of go along with what he says about character. It ain't what a man's born with, it's what happens to him."

"Why didn't Grampie go under then, Russ? He's had things worse than Guy ever had."

"Old lady Ellis brought Guy up, Jen. She laid down the law to all them kids that self-respect was money. She never let on to them what would happen if they lost the money. Johnny was figuring he was a little mite hard on Guy. He figures maybe he was part to blame, kicking him out of the business, like that. We, any of us, ought to've known Guy couldn't take it. We'd like to help you out some, Jen."

"You are helping," she said. "I don't know how to thank you, Russ."

"No, I mean help you," he said soberly. "It's too much for any woman with all them kids. Johnny'd feel a whole lot better if—"

"You beat all, the two of you," she said. "Nobody knows how much Guy cost Johnny. And you—after all you've done, you come apologizing to me because you didn't do more. I know how you feel, Russ. Me, too—I've racked my brain wondering where I went wrong, what I didn't do for him. And Grampie's doing the same thing—I've been worried to death about him lately. But, Russ, we've all got to look at it the way it was. With somebody like Guy, sick or a drunk, whatever you want to call it, no matter what you did for him, or how far you ran yourself into the ground, there'd never be any end to it until he died."

"Promise me you'll come to us if the sledding gets too tough," he said, not looking at her.

Jen shook her head. "Here, already, you've bought a fishhouse you don't need," she said.

"I do, too, need it," he said crossly. "I'll give you the other five hundred any time."

"No, you won't. And you know I thank you for it, Russ,

94

and for letting Jeb borrow it. I'll tell him to get out of it as soon as he can."

"Women!" Russ exploded. "Yattita, yattita, yattita! If I had a wife, I'd tie her tongue to a brick. You let Jeb alone. He and I'll work it out between us."

Jen got out of the car. Russ got out the other side, irately yanking her bundles out of the back seat. He carried them into the kitchen for her, came back and got into the car without another word.

Jen watched the car move away down the hill. After knowing him so many years, she could tell that he wasn't really sore—only more deeply moved than he wanted to show. She could hear him and Johnny now, having it over—knowing that they didn't owe Guy anything, but both of them as sure as they stood up in their boots that a little arguing would convince her that they did. It was decent of them—so decent that she had all she could do to keep from putting her hands up over her face and starting in to howl.

That night, after everyone else had gone to bed, she handed Grampie the receipted grocery bill. They were sitting by the kitchen table, he with his paper, she with her mending. All evening, while she had been waiting for Candy to go to bed, Jen had been working at a great heap of the boys' socks in the darning basket. It beat all how they did it—a sock would be new one day, and the next, it would have a foot and leg, but a great, yawning, scraggled-out maw where the heel had been.

Candy always seemed to know by instinct—or maybe a sense of smell—when something was in the wind. Ordinarily, she went to bed at nine o'clock, but tonight it was nearly eleven before she picked up her embroidery and went to her room.

You might know, Jen thought, that I had something private to talk over with Grampie.

For a long time, after he had examined the bill,

Grampie sat looking off over the edge of his newspaper, thinking.

"Grampie," Jen said, at last, "can I be a camel in the tent and fill your house up with boarders this summer?"

Grampie started. "Why," he said slowly, "I don't know's there's need of that, is there, Jen?"

Something in her silence made him look over at her and Jen looked back at him. He flushed a little.

"You had to sell the fishhouse," he said.

She nodded.

"I'm sorry, Jen. I wish you hadn't."

"I'm sorry, too. I know it had been the Ellis fishhouse for a long time, Grampie."

"Things like that don't amount to a hoot," he said. "Not compared to people. I meant I was sorry you had to have the money."

"My soul, Grampie! Here I am like a mountain on you with six kids, and you say you're sorry you can't pay my bills!" She almost said "too," but stopped in time.

"And I was thinking about Jebby," Grampie said. "He's going to feel bad. He had plans for that fishhouse."

"I know he did. Russ says he can use it till June."

"That'll help some."

You could see Grampie didn't think it would help much.

"I expected to have a time with Jeb," she said, thoughtfully. "I hope he won't feel I did it because I don't want him to leave school and go fishing."

Grampie said, "Jebby's set his heart on going fishing, Jen."

"He can't leave school with only one year to go. I want him to study, Grampie. To—to train himself for something. Not to have things so hard."

"He'll keep his shirt on," Grampie said gruffly. "He's about as smart as they come, Jen. Well, maybe things'll pick up come spring. They're a mite slow now, I know."

9 6

He looked at the grocery bill that lay on the table by his hand.

"Candy's a sensible woman in a good many ways," he said.

The blood came right up into Jen's head. She fired off before she could stop herself.

"I wouldn't touch a penny of her money with a ten-foot pole," she said. "But she might at least pay for her own salted nuts at two dollars a pound."

For a minute Grampie didn't say anything.

"When I failed up with the boatyard in '32, it knocked the pins out from under everyone, about money," he said, at last. "I expect Candy knows that when I'm gone, that money of her grandmother's is all that stands between her and cold charity. I was kind of hoping I could fix things up for them all. Maybe I can yet."

"Oh, dear," Jen said. "Tell me to mind my own business, Grampie."

She supposed she sounded kind of short, but she was feeling too bad herself to stop and think how to say things. She didn't know how Grampie worked, inside, any more than she did his daughters; she only knew she loved him. But now she could see he was feeling much worse than he'd ever let on.

I shouldn't have paid that bill without telling him, she thought miserably. It's made him feel belittled.

After all, Grampie belonged to the generation of men-folks who handled the money matters themselves, took pride in not letting such things worry the women.

But ten of us, living on him like a lot of suckers!

She hoped her feelings didn't show in her face, but apparently they did. Grampie glanced at her. Then he looked away.

"I never thought when my children was growing up that they'd need to turn their hands to anything," Grampie said. "Their grandmother didn't want them to work, so I never put my foot down. Even with Guy. He had schooling. He had the best of everything I could buy. I always said I—didn't want him to have things so hard."

He stopped, and for a moment Jen heard the echo of her own words dying in the room.

"Pa and I between us," he went on, "we made a lot of money in our time. I guess I thought the best way to use it was to make things easy for my kids. I never learnt them to work. So now they can't. The girls can't turn a hand over. Chris killed himself with a car. Guy was a drunk."

Jen tried to think of something she could say. He mustn't be let to feel like this. She said, "Well, I know how to work, Grampie," and stopped; and then went on a little wildly, choking on it, knowing how foolish it would sound, "There's a cream cake in the cupboard I'd like to have you sample."

He looked over at her and smiled. "Never mind, Jen."

She went and got the cake and put it on the kitchen table by his elbow.

"See if you think summer boarders might not pay pretty good to have some of that," she said. "How about if I make up a pot of coffee, go with it?"

"Gorry," he said. "That'd go good."

Poor old guffer, she thought, moving between the cupboard and the stove. There he sets, after a lifetime of the hardest kind of work, with nothing to show for it but this great ark of a house eating up taxes, and three of the uselessest womenfolks it's ever been my bad luck to see.

Where did his kids come from, anyway? They sure must've got that way from old lady Ellis. They sure never did from him.

She thought suddenly of the men behind Grampie, the men like him, going back through the generations to the time when people first came to Candlemas Bay. You saw their tracks all over a town like this. The schoolhouse. The church. The town hall. This house. They built big.

and they built strong. Some of their buildings had lasted for two hundred years.

Nathan, Daniel, James, Malcolm, Jebron.

Oh, Lord, she told herself, the tears running down her face. I've worked up a good one. I better stop. Right now.

But to think of all that, petering out into Guy.

Into Guy, and men like him, because if you looked around, you couldn't help but realize how many there were like Guy. Irresponsible. Grabby. Dishonest. Everywhere you looked. The radio news and the papers full of stuff that made you ashamed to read about human beings doing it.

A man who wouldn't take an honest job of work when it was offered, because he had unemployment insurance coming. Farmers selling surplus crops to the government for a dollar a bushel and buying them back for a cent to use for cattle feed; only before the government sold them back, it had to dye them blue, so that no one could sell them for surplus again and collect twice. Men who said outright that any deal was all right, just so you made money; men who said, what the hell, if you wanted to stay in business, you did what everyone else did.

What kind of works was that, to take a good thing like a potato and dye it blue? There were a hundred other things you could do with it, even if you only sliced it in two and used it to take the dirt off a dime. A family of eleven could eat a peck of potatoes to a lick, and that cost you fifty-eight cents. And there were places in the world where if a man had a peck of potatoes, he'd be considered the well-to-do man in his town.

Why, there ought to be a big monument with a baked potato on top of it, set up where everyone could see, to remind people of the things that really kept them going. For when you came right down to it, what was there better on earth, or needed more, than a good baked potato?

A tear dropped down and sizzled on the stove.

Oh, stop it, you fool! Jen told herself. Howling over potatoes!

But she couldn't stop. Because it wasn't just potatoes. Something was coming out that, through all the years of living with Guy, she'd kept firmly pushed down out of sight. If you had something real to fight, you fought it and it took up your mind. But now you couldn't help but wonder if it wasn't not just Guy's dishonesty and waste, but the same thing loose in the whole world. Things like blue potatoes, that made your stomach roll right over.

Jeb? she thought, with a clutch at her heart.

Neal, Andy, Clay?

They ought to grow up to be good men. But what kind of men could they be, in the world as it was now, as it was to come? Because, if you looked around you, you couldn't see, anywhere, a man like Grampie.

Jen made furtive swipes at the tears, because if he ever saw her crying, she'd go right through the floor. She took a firm hold of herself. She grabbed the coffeepot and poured out, and took the cups over to the table.

"You reading about all the potatoes being dyed blue?" she said brusquely, more to hear the sound of her own voice and get her common sense back than to know what he was doing.

"What?" Grampie said.

He hadn't been reading, only thinking behind the paper; but now he looked at the headline.

CONGRESSMAN SAYS ATOM BOMB WILL BE USED IN TIME, it said.

It was in smaller print, about the potatoes.

"Oh. Ayeh," Grampie said. "No telling how much of that is politics. Whichever party's in, the other one tries to make people think the country's on the rocks, and they've sure done a job of it this time." He folded the paper, tossed it into the woodbox. "It don't make sense, does it? Makes you feel as if the whole world's gone to pot—stock's run to weeds, like mine did. Maybe they just better go ahead and blow her up. But if you think about it, you get scared of the time to come."

Something in Jen jiggled back into place. It was partly the shock of hearing Grampie agree with her, partly the realization that what had started her off in the first place was the sight of a good man like him sitting there, old and discouraged, without anything he could lay his hands on.

What had ailed her, anyway? Of the men she knew, there was Grampie and Russ Allen now and Jeb to come, who could be trusted with any treasure you might care to name. And Jones Keppel had been as honest as the summer sun. You got overwrought, you forgot about the millions of others there must be.

How many men did she actually know who weaseled on their unemployment insurance or their surplus crops? For the one who did and got himself in the papers, how many must there be who didn't—only no one heard anything about them.

If you were the kind who could talk out such things with someone, you might get reminded that you were looking at one side of a thing that surely had two; that as far back as history had ever been written down, people in bad times must have felt the way you did, at some time or another.

"Well, I ain't scared," Jen said. "I *look* to the time to come. Maybe your stock's run to weeds. Mine ain't. I've got my kids, and they're part Guy, but there's me in them and you in them, and the old fellers who settled this place and made something with nothing but just their hands. I don't doubt the good times is gone and the world will be blowed up, if enough people set around on their arses and think so. Maybe we'll be blowed up, too, but we might's well live till we are. And if me and my kids and you happen to be amongst the ones left when the dust settles, we'll start in again, if all there is left to do with is a bent nail and a breadcrumb. They make me sick, squalling around. It's all I can do to keep from going out to puke."

"Jesus!" Grampie said. "That sounds good."

His face turned red. "Excuse me, Jen, I swore, but I ain't heard talk like that for a long time."

Jen's face was red, too. She guessed she hadn't minced words any, herself. But that was the way it was with her—if she got too wrought up, things sometimes came out rougher than she meant.

She glanced over at Grampie.

He had taken off his glasses and put them in their case, holding it in his hand. After a moment, he closed the case with a snap. She was pleased to see signs of his old spirits back in his face, but she wasn't prepared for the force in his voice when he began to speak again, nor for what he had to say.

"Jen, Jebby's building himself a string of lobster traps down in Guy's fishhouse."

"What?" Jen said, staring at him.

"Guy left some trap stuff in there. You know how Guy was, he never salvaged nothing—just got through with it and dropped it where it was. If he needed more, he bought new. I guess he figured there'd always be more where that came from. Well, he had rope and laths laying around from the time he went lobstering. Jebby, he cut his trap bows in the woods, and he traded work with Jerdon's mill for some sills. He'll have thirty-five traps, time school lets out in June."

"But he hasn't had the time—"

"He's used his spare time. He ain't played football or basketball, or any of them extra things high-school kids do. I don't say that's good, Jen. He's young. But most of our folks went to work before they was as old as he is."

Jen's jaw came out. "He'll go back to school in September. He ain't old enough to—"

"He's a man right now, if you let him be one. I see him do a thing last September that most men wouldn't, for an old chart that kids he's in school with couldn't read north on. If a boy wants to work, Jen, let him, not set around taking hand-outs from his folks."

"We'll decide it next fall," Jen said. "Besides, he hasn't any boat."

"He wants to fish double strings with me, till he can lay hands on a skiff." Grampie glanced at her slyly. "Some of them trap nails he's using are pretty bent. He straightens them out."

"Why, you old limb!" Jen had to smile in spite of herself.

He grinned at her, got up and started through the door to his room at the back of the L kitchen.

"Don't ask anyone else if you can take boarders, Jen," he said over his shoulder. "Just up'n do it. Because Candy's going to throw one hell of a whing-ding. Er . . . that was the best cake I ever et."

So here she was, Jen thought at the breakfast table, taking care of Candy's whing-ding, because if there was ever one on the way it was right now.

Lynnie still wasn't up, but Evelyn was sitting opposite Candace, already looking green around the gills. Poor Evelyn. She did hate rows. She had come casually in to breakfast, and had walked right into this one.

"You are not going to put boarders into this house," Candy stated, spacing the words evenly.

Jen said, "Yes. Yes, I am, Candy. I wouldn't if I didn't have to earn some money. But you know your father's failed some in the last few months—"

"If he has, I haven't noticed it."

You wouldn't, Jen thought, setting her teeth. He could wear himself to a shadow and you wouldn't notice it.

"It ain't fair to ask an old man to go on taking all the expense of this great family. There's eleven of us."

"Whose fault's that?"

"Partly mine," Jen said steadily. "I'm sorry I haven't any other place to go. But I do do the work and the marketing and run the house—"

"I hope you don't think that pays your way. All those children."

Jen felt herself beginning to go hot behind the eyes. It meant she was going to get mad, and she'd hoped she wouldn't. She glanced at Evelyn, who was staring at her plate, a kind of glaze over her eyes.

"Evelyn, you wouldn't like to see what the kids are up to, would you?" Jen asked. "I don't doubt, by now, they're boiling up each other. And please ask Neal to be sure the fire doesn't go out? I've got to wash, after breakfast."

"You sit right there, Evelyn!" Candace snapped. "I don't want anyone to miss a word of what's going on here. Now, you listen to me, Jen Keppel."

"I'm listening," Jen said grimly.

"I don't suppose it would mean much to you, your folks being foreigners, but this house was built in 1810. A respectable family's always lived in it. People who never scratched the backs of anyone, and who are not going to start now."

Jen thought, That does it.

"Some of you lovely respectable people better start scratching gravel, then," she said. "Or you'll get a court order for some grocery bills. Grampie Keppel might have been nothing but an old Dutch cobbler, but, by gorry, when he died his bills was paid."

Candace took a deep breath, leaned over and shook a lean finger under Jen's nose. Jen grabbed the finger and closed her big fist on it.

"Now, you wait," she said. "It ain't often you have to listen around here, but now you listen to me. I know my being here's partly responsible for the size of the bills. But I ain't responsible for being here. I fought Guy for years about coming here to live, and now I'm stuck. What I'm trying to do is the best I can, and keep Grampie from working himself to death. I know who built this house, Candy. Old Smackover Ellis built it, to run for a tavern."

Candace yanked away her finger.

"It was *Daniel* Ellis! And this house was *never* a tavern of any kind!"

Jen smiled briefly.

"Whatever Ellis built it, he was pretty nigh as close to being a foreigner, in them days, as the Keppels ever was."

"That, if I were you, I shouldn't wish to discuss."

"I'm a cook," Jen said evenly. "I've understood for years how you felt about Guy's marrying a common cook. Well, I ain't a common cook. I'm an uncommon one. When Guy married me, I was making more money in a week than he could in a month. Now he's dead, and he ain't left me nothing but a mess of bills."

"You're *speaking* about the dead," Candace said icily.

"I respect the dead as much as you do. But I don't feel a call to be sanctimonious about what they did while they was living. Now, Candy, I won't live on Grampie for nothing any longer, you can put that in your pipe and smoke it."

"Kindly watch your tongue. I don't care to be spoken to like that."

"I'm sorry," Jen said. "The way you're talking to me, as if I were the hired girl, ain't pleasant, either. I didn't intend to say so much, when I started. I've talked to Grampie, and he says to go ahead and use the house."

"He couldn't have! He's crazy."

"I'll try not to disturb you any more than I have to, Candy. But I've got to do it. There ain't another thing, and don't think I haven't tried to think of something else, either! Why don't you help me, and we'll go into it together?"

Candace stiffened where she sat.

"You've been talking money matters with Pa behind my back."

"Somebody had to."

"Then I think you should mind your own business."

Jen eyed her.

"This house has twenty-five rooms in it. There's a hundred and sixty acres of land. You tell me what the taxes on it are."

Candace got up and walked out of the room.

Taxes! she thought.

Of course she didn't know what the taxes were. Taxes were the men's business in any decent, well-bred family. Respectable womenfolks never bothered to find out about taxes.

She shut her bedroom door behind her, poked up the fire in her stove and sat down close to it, trembling with rage.

Boarders in this beautiful house that Grammie always took such care of! All those transients from the cities, whom you saw downstreet in the summertime, running in and out of the restaurants, jamming the roads in their cars, crowding the grocery stores until decent people who had some right there couldn't get to the counters. Right in your own home! It wasn't to be borne, and Pa ought to have told Jen so. He would have, if she didn't have him wound around her finger, the doddering old fool.

Maybe she's only after my money. When she finds she can't make me pay the bills that way, she'll try something else. They always have been after it, the whole kit and boodle of them.

Well, they won't get it. If I'd ever given one inch about that money, it would all be gone by now.

There it was, sitting in the bank, gathering interest every day. Not a cent had been touched since Grammie left it—fifteen thousand dollars, to begin with—seventeen years ago. It shouldn't be touched until there was need.

For who had she, Candace Ellis, to look to, now that all the menfolks were gone except Pa?

She thought of the old, strong men, Gramp Malcolm, Uncle Eben, Uncle William, Uncle John. They had looked after things, seen their womenfolks had enough. Not Chris, her elder brother, dead now like all the rest. Not Guy. They were like this younger generation. But even they would have been a little something, and they were gone, too.

Only children were left. Jeb . . . she didn't like Jeb. For all she could see, he was a Keppel. The little ones were nuisances, all under Jen's thumb. Neal . . . it was possible something might be done with Neal. But he was still a child, twelve years old.

Pa was failing. She had known it. Jen had put into words what Candace had refused to admit, even to herself. He was failing; and when he was gone, everything would go. This house, this land, where the Ellis family had stood on its feet for two hundred years.

Grammie's house.

Little Candy, Grammie's little dove, come straight down through the centuries from the blood of a king himself. Don't let anyone ever touch this house, Candy. People go, but a house abides. Once the house is gone, it's all gone.

Oh, Grammie.

The house was starting in to go right now, the way all the fine old houses went, as surely as if red rot had got into its solid beams and were eating it hourly down. Jen and her kind were everywhere. To them the wonderful heritage of a house and land meant nothing but how they could use it to make money out of the summer people. Sell the land for summer cottages. Fill up the house with boarders for a season or so, remodel it into a hotel. Then would come a bad year when the summer trade didn't show up, and the hotel would fail. There it would stand, windows broken out, doors banging in the wind, paint scaling off, an eyesore on the countryside. No good to anyone. Like the Griswold house.

Old Randall Griswold, in the '80's, had been one of the well-to-do men of the state, several times a State Representative, a power in all the political and money-making pies in the town.

And where were the Griswolds now? Their land was sold, the money spent. The womenfolks of the younger generation were working in the sardine factories, trying to keep their families' heads above water; or they were cooks and maids in the summer cottages. Their menfolks were caretakers or gardeners or deckhands on somebody's yacht. In the wintertime, none of them had any work. They lived on credit from the grocery stores, and during the depression they'd had to take food from the government.

Old Randall had lived to see the land go out from under him, and then he had died. Candace remembered him—a senile, tobacco-stained driveler, without two cents to rub together, prattling about his deals in shore property. The Griswold shore property, whose deeds dated back to the Revolution.

Candace glared at the stove as if she wanted to smash it, though, actually, she was not seeing it at all.

Pa must be failing or he'd never permit anybody's foot to get in the door with the Ellis property. And when he's gone, I'll be the only one left to hold the land. I'll need all Grammie's money to hold it.

Lynnie was a fool on wheels, there was nothing in her head but men. Soon she'd marry and be gone for good. Maybe she'd marry Russ Allen. Pray God she did. But Evelyn—I'll have to support Evelyn. She can't turn her hand to anything and she isn't even company. She's nothing. She's a child. She'd been better off if she'd died young.

Candace looked back through the years, seeing Evelyn.

Little sister Ev, with the "secrets," silently crying the round, clear tears. Ev, at sixteen, with her "secret" diary, that hadn't stayed a secret long. Ev, at twenty-five, nervous with people, happy only when she was alone.

Oh, the interminable hours Evelyn spent alone! Until Candy couldn't stand it any longer and went into her room. And then, scrabble, scrabble would go something over what Ev was doing, so you couldn't see. She kept that big old wardrobe of Gramp Malcolm's in there, locked, and the key on a chain around her neck.

Spending her time making toys out of clay, or whatever else witless and worthless they'd taught her at that art school.

Art school! The old fury Candace had felt when Pa let Ev go away to art school, came over her again. It was one of the few times Pa had stood up to Grammie, and Grammie had been right. A waste of money, she'd said it would be; and a waste of money it had been. Because if Ev had ever learned anything, no one ever found it out. Playthings for children was all it amounted to; and she had come home more unapproachable than ever.

Evelyn, at thirty-two, was as inaccessible as a rock. She kept a whole secret life that no one could touch, that clung inside her like a Chinaman's-hat seashell to a ledge. It drove you wild. You could spend a lifetime and not find out what went on behind Ev's pink, vague, foolish face.

She's nothing. She's a child.

She and Lynnie won't forgive me for not letting them have part of Grammie's money. But what would Ev know about money? And Lynnie—five minutes, and she'd fritter it all away.

So there it was, untouched, a fire against the cold, a roof against the night, when other fires and other roofs should fail. If you kept it, you could keep other things that, once lost, were gone forever. So long as it was there, you could bear to grow old.

The stove wasn't very hot. It was cold in Candy's room and the woodbox empty. Oh, for the old dear days back again, when Grammie ran the house like silk and saw that Jossie Evans kept every woodbox full! This March weather was worse than December when it came to burning out wood. Candy'd see herself, though, asking one of Jen Keppel's kids to bring her an armful.

Unless, maybe— She hesitated. After all, they were Guy's children, too.

No, sir! She'd wait until Pa got home.

After Candy's door closed, Jen got up and started to stack the dishes. She saw with a grim smile that Candy hadn't flung off before she'd finished her coffee. She said, "You through, Evelyn? I'd like to clear away."

She must have spoken more briskly than she meant, for Evelyn grabbed up her cup with a flutter.

Jen sat down again.

"Evelyn, for heaven's sake, there's no bones broke. She can't hurt you, can she?"

Evelyn's face, which had been red, became quite white, but Jen did not notice.

She went on. "Talk's all. Talk never hurt anyone."

Evelyn said, "Whoever said it did?"

She spoke in a clear, firm voice and Jen jumped.

"Well," she said, looking uncertainly at Evelyn. "Stand up to her sometimes, why don't you?"

"Oh, no," Evelyn said.

Oh, well, Jen thought. What can you expect? The poor girl's been buffaloed all her life. I suppose she and Lynnie'll both feel the same way Candy does about the boarders. Or will they?

"Ev," she said, "I don't know how many boarders I can get, but I'll likely need to hire some help."

"Oh, I'll help you," Evelyn said. "Gladly."

She got up briskly and began gathering the dishes. Her face was the same as always, round and mild, the cheeks pink, the gray eyes quiet behind the glasses. "Lynnie'd help, too, I should think, if you paid her, Jen."

Evelyn started for the pantry with a leaning pile of oatmeal dishes. On the way, she dropped a spoon, which she didn't come back to pick up. Jen heard the pile of dishes go crashing into the sink.

And a great help you'll be, miss, she thought.

She picked up the spoon. Sometimes you couldn't help but wonder if Evelyn was quite so buffaloed as she made out to be. There certainly wasn't any way to tell.

In the front part of the house, Candace's door snapped open.

"Neal!" she called. "Bring your Aunt Candy an armful of wood!"

Out behind the barn, on the five long lines that sparkled with frost, Evelyn hung out the clothes. It had been a cold night and was still cold, so that the light snow which had fallen before daylight was little more than an inch of frost crystals, blown into the air with every puff of breeze.

Crunch! went the old snow under it, when she stepped off the hard path under the clotheslines. As if she were stepping into a good boiled frosting which had hardened just right.

In the lee of the barn, where the sun reflected off the white clapboards, the snow was beginning to melt. On the barn doorstep, it was just right for a snowman, and the wet wood of the step showed brown in streaks. Standing there, you got a taste of spring, even though, out under the lines, the clothes had frozen before you got them out of the basket.

There they hung, stiff as shingles, the sheets in blue-shadowed planes and angles, the children's little pants and Pa's long-handled underwear caught in a frozen dance.

There was something, there was something, about clothes hanging on a line.

Here on the hilltop, you looked down across white fields to the ocean. Day by day, now, the gray-green winter color was leaving it. Soon it would be blue as cornflowers. March. April and May. All to come.

Now the wind was blowing snow out of the spruces; crystals that whirled and shone in the air like dust off the moon. Soon it would blow pale green dust of alder catkins.

Oh, thank whatever Ellis it was who built the house on top of this hill!

Jen. Dear Jen. She was going to take boarders and offer wages for help.

"Sucks to all their money," Evelyn said aloud.

She glanced sharply and quickly around, but no one was near. The children were over sliding on the hill, Jen was finishing the washing, Lynnie was still asleep, Candy pouting in her room.

Oh, Candy, Grammie's sugarplum Candy! Little Big Sister, forever ten years old, preserved in the years like a yellow quince in a jar of glass! You wouldn't care for "sucks," a fine word indeed, which little boys use.

Jen mustn't be hurt. And Candy would get back at her if she could. Candy always got back at people, sometimes taking years in the process.

Jen doesn't know how Candy does that. If I had the time to be forever on the look-out, maybe I would bother to stand up to Candy.

Maybe—Evelyn smiled, a little grimly. It looked as though Jen were able to take care of herself.

The little cats came tearing across the yard, one chasing the other. They skidded into a small drift, almost out of sight, a tangle of gray-striped and tawny tails and paws. The sparkling crystals flew.

Evelyn smiled. Once, long ago, she had wanted to be a cat, an independent, unassailable cat, free to run when the clamor started, to run from Grammie and Lyn and Candy; to be alone beneath trees, in mossy holes, under the lumber pile.

But a cat lived such a little while, a tick in endless time. Eight years? More only if it were lucky.

And would you spare even one year of a possible seventy, each containing winter, thundering winds and blowing snow in the sun? Or spring, thin green in the meadow, the cow stumbling out of the barn on the first warm day, the smell when you looked in the rock garden to see what had winterkilled?

Not now. Not now, that you had learned to be secret, to live in a world where everyone else must stop at the threshold of your door.

"Oh, live long," Evelyn said to the little cats. They burst out of the drift, plowing, with snow crystals caught in their ruffled fur. "If I were God, cats would be like turtles and live a thousand years."

She knelt on the barn doorstep, looked thoughtfully at the cats, then scooped up a melting pile and began to model a cat of snow.

And children would stay children forever. No one would be old and nosy, with gray-streaked hair over thin temples and a turned-down sour mouth; to take and take and worm and worm to get inside and take some more, so that you made your face a foolish blank and hid behind it from everyone but cats and children.

Evelyn's fingers flew.

The snow cat was asleep, paws tucked under, tail curled over, its small rump round and tight and smooth as a stone.

"Live forever," Evelyn told it, "to lay your lovely side against the rock and never sleep the years of milk and fish and sun and new green leaves away."

Jen called cheerfully from the L kitchen door. "Last basketful's ready, Evelyn."

Evelyn got up, picked up the basket and went into the house without a backward look.

For a little while the snow cat slept, relaxed and tranquil, then it softened and ran down in trickles over the wet, brown-weathered wood, steaming lightly in the sun.

THROUGH April and May, Jen cleaned the house. On a Saturday, she got the boys to help her take away the beaverboard partition from the front staircase and bring wood for fires to get the damp and chill out of the upstairs rooms.

To her surprise, she had a tussle with Neal to make him help. Usually, he was accommodating about chores; but about this one, he seemed to have a real chip on his shoulder. He sat right back and dug in his heels. When Jen insisted, he started in working; he dawdled when her back was turned, and the first thing she knew, he had skipped out. He didn't show up at home until late afternoon.

The other kids, though, helped like Trojans. Mertis and Maggie helped scrub, and while they weren't exactly efficient, Jen was pleasantly surprised at how much they could do. Andy even got in his two pals, Larry and Joe Palmer. Jen had to admit that willing kids, enthusiastic over a project, could certainly accomplish a lot. But upstairs in the old Ellis house, that morning, the joint was jumping, and at noon, for the sake of her sanity, Jen got rid of the lot of them. They were dying to see the Saturday afternoon movie; so she gave them all movie money and sent them off to the show. It was the least she could do, she thought, after the way they'd duffed in. She'd just have to afford it, that was all.

When Neal came home, she was laying for him.

"Where've you been?"

"Down to the shore," Neal said. "What can I have to eat, Ma?"

"Nothing," Jen said. "People who won't work, don't eat."

"Aw, Ma. I had to—"

"Your part of the job's up there waiting for you. When you've done it, you can come down to supper."

Candace said, "The boy's hungry, Jen, for heaven's sake!"

A glance passed between Neal and his aunt.

"I know he is," Jen said shortly.

If there was one thing she wouldn't put up with, it was being interfered with when she was correcting her children.

"You do as you're told, Neal."

Neal had his mouth open, but at the look in his mother's eye, he closed it and started toward the front hall, dragging each foot as if it weighed twenty-five pounds.

Jen went after him.

"That beaverboard has got to be carried out to the barn," she said. "Then you can take out the storm windows and stack them. I want to see you move, Neal."

"I'm so hungry, I can't," he whined.

"I don't doubt you are. But dinner was ready at noon for those who bothered to come home to eat it. You know I'm too busy now to fool around waiting meals."

Jen had no illusions about the terrible, unfillable abyss which was the stomach of a twelve-year-old boy. But if she let him get away with this performance, the next one would be worse. She knew Neal.

She sensed Candy's presence in the hall behind her.

Neal said, suddenly, "I won't help us fix up to take boarders."

"What was that?" Jen asked grimly.

"I won't help us to take boarders."

"Why not?"

"Well, it's cheap. You lower your whole family, that's all."

Jen's hand shot out and fastened in the front of his shirt. "Who did you hear say that?"

"No one," he mumbled. "I just think so."

"Look here, Neal. How do you think the seven of us are going to eat if we don't work?"

"*I* don't know." He shrugged.

The implication that it was *her* problem—that it had nothing to do with him—was too much for Jen. She boxed his ears soundly. While she was doing it, she saw Candy go by her like a shot and into her room, slamming the door behind her.

Mad, because I'm smacking Neal, Jen thought. Well, she herself's as much to blame as he is.

The thought of that lightened her hand.

"You can get that idea out of your head so fast it sizzles, Neal Ellis. You're going to work and help me, and don't you forget it. Jeb works hard and Andy's duffed in here all morning. Even the little kids have helped. If you think there's a place around here for a slacker, you've got another think coming. About the best way there is to lower your whole family is being a loafer and sneaking out on your job, if you ask me. Now, you go do that work, and don't you show up to eat till it's done."

She watched him as he went out of sight around the landing of the front stairs. The set of his shoulders, stubborn and sulky, bothered her. What had Candy said to him?

She better not start pouring into my kids that stuff about work that ain't good enough for nice people, Jen said to herself.

She went thoughtfully back to the kitchen. If she could only get out of here, into a house of her own! Maybe she could, at the end of the summer, if all went well. In the

1 1 6

meantime, she could keep her eyes open for some house she could rent.

Neal was in the upstairs hall, sullenly hauling away at the pieces of beaverboard, when he heard someone coming up the stairs. It was Aunt Candy, he saw, peering furtively over the banisters. The licking hadn't been much—Ma had hardly made his eyes water—and the beaverboard was in sections, so that it wasn't heavy. But now Neal blinked his eyes hard to squeeze tears out onto his cheeks; he tugged at the beaverboard, groaning, and, as he lifted a section of it, he staggered.

Aunt Candy came straight over to him. She took the beaverboard out of his hands and set it down. She wiped away his tears with her nice, clean, sweet-smelling handkerchief.

"Aunt Candy's poor little boy," she said. "There, now, Aunt Candy's little Neal. Does your face hurt where she slapped you, dear?"

Neal's tears began to flow in earnest. He sobbed.

"Ssh! Don't make a sound, Neal. Here!"

She pulled a handful of dates and salted nuts out of her dress pocket and slipped them into his grubby hand.

"There, now," she said. "Don't you cry any more."

Neal could have stopped any time, but he thought it might be sensible to go on crying, just a little, to see if she would offer him anything more. She was plenty mad about his licking, he could see that.

"They all plague you," she said. "And you're the best and smartest one of them all. You're my favorite, over the others, Neal. Don't you forget that, because I shan't."

He took a short, hiccupy breath.

"When I die, you'll have all—"

Aunt Candy stopped dead. Her eyes narrowed and her face got a funny, thin look. She went back downstairs with a light, soundless step.

Neal crammed nuts and dates into his mouth.

1 1 7

Gee, they tasted good!

He ate every one, running his tongue around his watering mouth to get the last sweet, sticky, salty, nutty taste.

Jiminy crikey, Aunt Candy's favorite! What did she mean, saying I'll have "all" when she dies?

She means all her money. Oh, my gee! She's got thousands and thousands.

The idea struck him all of a heap, so that he sat down, weakened, on the pile of beaverboard.

But she sure had looked as queer as an old duck when she mentioned it.

The first days Jen worked upstairs with her scrubbing rags and pails of suds, to her surprise, Evelyn and Lynnie came along too. They weren't much more help than Mertis and Maggie had been, but they were willing. Evelyn was likely to lose herself between one job and the next, and Lynnie loved to talk. She would settle down by the fire, in whatever room they happened to be cleaning, her scrubbing cloth dangling from one hand, her tongue running, while Jen worked. And though Lynnie was entertaining—she always had the latest gossip on tap—Jen wasn't one who could work well and talk at the same time. But it was something to know that she had Evelyn and Lynnie behind her.

Candy hadn't given an inch. She was never far from the cleaning operations, hovering resentfully in the hall or the next room. If Jen started to move any of the furniture around, she would pounce like a hawk.

"Grammie kept that there for years," she would say, her black eyes snapping; or "That was Grammie's place for that, and I don't want it moved."

Jen humored her, but it was hard to, sometimes. In the end, the only changes she made in the arrangement of the rooms were to put bedside tables, with lights, alongside each bed. The old-fashioned way was to have the light glaring down from the fixture in the ceiling, a thing Jen hated, herself. And anyone who read in bed as much as Candy did might realize that bedside lights were necessary to people on their vacations. But there was a battle royal about the tables, since Grammie's "stands" had always been kept by the windows. Then, after Jen was through, Candace went around in each room and put the stands all back in their original places. She put all the lamps back where she thought they belonged, and connected them up to their original plugs.

Jen let it go. There'd be time enough, after the boarders came, to shift a few tables. And if she knew summer people, they wouldn't hesitate to ask for any kind of rearrangement of their rooms.

The old house was beautiful, after Jen finished. The big, sunny upstairs rooms paid back in full any time spent on them. Light and air streamed through them now instead of musty dampness, and Jen discovered a curious thing. In every one of them, there was a sweet, elusive smell. It was not alone the smell of a freshly cleaned house —Jen knew that well enough. She couldn't always detect it; but after she'd closed the windows and gone downstairs, if she had to go back up for anything, there it would be.

"What's that smell, Evelyn?" she asked, one morning.

They were putting the last touches on one of the rooms, making the bed.

"It's home sickness," Evelyn said promptly, making two words of it.

"It's what?" Jen asked, looking at her curiously.

That was a funny thing to say.

But Evelyn just went on tucking in the sheet.

"Don't be such a fool, Evelyn." Candy spoke from the hall, in a voice like a rasp, startling Jen, who hadn't known she was there.

Candy appeared in the doorway. "It's lavender," she

said. "I'm not surprised you don't recognize it. Grammie used to grow it and keep it in the closets and bureau drawers, but people nowadays don't bother. I notice you threw out all her bunches that were left here."

"I did?" Jen said, puzzled.

She hadn't noticed any bunches of lavender, which anyway must have been pretty old and crumbly by now. Then she remembered, suddenly, that Lynnie and Evelyn had cleaned out a good many of the closets and bureau drawers for her. She looked up at Candy, to be met with a glassy, frozen glare.

"Your transients will appreciate the smell of lavender," Candy said.

"I expect so," Jen said pleasantly.

She'll be lucky, Jen thought, if there're no more changes made here than a few old bunches of lavender, if I know summer people.

And Jen was right.

The first to arrive was Mr. Geoffrey Raymond, a painter, who simply scaled his hat at the bed and went over to look out of the window. He said, "Thanks, Mrs. Ellis, this is heaven. I'll stay forever." He wanted no changes made, nor would he have noticed if there had been. He was the least trouble of any man Jen had ever seen around a house. But the next to arrive, at the beginning of June, were the Clawsons and their Flora.

Jen had taken part of her fishhouse money and advertised for boarders in the city newspapers. She had been astonished at the response. She had thought it might take time to work up her trade. But in the years following the war, people had money and were on the roam. Jen's prices were lower than resort-hotel prices—she could have filled up her available rooms twice over.

She considered herself lucky, too, to have any trade at all in June. June was still spring at Candlemas Bay, with a lot of east wind and fog. Most of the people who had answered her ads wanted to come in July and August. She had been surprised when Mr. Raymond wrote wanting a room at the end of May; and then, a day or so later, she had had the letter from Mr. Clawson.

Neither of these two, it seemed, cared whether they were cold or warm, wet or dry. Rain or shine was all the same to them. Mr. Raymond sat out on the rocks with his paints all day. If the fog came in, he painted a picture of fog; if it rained, he put up an umbrella over his easel. At meals, he ate whatever was set before him; and Jen truly believed, if his bed weren't made up—as it always was—he would have crawled into it without knowing the difference. Mr. Raymond was a tall, graceful man, about thirty-five, with sandy hair and blue eyes; he was pleasant to talk to, when he stopped to talk, which wasn't often. Mr. Clawson spent all his time salt-water fishing. When the weather was too bad for his hired boat to go out, he fished off the ledges with a pole.

Mr. Clawson, according to Lynnie, who could be counted on to extract all available information from anybody, had some kind of a wholesale business from which he took a long vacation every summer, traveling around various coasts to see where he could find the best fishing. He had been all over the world, just sampling the fishing.

His womenfolks didn't care for his kind of vacation. Flora wanted to be at a resort where there were tennis and dancing, and Mrs. Clawson, too, would have preferred a hotel. But she was a student of people, she told Lynnie. Whenever she was stuck in some odd, out-of-the-way place, waiting for Mr. Clawson to decide about the fishing there, she whiled away the time studying the natives.

"She keeps a notebook," Lynnie reported in the kitchen. "And whenever she finds out about queer customs or people, she writes it down."

Candace snorted. "Study herself and that girl of hers, she'll have a notebook full," she said.

Lynnie said, "Well, I guess we all have our peculiarities. Mrs. Clawson comes from a very old, very wealthy family."

"So she says," Candace said grimly.

Lynnie and Candace were always having it over about the Clawsons. Half the time, Jen didn't bother to listen. She was too busy; besides, she had already formed her own opinion, on the day the Clawsons had arrived at the house.

Flora and Mrs. Clawson didn't care for their rooms. They wanted to look at *all* the rooms. They finally made a choice; but then, everything had to be changed around— the bed, the tables, the chairs, the bureaus. Jen felt, superintending the operation, a little as if she were trampling over a dead body.

They fussed over the food. Mr. Clawson fussed if he were given anything but fish. He was in fish country, he said; he wished to eat fish. Mrs. Clawson didn't like fish. Flora didn't like what the others had. She always wanted something else cooked.

Jen told herself she didn't care. So long as they paid their board, they could have fried goat, if they wanted it. The money was coming in, the terrible tension beginning to ease. Grampie was himself again. The first batch of boarders was settled in without another yip out of Candy.

Jen hadn't been able to foretell just what Candy might do about the changes in the upstairs front bedrooms; she had been more worried about that than she'd have cared to admit. There would certainly be one old humdinger of a row if Candy went up there sometime and started hauling Mrs. Clawson's furniture around. But so far as she could see, Candy did nothing at all.

Jen hadn't been present when Mrs. Clawson and Candy had thrown down the gauntlet.

Candy had been sitting in the sun on the glassed-in back porch. Mrs. Clawson joined her without an invitation.

The small porch had been built on the back of the house where it would get the morning sun and overlook the ocean. Candy felt, with reason, that it should be private to the family. The boarders had the big, sunny, comfortable front porch, also glassed-in, with all the good porch furniture.

But Mrs. Clawson felt that, since she was paying to stay in the house, any part of it should be accessible to her; she wished to be assured, also, that no one was receiving more consideration or being made more comfortable than she. It could also be said that she was inquisitive. She came up on the back porch and sat down in a wicker chair, with the air that if anybody were to leave, it should be Candace.

She said, "Good morning, Miss Ellis."

Candace said, civilly, "Good morning."

"I haven't seen very much of you."

"No," Candace said. "You haven't."

There was a brief silence, while Mrs. Clawson rocked and Candace went on with her sewing.

"Your sister Lynnie tells me you're very busy with your —er—social organizations," Mrs. Clawson said.

"Yes. I'm generally busy."

"I expect you are. I, too, when I'm at home. I don't have a moment to call my own. One organization after another, and *all* those committees! And the charity work, of course, which such a family as ours is always called upon to do. That's why I'm so glad to get away in the summer. I quarrel with Mr. Clawson about coming to these dead little towns, but, you know, it's such a relief to me to be away from it all, where there isn't one single thing to attract my attention, and no so-called *interests.*"

"Is that so?" Candace said concisely.

"Except, of course, the natives. I'm always interested in them. You see, in my small way, I'm a sociologist. I hope someday to have enough material for a book on rural customs and the economic life of these people."

Candace did not say what she thought of this, and Mrs.

Clawson glanced at her. The elder Miss Ellis, it seemed, was not sociable.

Gauche, Mrs. Clawson thought. And embarrassed at being asked to carry on any sort of sophisticated conversation.

Well, it shouldn't be too difficult to put her at her ease. One just went on talking, naturally, to even the most stand-offish of these reticent people, who, after all, were secretly flattered by your attention; and sometimes one often got some very good ideas for one's notes.

"We've been in many of these coast towns, Mr. Clawson and I," she went on. "I find their economic situation most interesting."

"Truly?" Candace said. "In what way?"

"Well, here you have some of the oldest towns in the country falling into decay because, with changing conditions, there's not enough work to support their people. I understand this entire region was once farming and fishing communities. Now, of course, it's largely summer-resident property."

"Yes," Candace said.

She put down her sewing and folded her hands in her lap, with an air of waiting which any one of her family would have recognized. "That's very true. As you say. Many of our local people have sold their land. They have no jobs in the wintertime."

Mrs. Clawson smiled.

"The solution would be so simple," she said, "if they only had a little gumption."

"You have a solution?"

"Certainly. Any sociologist or economist has. Your local people have no place here any longer. If there are no jobs, they should pick up themselves and their families and go elsewhere, where they *can* find work. But will they? No."

Mrs. Clawson was thinking of the paper she planned to read before her Club when she returned in the fall, and which was beginning to take shape in her mind. Often, she had used the notes for her book for that.

"They cling like limpets to their old way of life, the life their fathers set up here and which now is gone. They squabble like crows over the few paying jobs there are. And each year we come back, we see them still poorer, still nearer the—er—ragged edge than ever. They have only themselves to blame."

"Yes," Candace said. "They have only themselves to blame."

There was a brief pause, into which Candace spoke briskly.

"We're hospitable," she said. "We like to keep enough cooks and maids and chauffeurs around so that our summer visitors can be kept comfortable. A grocer, too. And one plumber and one electrician, so that lights and water in the cottages can be turned off in the fall and on in the spring."

Mrs. Clawson glanced over sharply. Was this woman being ironic? No, of course not. It was the typical, servile way of talking. They thought they could get more money out of you if they bent low.

"I'm afraid you keep too many," she murmured.

Candace said, "Our guests like a choice."

Conversation languished.

The Waltham children, having been sitting down at desks through the electric spring weather, passed the house on the way home from the last day of school. They had a game, which included making a noise like a burp gun, and then dropping dead with horrible squirms and yells of anguish.

Mrs. Clawson gazed after them distastefully.

"Don't you think, Miss Ellis," she asked, fixing Candace with a narrowed, sociological eye, "that inbreeding in these coastal towns is responsible for so many feeble-minded children?"

"Yes, I do," Candace said, pleasantly. "We've seen that theory proved so well since the summer people began coming. The old, wealthy families are inbred, of course, like royalty. I've noticed that a good many of them do have one or two feeble-minded children."

Mrs. Clawson's smile froze. She rose at once and left the porch.

What a rude, ignorant woman! she thought.

And Candace was thinking, Common cultch!

PART THREE
The Skiff

BEFORE daylight, on the day after
school closed, Jeb went down by himself to clear out Guy's
fishhouse and get it ready to turn over to Russ for good.
The job involved sorting out Guy's accumulations of a life-
time, for, as Grampie said, Guy never salvaged anything.
He had always bought the best, generally more than he
could use. Left-over stuff he either kicked under the work-
bench or chucked into the loft—no matter, so long as it
was out of the way enough to leave him work-space. When
he needed more, he bought new.

As a consequence, the fishhouse was a junk heap of old
and new rope, canvas, laths, engine parts, bolts and screws,
gangion, open cans of paint with brushes dried up in them,
tar, oars, calking oakum—dozens of different kinds of mate-
rials. Jeb had already salvaged enough to build most of
his thirty-seven traps, which were now stacked along the
beach outside the fishhouse. Twenty of them lacked heads.
He hadn't found enough heading-twine to knit heads for
them all. There might be some more twine in the loft. It
would take quite a while to sort out what was lying up
there, and what with his school work, helping Grampie
haul traps on Saturdays, working on his own traps nights
after school, Jeb hadn't been able to find time. He had to
admit, too, that he'd been putting it off.

Ordinarily, he would have enjoyed routing out the fishhouse. It was a job he'd been looking forward to, up until his mother had sold the place. The loft hadn't any window; it was dark up there, and when he wanted anything, he had to root around with a flashlight. The whole rear wall was stacked nearly to the ceiling with stuff, flung in helter-skelter. Turning it over, he never knew what he was going to find. For one thing, there was nearly a whole case of whiskey up there, hidden under a stack of crocus bags.

Cutting a window in the end of that loft was one of the things Jeb had planned to do first. He even had the window spotted—an old, eight-paned sash that was laid away in Grampie's barn. Well, no use to plan anything now. The place didn't belong to him any more.

It had been decent of Russ to let him keep his stuff here this long.

Of course, Jen had needed the money. But before she sold the fishhouse, outright like that, the least she could have done was talk it over, find out what Jeb's plans were. All spring, he had gone on doggedly building his traps, waiting for school to be done, when he would have six more precious hours a day. Now he had the six hours, he was going to have to use them cleaning out the fishhouse, when every minute counted. No one seemed to realize how carefully he'd planned his time; or to think that what he did with it was very important.

He stood glumly over the stove, waiting for the fire to burn up through the kindling so he could close the drafts. The stove was a corker—a camp cookstove Guy had bought new last summer. The old stove had been a good heater, but now it lay, bottom-up and rusted, down on the shore where Guy had rolled it. He'd wanted something he could cook a snack on when he came in hungry and didn't want to go up to the house. There were still many cans of coffee, soup, beans, condensed milk in the big box-cupboard in the corner, part of the supply Guy had laid in.

"Oh, don't bother with two or three," he would say.

"Just give me a case," going in debt for it if he didn't happen to have the cash handy. The storekeepers all knew that if he didn't pay old Jebron would.

Jeb and Grampie had been using out of that supply all winter. It had come in handy on cold Saturday afternoons when they'd got in from hauling, chilled to the bone. They'd warm up the fishhouse and have a mug-up, before Jeb went to work on his traps for the rest of the daylight. It had been fun.

Now he got down the percolator from the cupboard, put in coffee and cold water and set it on to heat. There was barely enough light in the room for him to see what he was doing; it couldn't be much more than half-past three or four o'clock. When he had left the house, there hadn't been even a streak of light in the sky. But it was nice here in the warm dark. The red squiggles from the stove drafts, jumping on the walls, were enough to see by to make a little coffee.

On the way out through his mother's kitchen, Jeb had rifled the icebox of some butter and a jar of jam. He had got himself bread and half a dozen doughnuts from the pantry.

Later on, Neal and Andy would be down to help him. At least, Jen had told them to. Jeb meant to get rid of them if they came down early. They could take the punt and some flounder lines and go fishing off by the moorings. Jen could always use a mess of flounders. Mr. Clawson would eat flounder filets by the dozen. What a guy he was for eating fish! And now in June, before the fish-packing season got really under way, the harbor flounders were hard-meated and good. The kids could help Jeb this afternoon, when there might be some lugging to do; but the sorting-out he wanted to do by himself.

He sat down in the creaky chair by the window to wait for his coffee. It was already starting a cheerful rumble inside the pot. In a minute, he'd be able to smell it. The fishhouse had got warm and comfortable; it was just the place for a man to be in the early morning, alone, sitting for a few minutes while he planned his day's work.

Such a place his mother wouldn't understand. She was always so surrounded by kids and people. Maybe no woman would understand it, seeing it was a man's workplace, cluttered and dirty, its brown beams blurred by the cobwebs of years. Nails driven into its worm-eaten two-by-fours held coils of rope, nets, gaffs, old buoys. It smelled of paint and tar, shavings and oakum. Under Guy's mess of paint cans and boxes of trash, the top of the workbench was black and greasy with age; the front edge was worn round, scarred, scraped, scored, dented by tools, until the wood was polished and layered like fish scales.

The workbench top had been made out of a single two-inch plank, three feet wide. The tree it had been sawed out of must have been a mighty one. Near the back of it, on one corner, were the deeply burned initials "M.D.E.," where Great-Grandfather Malcolm had once tried out his trap-branding iron. Grampie's initials were there, somewhere, too, for the fishhouse had been Grampie's before he had turned it over to Guy. One of them had had to give, because they couldn't get along. Of course it had been Grampie. And a man, anyway, ought to have his own fishhouse, seeing it was the only place he had to be alone in. Things like that a woman couldn't understand.

"Now, Jeb," Jen had said last night, "I ain't said much about it, because I wanted you to get school settled away. But tomorrow morning, you start clearing out that fishhouse for Russ. You've been mooning around over that job all spring."

She hadn't meant it to sound the way it did; but once or twice, since March, she had mentioned the fishhouse, and he just never did seem to get under way on the job. Besides, her conscience was still bothering her about him.

She'd never been able to get him to say anything; the matter had grown until it stood up black between them. She didn't see how he could blame her—the money had gone for groceries, mostly; she'd been able to clean up a few of Guy's bills. But Jeb had clammed right up. He hadn't even mentioned his lobster traps to her.

He said now, not looking at her, "Russ isn't in any hurry."

"We've traded on his good nature," she said shortly. "I made a bargain with him. It's time he got what he paid for."

"All right," Jeb said.

"I've told Neal and Andy they'll have to help you."

"For the Lord sake, Ma, I can do it. I'll tend to it."

"Go down there and moon around and not get it done, you mean," Jen said. His stuffiness just picked her right up, that was all.

"I guess you can trust me with that much," Jeb said, hot-eyed.

His flare of quick anger was exactly like her own, if Jen could have recognized it.

"Of course I trust you," she said. "Jeb, I had to sell it. You know that."

"Sure. I know, Ma."

"You can have whatever's there," she went on.

He glanced at her, startled. "I can? Everything?"

She nodded.

Maybe it would make things up to him a little. Of course, he'd used most of the stuff already, building his traps. There couldn't be too much left.

"There're a lot of things down there, Ma."

"Well, see what you can salvage. I suppose, if there's anything new or valuable that your father didn't pay for, it'll have to go back to where he bought it. I've got the bills for a lot of his things."

Jeb said, with decision, "I'd better see those bills, Ma."

"What for?"

She certainly wasn't going to let him see that mess of bills and start in worrying over them the way she was.

"It might simplify matters, looking things over in the fishhouse, that's all."

"You won't have much trouble. Grampie said your father's new things were mostly aboard his boat. If you run across anything you don't know what to do with, you can ask me."

Jeb shrugged. A queer look came into his face. He got up and headed toward his room in the L.

Jen started to call him back. She had made up her mind to say that maybe he could use the stuff to finish up his traps; anything, just so he'd know she knew about them and was proud of him for going ahead on his own that way. Traps took work and skill; and Grampie said Jeb's were good ones.

But the look he gave her stopped the words in her mouth. If they talked any more, they'd both get madder; and that was no way for a boy to look at his mother.

Sitting at the window of the fishhouse, Jeb was thinking, She treats me like a kid. The way she uses Neal and Andy.

Just so long as you were in school, you were a schoolboy, or everyone thought you were. If you grew to be seven feet tall and could lift five hundred pounds, a schoolkid was what you'd be.

Jeb grinned wryly. He wasn't seven feet tall; he didn't know how much he could lift. He was near six feet though, and— He flexed his biceps, feeling with satisfaction the tough bulge under his shirt sleeve.

But to his mother, he was a kid. Like Andy. Like Clay, for all the use she made of him.

She'd wear herself out over those blasted boarders—already she seemed nervous and strained, and she was thinner. People, too, whom any right-minded guy wouldn't care to entertain in his house. Oh, Mr. Raymond was okay—seemed like a heck of a nice fellow; but the Clawsons . . . Holy smoke, who did they think they were? Treating everybody like servants.

Of course, Jen had to do something, and taking boarders was a good idea, if she didn't break her back over it. The thing was, she needed help—not somebody trifling like Aunt Lynnie or absent-minded like Aunt Evelyn. She ought to have somebody substantial, like Myrabel Evans, to come right into that kitchen and help take over. He helped, himself, wherever he could; but the things she let him do were nothing but kids' chores, that Neal or Andy could do just as well. Besides, if he didn't get his traps done and fishing, he wouldn't be able to bring her home any money, and that was the important thing. She didn't seem to think what he could do was worth anything, that was all.

She could have let him see those bills, given him some idea of how far behind the eight-ball Guy had left them all. How did you know what you could plan if you didn't know how much you owed? It didn't make sense.

Jeb let the chair legs down with a clunk, poured out his coffee and ate his breakfast. Then he picked up his flashlight and swung up the ladder into the loft.

The loft was dark as a pocket. It was hard to know where to begin. Guy's cuckoo's-nest was thrown together, stacked up every which way. Probably the best thing to do was to heave whatever wouldn't break down the stairs, sort it out where you could see what you were doing.

He began with some old squares of canvas and a couple of pairs of oars, which he boosted down the stairs. Then he rooted his way steadily to the bottom, every now and then carrying a load over to the trap door and dropping it through. To his amazement, he found a full keg of trap nails, buried in a corner, and he groaned, thinking of how he'd scavenged for nails all winter. He'd hunted for them up here, too; but he hadn't found these. Ought to have had the sense to turn the place out before; saved himself a lot of trouble.

There was a big pile of manila rope—six-thread, some of which he'd already salvaged for warps for his traps. Buried in it, only its top showing, was a long, new-feeling corrugated cardboard carton. Better not heave that downstairs until he found out what was in it. Might be something breakable.

He laid down his flashlight, and in the darkness slit with his jackknife the heavy gummed tape that sealed the carton. Whatever was in there was something new from a factory somewhere, never been opened. He peeled back the end of the carton and flashed his light onto the contents. There, slung in stout wooden cleats, was a brand-new, five-horsepower outboard motor.

"Oh, my gee!" Jeb said, in a voice that was almost a moan.

He propped his light so that the beam would fall inside the carton and pulled away a little of the excelsior packing. It was real, all right; the latest model. One of the best makes made.

What had Guy bought that for? He'd said something, once, about having a skiff with an outboard to go gunning with when the birds began flying in the fall. Gunning from a boat with a motor wasn't legal and Guy didn't own a skiff; but apparently he'd had his plans. At least, he'd got himself an outboard.

Had he paid for it?

Probably not. It would have to be one of the things to return to some Bellport store, as soon as Jeb found out where it came from.

Maybe Guy had, though. He'd paid for some things.

Blair and Sons handled the agency for these outboards, in Bellport. It would be easy enough to call them up and find out if Guy had left a bill there.

Jeb squatted back on his heels, staring at the beautiful object in the crate. With an outboard like this, on some kind of a skiff, he'd be able to run twice the string of traps he'd planned, because he wouldn't have to take the time and energy to row. He could build more traps—he had the stuff for at least fifty, except for the heading-twine, and he could get that somewhere. Run a string of seventy traps, say, make twice as much money . . .

To say nothing of the pure joy of having a new engine to tinker with, to handle.

He put out his hand and stroked the outboard. The metal felt cool, silky with some kind of fine oil.

"Which had you rather have, a hundred horsepower engine or an ash breeze?"

Jeb snatched his hand away. He could hear Guy saying it, almost as if he'd been there in the loft with him.

Of course it wasn't paid for. And if it were, Guy had left a big bill for other stuff with Blair and Sons, who were Bellport's main marine hardware dealers. So the outboard would have to go back to them anyway.

Cover it up, something whispered to him. Don't say anything about it. Wait till Blair's bill's paid. Maybe, somehow, you could get that one paid first.

It isn't as if an outboard was just for fun. It would be working equipment; with it you could make twice as much, get the bills paid faster.

Pay for it when you feel like it, said the echo that was Guy's voice. *Hell, it don't hurt them dealers to wait for their money. They're rolling, most of them. And if you don't pay 'em, anyway what can they do?*

Jeb's hands, as if of their own accord, pulled the carton shut, spread crocus bags on top of it, buried it deep under odds and ends. He picked up the flashlight and went over to the other side of the loft. Who was to know he hadn't started in there in the first place?

He flashed the light beam around to see what was next

to come to hand; and all at once he was so tired he couldn't seem to move.

If he could only be let alone to do his work as he'd planned it, if things would stay simple. But everything was against him, pulling the other way. He'd lost the fishhouse; he didn't know where he could lay hands on a skiff. And he'd lose this outboard, too, he might as well count on it.

Okay, clean out the damn fishhouse. Turn it over to Russ. Sell the stuff and get the money. No matter if it was all stuff you yourself could use in your work; you weren't going to work, now. Not at fishing, you weren't. Up at the house, you could tie on to Jen's apron string, help her feed a lot of boarders.

Sell the stuff. Use the money. And then where were you? Worse off than when you started. Left with nothing.

Money was the important thing. Not work; not being contented doing the thing you wanted to do.

Oh, to the heck with it!

He stepped back and his heel cracked against the wooden case which, he saw, turning lumpily and flashing the light on it, was Guy's case of whiskey.

Oh, damn you, Guy! he said under his breath, feeling the thick, heavy clotting come into his throat. Why couldn't you have stayed the way you were? What did you have to go and make such a mess for?

The heavy feeling suddenly seemed to explode. He grabbed up the case and hurled it with all his strength at the open trap door. It fell through, hit on the bottom ladder-rung, bounced against the opposite wall and split open, with a sound of breaking bottles crashing in all directions.

"Hey," said a mild voice, from below.

Jeb stuck a red, sweating face down through the trap.

Russ was standing in the door, surveying the carnage with a look of astonishment.

1 3 6

"Case of whiskey got away from me," Jeb said furiously.

"Seems so." Russ grinned up at him. "You toss it or throw it?"

Jeb swung himself heavily down the ladder, climbing over the mess at the bottom.

He said, "You won't get in here for a month, Russ."

"Well, what's the rush, anyway? I ain't worrying."

Russ went over, shook the coffeepot and beamed. "I smelt this fifty yards up the hill. You want any more?"

Jeb shook his head. He sat down by the window, mopping his scarlet, streaming face.

"You better. You go throwing heavy junk like that around, you'll need your coffee."

Russ, having filled himself a mug of coffee, laced plentifully with condensed milk, sat down, stirring.

"You got quite a clean-up on your hands, Jeb," he said soberly.

"Ayeh. Ma has. It doesn't seem to be up to me."

Russ glanced over at him thoughtfully.

"I don't need this fishhouse, Jeb. Leave it, why don't you? Clean it up piecemeal, when you have time."

"It's okay. I've got time now."

"Ain't your hands kind of full, finishing up your traps?"

"No. I can sell them for more'n I put into them."

"Not planning on lobstering?"

"What with, for gosh sake? A punt and a pair of oars?"

"H'm," Russ said. "I d'no. But there ought to be a new outboard stowed away in the loft somewhere. I see Guy lug one up there, last August. I figured you knew about it."

Jeb sat staring at the floor, his elbows on his knees.

Russ waited for him to say something, then went on.

"Going to use it for gunning, he said. He was having McCarthy build him a skiff, too, over to the boatyard. Didn't you know nothing about that, either?"

Jeb shook his head, staring.

"Don't your ma know about it?"

"No. She'd have mentioned it. No, we didn't know."

"Why, that louse!" Russ said.

"Who?"

"McCarthy. Guy'd paid him a hundred dollars down on that skiff, I know for a fact. You and I'll go have a talk with him, the son-of-a-gun!"

"You better take Ma, not me," Jeb said bitterly.

Russ said, slowly, "Your ma's pretty worried over things, Jeb."

"I know she is. So'm I. She might let me carry my share, not treat me as if all I was fit for was to suck on a bottle!"

His rage suddenly burst out again.

"What kind of sense does it make? A lunk six feet tall and weighing a hundred and seventy . . . sits around on his tail, learning Cicero wants the Romans to bust up Carthage! And his mother doesn't know where the next cent's coming from to feed him! What does that add up to? Hanh?"

Jeb thrust his hot face close to Russ's and Russ recoiled with a start.

"Hey! What—" he began, feebly.

"Compositions on 'My Vacation Experiences!' " Jeb roared out, his voice incoherent with fury. "Take three years to learn power tools and different kinds of wood, and then know what I built? A damn what-not!"

For a minute, his voice got away from him and he couldn't go on. The angry tears came into his eyes and rolled down his cheeks, and he let them, a part of the storm that was going on inside his frantic heart.

"Well," Russ said. "Was it a good what-not?"

"Damn right it was!"

"What I mean is, the cussid things ain't much good, Jeb, but they must be devilish to build, all them little shelves. If you can make one of them, you ought to be able to build almost anything else."

Jeb wasn't listening. He smacked his fist into the palm of his hand, rubbing it hard there, nervously.

"A hundred kids get out of high school, any year, and maybe two of them know what they want to do. Well, I know what I want to do. If I'd been born a hundred years ago, maybe I'd be let alone to do it."

Russ was looking at the big fist, the competent wrist attached to it, the spread of lean shoulders under the cobweb-smeared blue shirt.

"Don't be a dope," he said cautiously. "What would there have been for a man interested in diesels, a hundred years ago?"

"Sure, I know. I got sense enough to know that the best time to live in is the time you're born in. But Grampie had a boat and gear when he was twelve years old, and Gramp Malcolm owned his pinky before he was eighteen. Damn it to hell, Russ, Nathan Ellis was only nineteen when he founded a town. What does that make me? A schoolboy?"

Russ set down his coffee cup.

"It sure as hell don't sound as if you was," he said.

This was pretty unusual. But maybe a kid who grew up practically in the pocket of a man like Captain Jebron Ellis would automatically learn to think for himself. The kids you saw hanging around the drugstore didn't talk like this.

Russ pulled himself up short, remembering the war.

"Jeb," he said. "You recall Jasper Bemis?"

"Sure. Of course I do."

Jasper Bemis, nineteen. Killed piloting a plane over Japan.

"Kids," Russ said thoughtfully. "Well, I don't know exactly what that means, Jeb, except I don't doubt Jasper Bemis was as big a man in his time as Nate Ellis and them was in theirs. Different times, they call on a man for different things. And I don't doubt, either, that there was times in their lives when any one of them couldn't find

1 3 9

anything big enough to use his arm muscles on. Look, you feel the way you do, why don't you find out what it takes to go to diesel school?"

"Ma thinks there's nothing in the world but a high-school diploma."

"Your ma's got more sense than about any three other people you know," Russ said. "She'd be liable to listen to reason. Things been pretty tore up, up at your house, for a long time. She's got a job on her hands that would scare most men."

"Sure. Why won't she take help with it? She gave me what was here in the fishhouse, but she said anything new I could salvage would have to go back to the stores. She won't even tell me what Pa's bills amount to. That outboard—I can't even keep it, and it would be part of my tools."

"Well, there's salvage and salvage. But you're right, a man's a fool not to keep his tools. Sort out what's here, keep what you need, sell the rest. There's a mess of good stuff here. Johnny would know about what such gear's worth secondhand. Take a lot of it off your hands, I wouldn't wonder. When the junk's out of here, there'll be room for the two of us. I'll move in what I need to, you can have the rest. Stick up a partition, if you want to."

"Ma's gone stubborn about that, too," Jeb said. "She says for me to get out of here."

"Womenfolks are all stubborn," Russ said. "What they don't know, won't hurt 'em. If you can't walk through 'em, walk around 'em."

Jeb grinned. It was the first ray of light Russ had seen and he grinned back.

"About them bills," he went on. "There's a good way to handle a mess like that, you might suggest to your ma. Lump them all together and get a bank loan to pay them. That gives the dealers their money and shows them you mean business. I figure the interest you pay the bank's a small amount for getting your credit fixed up."

"How's that again?"

Russ explained it, carefully.

"You might mention it to Jebron first," he finished. "What say I help you sort out and clean up today? I was going out, but all of a sudden I've got a notion if I dragged up a fish today, I'd be likely to spit in its eye. What if you was to make a couple or so trips dragging with me, anyway? Earn some money towards that outboard? I need a man, you know that, and damn, I get fed up, dragging alone."

"Okay," Jeb said. "Tomorrow?"

"Uh-huh. And how about the movies tonight? Hey, for godsake, Jeb, how long's it been since you was to the movies?"

RUSS was driving past the Ellis house on the way to the shore when he saw Jen leave the L-kitchen door and go up the walk to the barn. On the way to feed the hens, he decided, craning his neck, for she had a dish of feed in one hand and a pail of scraps in the other.

He pulled into the driveway and started along the walk after her. It would be a chance to catch her alone; he'd been wanting a chance to talk to her about Jeb. He'd given up, months ago, trying to make her take the second five hundred dollars for the fishhouse; but that was all right with him, now that he saw there were other ways he could help. He had dropped in at the house a couple of evenings lately, but she was always surrounded by a gaggle of kids or boarders. And there was generally someone talking to him, too.

He had to grin, sometimes, wondering what would happen if a man ever wanted to do anything private—his courting, for instance—at the Ellises'. If he had been interested in Lynnie, or she in him, any more than to be good friends, they would sure have had a tough time finding a corner to be by themselves in. The minute he arrived at the house, the kids converged on him; Jeb and Jebron wanted to talk fishing, or have him listen to the draggers on the short wave. All the Ellises took it for granted that he and Lynnie were going together; yet when he went there he seldom saw her, any more than to say hi to.

If the day ever came when the family finally got it through their heads that there wasn't anything between him and Lynnie they'd probably break their necks to shove the two of them together. People were funny that way.

It was last summer's business which had started them to linking him up with Lynnie. She was like a sister to him, of course, since he and Johnny had always run in and out of the Ellis house. Lynnie had asked him if he'd mind taking her to dances. He needn't do anything else, she said. Just take her and bring her home.

Candy, it seemed, had got it into her head that the summer crowd Lynnie went with were fast—"a barroom bunch," she said. She was following Lynnie's scent like a bloodhound, nose down.

"Tell her to go drop down a hole," Russ said, surprised.

It wasn't like Lynnie to knuckle under, to Candy or anyone else.

"Well, I can't make her mad or I'll never get my money out of her, Russ," Lynnie said. "And I may be going to need that money pretty soon."

Russ could guess what she needed it for. He had met her friends. They seemed like nice enough people to him—doctors, teachers and such, on vacation. There was one of them, Ralph Strong, a lawyer from Wisconsin, whom Lynnie would probably marry, if nothing happened to prevent it. Russ hoped nothing would. Marrying Strong was the best thing that could happen to a girl like Lynnie. He was a nice guy, and he'd take her far enough away so that she needn't ever see Candy again, if she didn't want to. Strong wasn't well-off. Five thousand dollars would make a lot of difference to Lynnie.

They hadn't got married last summer, but they'd got engaged. Strong would be back this summer; then things would probably depend on whether Lynnie could pry her money out of Candy.

If she couldn't, Russ thought, well, Strong's a lawyer. If I were him, I'd help Lynnie sue the old girl.

Funny about Candy, he thought, coming up on the barn doorstep and looking around to see where Jen had gone. You can't dope her out any more than you could Guy. Some things about her you had to admire—like the way she'd gone single-handed into Almira Lothrop's house when Almira was taken crazy and no one else had dared to go near her for fear of getting a kettle of hot water in the face. Candy had marched straight in the front door. She'd quieted Almira down, so that the three selectmen who'd been hanging around outside waiting for each other to be the first one in, could get her into a car and taken away to the asylum. Candy had gone along, too, sitting as stiff as a stick beside Almira, with Pete Waltham in the back seat.

You had to hand it to her for nerve in a righteous cause; but once let her get down on you and God help you. Russ felt a slight prickle on the back of his neck, thinking what would happen when Candy found out how he and Lynnie had been fooling the lot of them.

He grinned, a little ruefully, to himself.

Oh, well, everything blew over in time. Candy'd have to have her say, though, once she found out he and Lynnie never had been interested in each other.

There's the only thing around here that would ever interest me, he thought, catching the flick of Jen's blue dress through the glassed-in wall of the henhouse; and the idea, coming to him unexpectedly, jolted him to his boot heels. He stopped dead in the middle of the barn floor.

There was no one in the barn but Clay, who came out from behind the feed barrels, smiling a wide, amiable smile of toothless greeting. He carried in his hands a large, unsprung rattrap, which was baited with a piece of doughnut. Someone, apparently, had set the trap and left it behind the barrels.

Good Lord, Russ thought, turning cold. If that thing ever snaps on his hand, it'll cut his fingers off.

He restrained himself with an effort from grabbing at the trap, realizing that Clay would probably shut to on it and spring it.

"Hi, Clay," he said cautiously. "Give me the rattrap, will ya?"

"No," Clay said, retreating.

"Aw, come on, be a sport."

"It's my rattrap and I'm going to catch a rat in it," Clay said firmly.

"Good enough. Where'll we set it down?"

"I know," Clay said. "You go away. I'll put it there."

Being the youngest in a family of six, Clay well knew the situation of having something taken away from him. He eyed Russ with distrust, edging farther away from him.

Where, for the Lord's sake, was Jen? She'd been right there in the henhouse. Why didn't she come in? Still, if she did, and hollered at Clay—

"Want my watch?" Russ said desperately. He pulled it from his wrist and held it out.

"Nope," Clay said. "I want my rattrap. It's got doughnut on it."

He lifted one small fat hand and patted the bait affectionately.

The bait-patting was too much for Russ's nerves. He made a leaping grab. His hand went over Clay's and the trap snapped, not on Clay's fingers, but on Russ's thumb. Clay sat down with a thump.

Russ said, "Jeez-us Ker-ist!"

1 4 4

He slatted his hand and the trap flew with a crash of glass into a pile of stacked-up storm windows. He danced up and down, holding onto his thumb.

Clay let out a deafening, wide-mouthed yowl.

"My soul!" Jen said, coming in from the henhouse. She stopped and stared. "What in heaven's name—"

"For the love of Pete, why don't you look out for your kids?" Russ roared, into her astonished face. "What's the idea, letting a two-year-old kid fool around with a baited rattrap? He might have lost his hand. Instead of me losing my—"

He grabbed his thumb between the thumb and fingers of his other hand, massaging it vigorously.

"Holy jumped-up bug-juice! *Don't* that hurt! F-f-f-t!"

Jen took in the situation at a glance. She had set the trap herself, in so hidden a corner behind the barrels that it had never occurred to her Clay would find it. But it was lying, now, sprung, beside the shattered windows.

"Clay!" she said. "You set sail for the house! Don't think you won't get your britches dusted, if I catch up with you on the way!"

Clay's roar cut off in the middle. He put both palms on the floor and helped himself to his feet. His bottom grew visibly smaller as he sidled past his mother. He vanished, his short legs pumping briskly, in the direction of the house.

"Here," Jen said. "Let me see that thumb."

"Don't touch it," Russ howled. "It's broke in six or seven places."

She plucked the thumb out from between his frantically massaging fingers, and felt it, at first gently, then with a steady, increasing pressure.

"Does that hurt?"

"Ouch! Take it easy, Jen, for godsakes!"

"It isn't broke, Russ. There's a welt on it and it'll be stiff. That's all, thank the Lord."

He held the thumb upright, regarding it sourly, then wiggled it once under its own power.

"No," he said. "I guess maybe it ain't *broke*."

"I'm awful sorry, Russ. That baby's a hellion on wheels. I reached that trap back in there as far as I could and then shoved it into the corner with the broom. How he ever got it out is a mystery to me."

Russ stood testing the efficiency of his thumb; then he glanced at her with a sheepish grin.

"I'm sorry, Jen. But, my gorry, that sure did touch me off for a minute."

"I should think it might most anybody," she said, looking at him with concern. "You never could stand pain in your hands, anyway."

"That's right, I can't."

It was true that his hands were sensitive. He'd frost-bitten them once, out skating when he was a boy. But he didn't know he'd ever told Jen that; or if he had, that she'd remembered it.

"Grampie's got some old-fashioned liniment here somewhere," she said, rummaging around on the shelves of an old box-cupboard, pushing aside bottles and cans till she found what she wanted. "He keeps it out here, because when Candy finds it in the medicine chest, she throws it out," Jen said, coming back with a bottle. "The doctor told her it's no good. But I know it'll take out soreness. I used it on Andy's knee, just the other day. Le's see that thumb."

He held it out to her gingerly, wincing as the strong liniment came in contact with a hidden abrasion.

"Oh, is the skin broken there? Never mind, it never smarts for very long."

"I must have looked funny, hopping and hollering like a stuck turkey," he said. "Most women I know would've laughed their heads off."

"Well, they've got a peculiar sense of humor, then," Jen said.

She was standing close to him, her head bent over his hand. Russ could smell the clean smell of her hair, blended with the acrid sharpness of the liniment. Her hands felt smooth against his, cool and comforting.

"If a man risks disabling himself to keep my baby from getting smashed fingers," Jen went on, "I can't see it's very funny."

Russ stopped feeling like a fool. Apparently, it didn't seem to her that he'd made much of a touse, after all.

"Hey," he said. "That's a good handkerchief."

She ignored him, tying her handkerchief, soaked in liniment, in a neat, workmanlike bandage around the thumb.

"There. Keep that on a few hours, Russ."

"Thanks a lot," he said, grinning down at her.

He didn't have to look down a great way, either, he realized. She was darn near as tall as he was.

Guy had always said, bellowing laughter, "Don't marry a big woman, Russ. Get somebody you can put across your knee, if she needs it," and Russ would answer, "Hell, you know I'll never get married, till I can find somebody like Jen." He'd always said it, automatically. It had been a joke between them for years.

"Well . . . what is it?" she asked. "Does it still hurt a lot?"

Russ started a little, realizing he was standing with his thumb stuck straight up into the air, just as it had been when she'd taken her hands away from it.

"Hell, no."

Hastily, he shoved his hand deep into his pocket, and that did hurt, so he took it out again.

"I was thinking I came in here to talk to you about Jeb," he said. "Touse kind of knocked it out of my head."

Jen instantly looked anxious. "What about him? Is there anything—?"

"If he was my kid, I'd be proud of him."

"Well, I am. Of course I am. Only I've hardly laid eyes on him, except for meals, since school closed. He doesn't tell me a thing."

"He's all right. He's busy."

"Busy at what?"

"Well, you know, he's been three trips dragging with me, don't you?"

"Yes. But he hasn't told me—"

"Hasn't told you all his business, that it?" Russ eyed her quizzically.

"Oh, that's only part of it, of course, Russ. But after all, he's only seventeen. I've got to keep an eye on him."

"I wouldn't worry," Russ said, "if I was you."

"Well, I do worry. I've seen enough of what happens when kids run their own rig without any rein on them."

Russ grinned at her. It hadn't been any part of his scheme to make her mad.

"You know," he said, "it depends on the kid, Jen."

"Well, yes, but—"

"You remember," he went on reflectively, "how many kids of seventeen and eighteen and nineteen you heard about being in the Battle of the Bulge? And in a bunch of Air Force pilots, a man over nineteen looked like a grandfather."

"They were trained. Jeb isn't."

"How's a boy going to get practical training in peacetime, then?" he asked. "It don't make sense to me, Jen. Send kids to fight a war, but in peacetime set them to building what-nots. Jeb's old enough to take some responsibility."

Jen flushed hotly. "You know as well as I do that he learned to use power tools, making that what-not in his manual training course," she said. "You ought to know better, Russ. If Jeb has got you to come in here and argue with me over his going back to school—"

"He didn't even know I was coming. His school's none of my business. Though if he was my kid, I'd let him go to diesel school. What I came in to say, on these dragging trips, I've been able to pay him a man's wages. When he'd take them."

"Well, he can't be worth a man's wages to you."

Russ felt himself getting hot under the collar. Darn a stubborn woman!

"He's hefty and strong and quick, and he cares a damn whether he does a good job."

"Russ, I know it's good-hearted of you, but you haven't ever given in about that extra five hundred dollars for the fishhouse, and I don't trust you not to give us money we don't earn."

"Well, I'll be damned!" Russ said. That really did make him mad. "So that's what you told Jeb. Now he thinks I'm dealing him out charity, when I only want him to take what he earns. By God, Jen, you better fix that up with him. Fast. He's as blue as a whetstone over it."

"Easy money—" she began.

"Easy money!" Russ said. "Like to have you make a trip out with me someday, see if Jeb earns any. Look, Jen, you've got a man growing up there, not a what-not builder. If I was you, I'd give him a little credit for his brains, or you'll have him hanging around the drugstore corner."

He hadn't meant to say so much, but he'd come out with some ideas he'd been mulling over, ever since Jeb had refused to take a third of his last day's pay.

Jen looked him in the eye. "I know you so well, Russ Allen," she said. "All this blustering around, and what it means is, you're trying to find some way to slip me that extra five hundred dollars. I never in my life saw such a stubborn man!"

"Stubborn!" Russ howled. "Why, that makes me mad!"

Maybe he had paid Jeb a little better than he would have any other boy; it didn't help his temper any to know that Jen had seen through him.

"Why, you don't even know what he did with the money," he went on, furiously. "You think I'm so big-hearted—he took it over to Blair and Sons and paid it in on his outboard motor!"

Jen froze. "What outboard motor?"

"The one in Guy's fishhouse. Guy had one."

"I know. I saw it on Blair's bill and thought likely it sunk with the boat. Jeb ought to have told me about it."

"Well, keep your shirt on. He intends to."

"He can't have it, of course. It'll have to go back to the store."

"There you are," Russ said. "Going off half-cocked without listening to things. Jeb needs that outboard. It ain't no plaything to him. It's practical for him to have one, lobstering. He'll make twice the money."

"We owe Blair and Sons too big a bill for him to go buying outboard motors now."

"Okay," Russ said. "I hadn't any right to tell you about it, Jen, so please don't let Jeb know I did. He'll mention it to you in his own good time. Then you can make him take it back." He exploded suddenly, "But if there's anything any stubborner than a woman, I'd like to know what it is!"

He turned and strode irately out of the barn.

Jen heard him yell, "Hey, for godsakes!" and she went after him to the door.

Clay was coming up from the brook, putting along at full speed. Three strides behind him came the big Rhode Island Red rooster. Clay was not crying this time; but his mouth was wide open in soundless horror. He ran full tilt into Russ and climbed his leg like a tree.

Russ took a kick at the rooster, who ruffled up instantly, with a hoarse squawk, and flew at his boot.

To Jen's amazement, Russ retreated precipitately. He came into the barn, carrying Clay and spitting fire.

"I'd just as soon stick my head into a nest of lions as outdoors around here," he roared. "You take this baby and look after him, for the sweet loving Jesus's sake. It's a wonder that cussid thing didn't pick his eyes out!"

"I didn't know the rooster was out," Jen said indignantly. "He's supposed to be shut up in the yard."

He thrust Clay into her arms.

"Anything under God's heavens I can't stand, it's a hen," he spluttered.

Jen watched him go down the walk, making a wide circle around the rooster, and climb into his car. Now that she thought of it, she remembered hearing Guy say once that Russ would rather walk through a flock of rattlesnakes than a flock of hens. Thank the Lord she hadn't laughed at him for running from the rooster. Another time she might have, but now she felt too stirred up to laugh at anything.

Both Russ and Grampie, then, thought she wasn't being fair to Jeb. Maybe she wasn't. Maybe worry'd made a fool of her.

You get the habit of your kids being kids, you don't let go quick enough when they start to grow up. Lord, there's so many things to think of now.

But that outboard . . . of course Jeb can't afford an outboard motor.

Into her head came the picture of all the gadgets—the brass compasses, the radios, electric boat horns—the unneeded and unpaid-for stuff listed on Guy's bills; and in front of it all the big, black four-figure total that somehow, now, had to be earned and paid over to his creditors.

Worry may have made a fool of me over some things, she thought. But I know I'm not wrong about that.

Down at the shore, Russ pulled up with a screech of brakes. He banged open the fishhouse door and went in, kicking an empty box forcibly out of the way.

Jeb, who was standing at the workbench over a half-finished lobster trap, looked up, startled.

"What's the matter with *you?*" he asked.

"I've been up talking to your mother," Russ said shortly.

A slow grin spread over Jeb's face. He looked at the broad, stubborn shoulders, at the back of Russ's neck, on which he could have sworn the hackles stood straight up.

"Well," Jeb said, "if you can't walk through 'em, walk around 'em."

"You shut up," Russ said, "or I'll souse you off over the wharf."

JEB laid the cigar box containing the $325.46 on the table beside Jen's elbow.

"There's what I got for stuff I sold out of the fishhouse, Ma," he said.

"Oh, you found something you could sell down there, then," Jen said, glancing at the box.

It was an old box, black with fingerprints, which had seen hard usage since the day Guy had bought it, full of foil-wrapped perfectos.

Why, bless his heart, Jen thought. Jeb's brought me his cash box.

She didn't suppose there was much in it, but the idea of his turning over his cash to her made her beam up at him with affection and pride.

"How much did you make?"

"Well, I wish you'd count it, see if your count totals up with mine," he said, keeping his face carefully dead-pan.

"He figures his bookkeeping's a little shaky," Grampie said from behind his newspaper. "But I can't find nothing wrong with it."

If Russ and Johnny, or any of the fishermen, had overpaid Jeb for secondhand fishing gear, Grampie didn't know it. Materials were expensive; there had been a lot of good stuff in the fishhouse; Jeb had sold it below first-hand prices, and everybody was satisfied.

Jen reached for the box. She opened it and there was a dead silence in the room.

For a moment, Jeb thought she wasn't surprised or even pleased. It was almost as if she were horror-struck, staring at the boxful of bills and change.

Then she glanced up soberly. "Where'd you get this?"

"Nothing to do with me," Grampie said, lowering his paper. "Jebby got it."

He looked as proud as Punch, Jen saw, and relief washed over her, which she hid at once, hoping Jeb hadn't noticed anything. If Grampie knew, then this was all right.

Of course it was all right!

I've got to be a regular fool about money, she told herself.

But through the years there had been so many "deals," so many unexplained wads of bills. It would have been just like Guy when he was flush to leave bills around in an old box for her to find; or maybe wrap them up in a new pair of sheer stockings. And nobody would have appreciated it more than she, if she could ever have been sure the stockings were paid for, or the wads decently come by.

The first thought that had come into her head as she opened Jeb's box was, Oh, Lord, *what's* he been up to?

The rusty habit of years had caught her unawares and it was horrible. She could trust Jeb.

"Well, you can't blame me for being surprised," she said. "For a minute, there, I thought I was seeing things."

"For a minute, I thought you were, too," Jeb said.

She looked up, meeting his clear, troubled gaze, in which, after all, there was nothing of Guy.

1 5 3

"I guess it just wasn't the time to surprise me," she told him. "I've had a day the like of which I can't remember."

She had, too. Lynnie had taken the day off to go on a picnic with some of her friends. Along about noon, Evelyn had come all over vague and couldn't be depended on for anything. Jen had had the whole brunt—boarders, children, meals, clearing away, and the rest of it—all day.

"I was sitting here wondering if my feet would hold to get me up to bed, or if I'd have to walk on my ankles," she said, smiling, so they wouldn't think it really was that bad. "And in come the two of you, with this great wad of money. It's a wonder I didn't fall flat on my face."

"Count it," Jeb said, his face clearing.

It was all right. She'd only been tired.

Jen sorted the bills. She stacked the silver. And as she worked, she became aware of a deep contentment in the room, almost audible, like a cat purring.

Menfolks! she thought. You'd think they'd laid an egg, and I guess they have. Bringing home money—for them, it's like I feel when I spread a good supper and know the sitting room's warm and clean to rest out the evening in.

It came to her with a sudden shock that bringing home money was a great deal more to a responsible man than just satisfaction. It was something that had been bred into him, and into his kind over centuries of time, until it was almost as strong an instinct as to eat or to get children. It was the tape around his self-respect and pride which measured him to the rest of the world and to himself.

So that when a woman held in her hands the money her menfolks brought home, she was holding more than just tens and fives and ones. She was holding her husband's or her son's ability, and his ambition, and his dreams; and what might be behind one of his greasy, crumpled-up dollar bills was worth a thousand times over anything it could buy.

She stole a glance sideways. Jeb and Grampie were both

watching her like hawks, and as she got the total, she let out a good squawk of astonishment—that wasn't put on, either, she realized.

"Jeb, there can't be so much!"

"Uh-huh."

He looked at Grampie, his face red with suppressed laughter, his eyes squinted and dancing; and then they both burst out laughing.

And I pretty nigh spoilt that, she thought grimly. Well, give me time. I'll learn.

"I hope you didn't sell all the stuff, Jeb," she said. "I hope you kept enough of it so's you can finish up your traps."

She caught the electric quality of the look that passed between Jeb and Grampie, and turned away to hide a smile.

"I'm flabbergasted," she went on, quickly.

No use to advertise it, if you'd yielded a point.

"It don't seem possible," she went on, "I ain't going to go crazy wondering where my payments are coming from, this month."

"Well, now, that was something Jebby and I wanted to talk to you about," Grampie said. "Them payments on Guy's bills."

"I don't expect there's much to say, Grampie. There they are and they've got to be paid."

"There's a lot to say, Ma," Jeb said. "How much are they? We want to start paying them."

"I've started paying them. Jeb, your grandfather's done his share. We are not going to depend on him for one other thing. Between us, we've run him just about into the ground, and no more!"

"But look, Ma, before you fly off, will you listen to a plan I've got?"

"I don't want to listen, if it's anything to do with taking money from Grampie, Jeb."

Grampie got up and stood on the hearthrug, his hands thrust deep into his pockets.

He said, "I want you both to listen to me."

They both started, turning to stare at him.

My goodness, Jen thought, he's a big man.

She couldn't recall having noticed, lately, what a big man Grampie was. She had thought of him as an old man and a tired one, because for so long he had been going quietly about the house without much to say. In the past months, his clothes had seemed too big for him, his shoulders stooped a little. But now he stood up, the tremendous frame of his back as square as a box.

"When a man's folks stop depending on him, Jen, he might as well shut up shop and let them bury him. I'm sixty-nine, but I don't believe I'm done."

Jen flushed.

"Nobody thinks you are," she said, in a shocked voice.

My soul, she'd never meant *that!* Not to have him know she thought so, anyway.

Grampie looked at her meditatively.

"All our pins was knocked out for a while," he said. "We hoped, most of our lives, that Guy would straighten out sometime. There was a good deal *to* him, when he was young."

"I know," Jen said.

"I know you do. We can't, neither one of us, abide waste, and the waste of a man is the worst there is. When he went, in the useless way he did go, we took it hard."

Jen nodded.

"If he'd sunk in a storm, the way other Ellises have, we could've stood it better. The Weaver's out there, we all know, ready if we give it a chance. But the Weaver wasn't the rock Guy split on, Jen. There was one in himself that he never bothered to steer out around."

There was no sound in the room but the soft, furry snapping of the dying wood fire in the stove. Then Grampie went on.

1 5 6

"For a while, I couldn't get that cussid great rock out of my mind. Nor you couldn't. Nor Jebby, here."

He smiled at them.

"Well, it's over and done with. Now, we've got to write Guy off and forget him. Looked at on the surface, his life never meant nothing, and that's a hard thing. What you could say, it's pointed some things to look out for, and it's made a man out of Jebby before his time. He's young to be a man, but he ain't the first boy that ever happened to."

Jeb was over on the other side of the room fiddling nervously with the papers on the stand. Jen noticed that the side of his face and the ear that she could see had turned bright pink.

"We've got the pieces to pick up," Grampie said. "That's for all of us to do, Jen. What Jebby and I want to say, Guy wasn't only your husband. He was Jebby's father. He was my son. We don't like to see you so tired you have to walk upstairs on your anklebones."

"Darn right we don't," Jeb exploded.

"I guess you better tell me what you want to do," Jen said.

"Well, you've taken over running the house," Grampie said. "You ain't called on me for a cent since your boarders came."

That was right. She hadn't. The four boarders paid her thirty dollars a week apiece and the $120 was ample to run the house. She paid wages to Lynnie and Evelyn, and that didn't leave a great deal to apply to bills, but it left some, and when she had more boarders she'd be able to go faster.

"There's my main responsibility gone," Grampie said.

"I should think you'd be glad of it. I figured it was the only way I had of paying you back what you lent Guy."

"Don't think I don't appreciate that. I do, Jen. God-almighty, I do. But Jebby and I, we're menfolks. It's up to us to work and earn. We like to. You take away our reason for it, you put me with my foot in the grave and Jebby with his in the cradle. Run the house, for your share. Take your extra money and hire some decent help, so's you won't be wore out before your time. And let us tend to Guy's bills."

"I've *got* help," Jen said firmly.

"Where's your help today?"

"Myrabel Evans would come for twenty dollars a week and her board," Jeb said.

"Why, the two of you! You planned this all out ahead of time."

Jen didn't know whether to lay them low or burst out crying.

"Well, I did go to see Myrabel," Jeb said, shamefacedly. "She'd love to have her old job back. She was growling all the time I was there because she was going to have to work in the factory. Don't you, honest, want her, Ma?"

Jen saw a picture in her mind of Myrabel Evans, stout, sensible, hard-working, dependable and jolly, and of what it would mean, right now, to have her help in the kitchen.

"Oh, Lord," she said. "It would be heaven, Jeb."

"Well, let me call her up, right now." Jeb unfolded his long legs out of his chair.

"Wait, now. Let's think."

"What of?"

"Well, I promised Evelyn and Lynnie I'd pay them—"

"Evelyn don't know a dime from a hole in the ground," Grampie said, "and don't care. And if Lynnie wants pay for an honest day's work, she better put one in, not go tooting off on picnics."

"Let me call her, Ma."

"Well . . . all right."

Jeb came back from the telephone jubilant.

"She'll be up in the morning," he said. "Good old Myrabel. She was all ready to come tonight."

"Right now, there isn't enough to pay her and meet

steady payments on the bills," Jen said, with worry in her voice.

"Ma," Jeb said, grinning at her, "you don't listen to people. You just sit there, single-minded, like a clam. How much did Pa owe?"

Jen looked at them and her heart turned over. But she let them have it, and it rocked them both back on their heels.

"Just a shade under nine thousand dollars," she said. "Your three hundred and twenty-five, that'll bring it down to around eighty-six hundred, Jeb."

Jeb turned white around the mouth. "Holy Ker-istmas!"

Grampie stared at her. Then he smiled a little. "You're counting in what he owed me on the dragger, Jen."

"Of course I am."

"Well, he owed me forty-eight hundred. That's only thirty-eight hundred we've got to worry about in a hurry, Jebby."

"Phew!" Jeb breathed. "You had me sweating, there, for a minute, Ma."

Jen spun on him.

"You think what's owed your grandfather ain't as important as the rest of it?"

"Of course I don't."

But he was figuring on the margin of Grampie's newspaper, putting down numerals with quick little jabs of his pencil.

"We can do it, Grampie, I think."

Grampie said, "I'll talk to Ebbets at the bank."

"Can we do it? Is it okay?"

"Well, summer fishing ain't as good as fall, and we'll have to allow for bad luck. But your ma's running the house now. Ayeh. We can do it."

"Okay. Look, Ma." He tore off the margin of the newspaper and thrust it into her hand. "Here's what we thought."

"I don't get it, Jeb."

She couldn't make head nor tail of his scrawled figuring.

"Grampie and I are going lobstering," he began.

"Yes. I know."

"Well, I thought first I'd go with him in his boat. But we can make more money if I have a skiff."

"But—"

"Pa left an order with Bun McCarthy, over at the Rocktown boatyard, to build him a skiff and Bun did. Russ told me. Bun wouldn't even lay down her keel till Pa paid him something, so Pa paid half and guaranteed to pay the rest when the skiff was finished. Well, I went over to see Bun."

Grampie chuckled.

"Bun was surprised," he said. "He figured none of us knew anything about the skiff, seeing Guy told him he was keeping mum about it. So Bun thought he'd lay low, hang on to Guy's money, and bime-by, if nobody said anything, he'd sell the skiff."

"Well, that was pretty cheap," Jen said indignantly.

"Jebby fixed him," Grampie said, still grinning.

Jeb said, "I figured it'd be bad business to lose Pa's down payment. So I took his otter drag over to Bun and traded it for the rest of the cost of the skiff."

"You did?" Jen eyed him. She'd completely forgotten about the otter drag, salvaged from Guy's boat.

"Well, you gave me the stuff," he reminded her. "I sold most of it—only kept what I'd need. Russ said that drag, if we sold it we couldn't have got near what it was worth in cash. So I've got the skiff," he said proudly. "She's down anchored off the beach right now. I want you to come down and see her, Ma. She's a dandy."

"And what made Bun McCarthy so big-hearted as to trade for that old drag?"

"Russ said it was worth it in trade. Bun can always sell

a secondhand drag. He won't lose any money. Anyway, he didn't kick, Ma."

"He didn't open his frozen-faced yip," Grampie said, with a short snort of laughter. "Serve him right if he lost on it, but it was a fair trade, Jen. Bun makes a helmonious profit out of them skiffs he builds."

"All right," Jen said. "If you say so."

Jeb drew a long breath.

"Pa had a new outboard stowed away down in the fish-house. I want to keep it."

Jen shook her head.

"It isn't paid for, Jeb."

"It will be. There's only forty dollars left. Grampie and I together can run two hundred traps, Ma, if I have an outboard."

"But you haven't got that many traps, Jeb."

"We've got a hundred and thirty-seven. We plan to build the rest this summer. Set 'em as fast as we get them done."

"What about school this fall?"

Jeb looked at her. "I won't fight you on that any longer, Ma. If we could leave it for now, make up our minds when the time comes. I want to go to diesel school, and I might be able to get credit on my high-school diploma for that. I have to find out."

"Well, I'd certainly be glad not to have to fight you over it any longer," Jen said.

She felt bewildered, as if things were moving much too fast, and tired as she was tonight, she needed time to think. Jeb's plans sounded too ambitious; but she couldn't help but be proud of the way he was trying. Of course Russ and Grampie must have helped him. It sounded very much to her as if the three of them had put their heads together. She was about to mention this. Then she changed her mind. Let him try it.

She said, "Well, all right, Jeb."

She was completely unprepared for the hug he gave her, and so was he. Both of them turned red, and he looked away.

Jeb said, flustered, "Russ was saying that if you had a lot of separate bills, Ma, it's smart to take them all to the bank and get a loan."

If he had given a good bucket of milk, he had proceeded to kick it over. Jen's jaw set like a rock.

"Borrow from the *bank?* No, sir!"

"Well, Russ—"

"Russ, Russ, Russ! I'll have a word with him," she said grimly.

"He was just talking," Jeb mumbled. "But it's fairer to the dealers to pay them, Ma. They need their money. And it keeps your credit good."

"Credit!" Jen said. "I've heard nothing all my life but a man talking fast about credit!"

"Jeb ain't talking about buying on tick," Grampie said. "He means a man's *credit,* what the people in his town think of him. He doesn't get through life very easy if his credit ain't good. Mine is," he finished quietly. "Now how about letting us take a peek at them bills?"

There was a measured step outside the door, and Candace came into the kitchen. Her black eyes were snapping with rage.

"Why, Candy," Jen said, startled. "I thought you'd gone to bed."

"I don't doubt you did, seeing what's going on here." She stopped in front of her father. "Pa, you are not going to mortgage this house."

"Who said I was?"

"I know well enough which way things are headed."

"Just don't worry, Candy. It'll be all right," he said quietly.

"So you say. I've heard you say that before. Well, I

1 6 2

won't let you risk the very roof over our heads. You've lost everything else."

Grampie stiffened. "You'd have been welcome to come in here, Candy, where we was all talking things over; not think you had to listen outside the door. Then you'd have heard it all, not just half enough to go on."

"I heard enough to know that Jen's handing Guy's bills over to you to pay."

"I wouldn't think of your father's mortgaging the house! My soul, it never entered my head!" Jen's voice was so full of outrage that there could be no doubt as to how she felt.

"This house doesn't mean a thing to you," Candace said, turning on her. "Look at the disgraceful way you've used it. When I think of Grammie's beautiful rooms and the riffraff that's in them now, I could set the whole shebang afire and burn it down. Next fall, we'll have to disinfect before we can live again."

"Candy, that's enough," Grampie said. "You're making a fool of yourself."

"A fool! If there was ever a doddering old fool, and has been, ever since you ruined us all in 1932—"

Grampie's voice cut across hers.

"Jen, I want them bills, if you've got them handy."

Jen took them out of the drawer of her sewing table and handed them to him. He began glancing through the thick wad of papers.

"When you've looked at them, I'd like them back, Grampie," Jen said.

"You mean you'd like them back receipted," Candace said.

Jen flushed.

"There's no need of a row," she said. "I want them back now, Grampie."

"In a minute," he said, absorbed.

He reached the last sheet, flicked the papers thoughtfully against his hand and passed them back to her without a word.

"And you might as well give up your worming around, because he's *never* going to mortgage the house," Candace said.

Grampie said, "What would *you* do, Candy?"

Candy recoiled as if she had touched something hot.

"It's nothing whatever to do with me!"

"All right. Keep out of it then. People who want a say in this world have either got to fish or cut bait."

"You think I'd let you muddle around and lose the house, too? What would you use for security? Grandfather Malcolm's reputation? You haven't anything of your own."

"I know what your grandmother learnt you, Candy. You don't have to peddle her notions to me."

"Your own mother!" Candy said. "I warn you, Pa—"

"You warn me of what?"

Jen had wondered how much more Grampie was going to take. Now he suddenly faced toward Candace, and she fell back a step, but she did not lower her voice.

"Our people were people of distinction," she said. "The line goes back, if you follow it far enough, to royalty, to the best blood in the world. Those people are all dead now. This house—"

"Our people were common, ordinary folks, like anybody else," Grampie said. "If you want to say they had the best blood in the world, I'll agree with you. Most common, ordinary folks do."

"This house is all there is left of them. I won't—"

"This house was built by a man who worked with his hands, Dan Ellis. His great-grandfather, Joe, was an Essex fisherman. I don't say we ain't all got reason to be proud of what they done. They was smart men, good men, most of them. But they wasn't descended from the dukes and lords and crowned heads of Europe, by God. Your grandmother made that up out of whole cloth, the time it come up in the D.A.R. that one of the early Ellises was hung. He was, too. For stealing a sheep."

She stared at him. "You've never in all your life said such things to me!"

"No, and I wouldn't now, if you wasn't making such a cold-hearted show of yourself. Not that somebody shouldn't have said them to you, years ago. Have you grown up in this house, with all there is back of it, and all there is to come, without finding out that things like a house ain't important, it's the people in it? Thunderation, Candy, have the sense you was born with! You can always replace a house."

PART FOUR
Evelyn

SITTING on the screened back porch, from which the glass windows had been removed for the summer, Evelyn sang to Clay, her plain voice accompanied by the soft and various creaks of her wicker rocking chair.

> *"Fly under, fly over, my dimity-doo,*
> *My little gray feather, my darling, my dear."*

The old lullaby had a sleepy swing, and Evelyn herself was more than half asleep from it; she only wished Clay were. But Clay kept rolling his head in an uncomfortable way on her bosom, bouncing his fat little buttocks up and down in her hard lap. Finally he sat up straight, looked into her face and said unmistakably, "Nuts!"

From the wicker chair's twin, a few feet down the porch, Myrabel Evans said, "My, that baby's old for his age!"

Myrabel was resting with her crochet work, now that the dishes from the boarders' dinner were cleared away and there would be an hour or so before she and Jen had to think about supper. Her feet in lavender crocheted bedroom slippers expanded in comfort on the grass porch-rug; her ample figure, clad in a Nile green housecoat, filled the chair with solid immobility. No one, seeing Myrabel relaxed, would have believed the way she could move around a kitchen.

"He picks it up from the older boys," Evelyn said. "Come on, Clay, put your head down."

But Clay shrugged her off. He stiffened his body so that he slid through her hands to the floor. He padded sleepily across to Myrabel, climbed up into her lap and laid his head against her vast, billowing amplitude, where he relaxed with a long sigh.

Myrabel stared.

"Well, shan't you die!" she said. "Trust a male to find a soft spot."

Evelyn said, ruefully, "I'm not much of a pillow."

"Well, you *are* thin, dear," Myrabel said, comfortably. "But you've got ample for all intents and purposes. I will say, though, that you are entering into competition when it comes to me."

She put down her crochet work and began rocking Clay.

"Oh, dear," Evelyn said. "That's my job, Myrabel, and you're having your rest-time."

"I don't mind," Myrabel said. "Rocking one of the cussid little pests always does rest me, and that's a fact."

She weaved the chair ponderously to and fro, and presently broke out in a fruity contralto:

> *"Oh, Ringgold was a pirate bold,*
> *Who sailed the seven seas,*
> *With silver buttons on his coat*
> *And gold ones on his knees—"*

A milky, contented expression came into Clay's eyes. The lids drooped. He shoved his thumb all the way into his mouth.

"Here!" Myrabel said, yanking it out. "Don't do that. that's nasty."

"Sing some more," Clay said.

"I do believe this chair walks, Evelyn," Myrabel said. "Either I spraddle out its rockers or they're uneven. I'm a foot further from that table than I was. My old gra'-mother had one once—"

"Sing some more," Clay said, jerking up and down.

"You keep your shirt on," she said. "Don't talk when the grown-ups is talking, and if you're a-going to set in my lap, you stop your bouncing. It makes my stomach rumble. If I was ever to have a fit of my rumbles come on me," she went on to Evelyn, "when I was waiting on that tableful of summer people, I'd go through the floor. I was going to say, my old gra'mother had one of them walking chairs, uneven rockers, went sideways like a crab, and it walked her right off over the end of the piazza one day, tail over crocket, into the flower bed. It took an awful jolt out of her."

"Don't you do that," Evelyn said nervously.

"Oh, mercy, no. I'd know better. But Grammie was deef."

Clay, who had waited until she was through talking, now asked politely, "Sing the Pirate?"

"You've charmed him," Evelyn said. "When I don't sing, right up quick, he gets mad."

Myrabel looked down ferociously at Clay. "He knows better than to fly into a spizzle with me," she said.

Clay smiled up at her, sleepily.

"Oh, all right," she said.

> *"He laid in wait for merchant ships,*
> *From Clyde to Scatteree,*
> *And he shot their bloody topmasts out*
> *And sank them in the sea,"*

she sang.

> *"Did Ringgold the Pirate, oh!*
> *Blow wherever the winds blow,*
> *With his crimson turkey feather,*
> *And his pantaloons of leather,*
> *And his black, black flag on the bloody morning, oh!"*

She went through three stanzas, her voice blurring and tapering off to a hum as Clay sagged in her lap. Then, as she stopped, his eyes popped open.

He said, "Sing loud, My'bel."

"My soul," she said. "Some people do hate to give up." She came out strongly with the fourth stanza:

"His topsails spun, his halyards run,
He let his cannon rip,
Four-score-and-ten foul-hearted men,
They poured aboard the ship.
They sank her deep, they sank her low,
They caught the lovely bride,
And all day long the bloody heads
Rolled down the bloody tide."

"There!" she said. "That settles you for a couple of hours."

She got to her feet with a windy groan, dumped Clay on the couch in the corner of the porch and pulled a knitted afghan over him. Then she went back to her chair and took up her crochet.

"I don't see how you do it," Evelyn said enviously. "When I put him down, I have to be so careful, or he wakes right up."

"Why, I don't do nothing," Myrabel said. "I take a good solid holt on them, which I notice you don't, that's all. And then, they always do like my singing. My Randall and my George and my Timmy used to go to sleep something wonderful to the Pirate."

"It's a good song," Evelyn said. "Not exactly a children's song, but—"

"What *are* you talking about?" Myrabel demanded, with asperity. "Kids have gone to sleep to that song since before the Revolution. How I did love to hear old Cap'n Malcolm sing that, when I was little. Didn't you? My, I can't do it justice. Not the way he could with that bass voice of his."

Jossie Evans, Myrabel's mother, had for years been the Ellises' hired girl, in the days when the Ellises could afford one, and Myrabel and the Ellis girls had pretty much grown up together.

"I hope you don't think that song you was singing was any child's song, either," Myrabel went on.

"Well . . ."

"Hnf, it never had no tune, in the first place, added *to* which, it was dirty."

"Dirty?" Evelyn asked, amazed.

"Some woman asking her darling, her dear, to fly under her apron, do."

"Apron?"

"Dimity—that's an apron. Or always was, to my knowledge, when it warn't a dress. It certainly started up my ideas, till I realized you didn't have no more idea what you was singing than the man in the moon."

Evelyn chuckled. "I don't seem to have, do I?"

She got up. "I expect I'd better see where the other children are, while Jen's resting. Thanks, Myrabel, for getting Clay to sleep."

"You're a thousand times welcome," Myrabel said.

She watched meditatively as Evelyn's slight figure, crowned by her enormous checked sunbonnet, diminished along the path to the orchard. Then she shook her head with a little, mystified "Tch!"

It was a living shame for as nice a woman as Evelyn Ellis to dress so peculiar. She wouldn't be bad if you took them sunbonnets off of her and them dreeled-down dresses, that without doubt was Candy's cast-offs. You put her into something bright and pretty and give her a permanent— maybe one of Freda's windblowns, instead of that pug knot that hauled her hair back so tight it bugged her eyes out, and you wouldn't know Evelyn Ellis.

How old was she, anyway? Candy was forty-five, Myrabel's exact age, they'd gone to grade school together, so Evelyn must be around thirty-two or -three. How Candy Ellis used to bat that poor little bit of a youngone around! And from all Myrabel could see, she hadn't outgrown it a mite, either. In fact, now, you wouldn't care to be anybody that Candy ever got the upper hands of. You didn't even care to get any closer to her than you had to.

She's certainly growed into one blind dungeon of a woman.

In school, she had been as stubborn as a dry stick, break before she'd bend, and now that she'd had a come-down, she was worse. It *was* considerable of a come-down, too, for the Ellises to be running a boarding place; all the more to have Myrabel here waiting on their summer trade. Because when Myrabel's mother had worked for Old Gram, it was the Ellises that took the waiting on.

Well, no point to use up your rest-time having over other people's business.

Myrabel went serenely on with her crocheting.

She heard a tentative step on the walk outside the screened porch, and Mr. Raymond, the painting boarder, came past the corner of the house. He had his paintbox and stuff, but he didn't appear to be going anywhere in particular, just wandering along aimless.

Myrabel craned up.

He don't look at all well, she thought.

Maybe he was sick. He hadn't been in to the dining room at noon, but nobody thought much about that, because he often stayed out painting all day.

At that moment, to Myrabel's embarrassment, he looked around and saw her craning.

He said, sadly, "Good afternoon, Mrs. Ellis."

"Evans," Myrabel said. "Myrabel Evans, Mr. Raymond."

"Oh, excuse me." He blinked. "It's the screens, I guess."

Screens nothing, Myrabel thought. If ever I saw a man hung, it's him.

She said, "You want something to eat, Mr. Raymond?"

Mr. Raymond flinched. Her experienced eyes took in his haggard cheeks, the pale-blue shadows under his lower lids. She got up.

"You come in here, Mr. Raymond. Out bareheaded in that hot sun's no place for a man's in the shape you're in."

"Oh, God," Mr. Raymond said. "Does it show that bad?"

He came in.

"They's a stout spring on that screen door," Myrabel warned. "It'll shut to with a bang if you don't hold it." She added, so as not to embarrass him, "The baby's asleep."

"Thanks," he said.

He sat down in Evelyn's wicker chair, which, being a rocker, rocked. He jerked himself straight, muttering.

Myrabel went off to the kitchen, from which she returned presently with a tumbler. She handed it to him and sat down again.

Mr. Raymond gazed at the mixture in the tumbler with a sick eye, smelled it and sipped it. Then, with an incredulous glance at her, he up-ended the glass.

"God love you," he said, after an eloquent silence.

Myrabel nodded. "My first husband was a drunk," she said.

"Oh." Mr. Raymond gulped slightly. "Will you marry me?"

"No," she said, with dignity. "Amos Coughlin's my friend now."

Mr. Raymond said, "I'm sorry, Mrs. Evans."

Myrabel chuckled.

"Oh, Bert always used to think the world and all of me for the first ten minutes after he'd had a swig of my private receet for a hangover. I don't take it amiss, Mr.

Raymond. What have you been up to? You don't give the impression of being a drinking man."

"I'm not. And I won't be again for a long, long time."

"Bert always used to say that, too, but nevertheless, the demon rum killed him. The doctor said his liver was like the meringue on a lemon pie, and I will say it was a relief when he was gone."

"It must have been," said Mr. Raymond faintly.

"Indeed it was. Bert knew it, but that didn't stop him from going to Bellport every Saturday night and hanging one on. It ain't a chance a normal man ought to take with his liver, Mr. Raymond. Have you a love affair on, by any chance?"

"No, I have not," Mr. Raymond said.

"I don't mean to appear nosy," Myrabel said. "But I was going to say, if it ain't anything serious like a love affair, you could get rid of it better by taking the ax and mauling the hell out of the woodpile. I used to tell Bert that, but with him, it was a love affair, he was running around with that Carrie Tourtelot, and of course he had me and my George and my Randall and my Timmy. So there wasn't no ordinary help for Bert, and he took to drinking. I will say, though, I took as good care of him as I could, knowing, as I did, what underlay. I always say, if you know what underlays, quite often you can't blame a man. You don't have nothing so serious as a love affair, Mr. Raymond?"

"No," he said. "I expect you'd have to blame me. I hung one on over a picture I was painting."

"Did you reelly?" Myrabel said, with deep interest. "What of?"

Mr. Raymond glanced over at her.

"Two rocks," he said, "and the bones out of a cow's head."

"My goodness." Myrabel smoothed out in her lap the bright pink square she had just crocheted. "I wonder if that could be Byde Palmer's cow," she said meditatively. "The one that took sick, three years ago, and he led her down on Barle's Point and shot her."

"I found the bones down on Barle's Point. It was a complete skeleton when I found it, if that's what you want to know," Mr. Raymond said.

"I always said 'twasn't right to shoot the poor cretur and leave her there, bare," Myrabel said. "The least he could of done was to bury her. Well, Mr. Raymond, what was the matter? Couldn't you paint her bones?"

"I paint beautiful bones," he said, "and very nice rocks. The trouble was, nothing would go together."

"All right. I blame you," Myrabel said.

He said, "I blame myself."

"Well, art," she said. "The other day, down to the Aid, I got to listening to Claudie Allen tell about how she combed out the bread truck for almost running over her long-haired tiger cat, them bread trucks they go through like everybody in the town was starving for store bread, cats, dogs and children ain't safe. Claudie was telling what she told the driver, and I got my chains too long, and what come out wasn't reelly a square but the map of Australia-like. But I never went out and hung one on. I undone it and done it over. A whole square."

Mr. Raymond opened his bleared eyes at the pink blob in her lap.

"What *is* that?" he asked.

"This is the hundredth-and-thirty-ninth pink square for my pink-and-yellow crocheted bedspread," Myrabel said.

"Hund— How many squares will it take?"

"Four hundred and eighty. Two hundred and forty pink ones and two hundred and forty yellow ones. It's for a double bed. The yellow ones is all done."

Mr. Raymond closed his eyes.

"I can see," Myrabel said stiffly, "that you don't think

such a thing would be very pretty. Well, I'll tell you, Mr. Raymond, I wouldn't have mentioned it otherwise, but anybody who makes up your bed once a day can't help seeing them pictures you have got around your room, and they ain't pretty, Mr. Raymond. Them purple and green and I-don't-know-what-all-colored stwizzles, they ain't a picture to me, and what a grown man is doing with two rocks and a mess of cow's bones, I can't think, but I would say, little."

"How right you are," Mr. Raymond said, under his breath.

"I am, ain't I? I wouldn't of been so outspoken, not to hurt your feelings, if you hadn't kind of flinched away over my spread. You ain't even seen it, and it's been an awful lot of work. Look," Myrabel said.

She hitched the walking chair back to the table it had crept away from, pulled a big suit box off the shelf and emptied it out in her lap. She said, "I got the idea from my pink and yellow tulip bed."

A river of pure colors poured down over her green housecoat and her lavender slippers on to the pale fawn of the rug, and Mr. Raymond rocked back on his heels.

"Mrs. Evans," he said respectfully, "you win. It's beautiful, and so are you. I'd like to put you on a five-foot canvas just as you are, and call it 'Portrait of Mrs. Myrabel Evans.' "

Myrabel blushed.

Telling Jen about it, afterwards, she said she blushed all over.

"I could feel it start down you-know-where, and come straight up to the top of my head," she said. "I said, 'Mr. Raymond! Now you are reelly making fun of me,' and he said no, by gracious, he wasn't, and he said he was going down on the shore and find a place to sleep off his hangover, and then, if he hadn't give up painting for good, he was coming back and start right in. But he said he had give it up forever," Myrabel said, laughing hugely. "I just told him to be sure to keep his head in the shade."

MR. RAYMOND went down to a place he knew, on the eastern shore of Barle's Point, in the woods of which he had discovered the bones of the in more than one sense ill-fated cow. He stretched himself out full length in the sun, on a warm, granite boulder, with his head in the shade, and fell heavily asleep.

A little way up the shore, Evelyn, with Mertis and Maggie in tow, came out of a grove of beech trees to the edge of the red, sun-baked rocks.

"I don't believe you made one," Mertis stated. "I made sure you didn't even know what one is."

Evelyn laughed.

"You thought you had me, didn't you? You'll learn. You've never stuck me yet."

She had her sunbonnet off, carrying it, basketlike, in one hand, and the sun glinted on her dark-red hair. The sunbonnet was full of water-polished pebbles and gray small pieces of driftwood weathered into delicate shapes.

"Well, I've stuck you this time," Mertis said. "You've got to show me, Aunt Evelyn."

Evelyn's cheeks were pink, her gray eyes twinkling.

"You used the dictionary," she accused.

"Well." Mertis looked crestfallen. "I couldn't stick you on my own. I had to have help."

Evelyn said, "I'll tell you a secret. I had to use the dictionary, too."

Mertis brightened.

"You did? It was the first animal in there, and it was a wonderful one. Wasn't it wonderful, Aunt Evelyn?"

Maggie said, uncompromisingly, "Wull, where is it? I want to see it."

"You have to find it," Evelyn said.

She sat down and leaned her back against a boulder. "You've got five minutes to find it, same as always."

The two little girls started out, ranging the beech grove like beagles. Their white T-shirts twinkled in and out among the trees. A few minutes passed, and Maggie let out a delighted yell.

"Oh, what is it? Mert, Aunt Evelyn, what is it?"

The animal, modeled out of clay, now partially hardened, was crouched at the foot of an ancient, rotten beech-stump, about six feet high. Years ago, lightning had struck a tree, snapping it off at its fork and ripping down its side a weird, long scar, which was now weathered to a silvery gray. The broken fork thrust out like a huge, brooding head, and a wood spider had anchored across it a big, pale cartwheel of web. Below it, was a grass-grown mound, into which the strange animal nosed its amazing snout above its fiercely clawed, round feet.

"Oh!" Maggie shrieked, dancing beside it. "What is it, what is it, what is it?"

"It's an aardvark," Mertis said learnedly.

"It is, truly. An aardvark," Evelyn said. "See, Maggie, his nose."

"What makes it so long? Oh, it's a lovely nose," Maggie said. "And *ears*, Aunt Evelyn!"

She put a grubby hand yearningly on the aardvark's back.

Mertis said in an urgent voice, "He isn't dry, Maggie," and Maggie took the hand away. Both of them knew well Aunt Evelyn's animals, which had to dry and dry, and then, unless you were very careful, broke too easily.

"It eats ants," Mertis said. "Doesn't it, Aunt Evelyn?"

"Mm-hm," Evelyn said.

"Where are the rel ones? Couldn't we find an anthill with a rel one on it?" Maggie asked. "One we could truly play with?"

"Well, they're far away," Evelyn said.

She had meant to notice, when she'd copied the picture in the dictionary, where anteaters lived, because it was a foregone conclusion that Maggie would ask. Maggie was practical. She liked her information classified, often finding Aunt Evelyn's unsatisfactory.

"But where?"

"At suppertime, we'll look up and see."

"I want to know now," Maggie said stubbornly. "We can't play with it, so I want to know where it comes from."

Mertis and Aunt Evelyn looked at each other, over her head, with secret smiles. As if, the smiles said, such things mattered, in the case of such a wonderful animal!

"Well, let's go look in the dictionary and find out," Evelyn said. "I expect by tomorrow he'll be dry enough to play with, Maggie."

She went back to the shore for her sunbonnet, emptying the stones and driftwood out of it onto a boulder with a hollowed-out top.

"But we hunted for those things all afternoon," Maggie protested. "I want my pink rock I found."

"We'll come back for it," Mertis said firmly. "Aunt Evelyn needs her sunbonnet now, if we're going back to the house."

The three figures merged into the greenery along the shore path, leaving the stranger in a strange land, the aardvark, sitting under the stump of the blasted beechwood tree.

Shrieks of joy from not far away had penetrated Mr. Raymond's sodden sleep, but not enough to waken him. He merely stirred, mumbled, and passed back to dreamlessness again.

The blue afternoon went over him; the sun set in a parade of gold like the passing of an emperor's train, not waking him. Out of the east, the June moon rose; a white river flowed across the sea. The wooded land darkened with mystery; and Mr. Raymond slept on.

But at last the hard granite ledge, cooling under him, caused him to rear up lumpishly and stare around at a lovely universe which, to him, now, was a personal insult.

I need to sleep in a bed, he told himself.

And, unprintably, he specified the kind of a fool he was, saying that if that kind of a fool hadn't left paintbox and easel on the Ellises' back porch, he would have had them at hand now to hurl forever into the sea.

He got himself to his feet and stumped up the path toward the house, a cold, hungry, disheveled man with a headache. And as he passed the beech trees, the white moon shone down on a veiled gargoyle, striped with black and unearthly pearl, at whose feet crouched an animal out of fantasy, an undeniable anteater, chased in silver light.

Good God, Mr. Raymond said, focusing. I didn't get *that* drunk!

Nothing moved in the grove. The hallucination did not change. After a second or two, Mr. Raymond stepped off the path and went through the soft June-grass toward the clay model and the white, dead, lightning-riven tree, whose moonlit cobweb now was strung with beads of dew.

"I'll be damned," he said. "I'll be double, triple damned."

Who could have done such a beautiful thing?

He couldn't see details very well, and he pulled out his cigarette lighter, noting the strong, delicate workmanship, the material, which seemed to be nothing but ordinary shore clay. The sculptor hadn't tried to do more than indicate an anteater's heavy, hairy tail, obviously because of the limitations of the medium; but it was indicated; it was sufficient. The thing had an air of self-contained humor and a secrecy befitting moonlight.

Gargoyle and Anteater, said his mind, beginning to take fire with possibilities. It ran ahead of him up the path to his paintbox on the Ellises' side porch, and to the white, untouched, infinitely pregnant canvas in his room.

EARLY as Mr. Raymond got up the next morning, someone had been in the beech grove before him. Across the center of it, in the June-grass laid low with dew, a dark line went where feet had dislodged the water drops and something—a skirt?—had brushed.

What have we got in this wood—dryads? he asked himself, hurrying to set up his easel.

We might have, at that, he added, for the just-risen sun was slanting through the grove already curiously occupied, and the footprints gave a feeling of mysterious presence only just gone away.

He began sketching furiously in watercolor to catch what he could before the sun dried off the dew, forgetting that he had meant to go back to the house for his breakfast.

His second sketch was nearly done when he became aware of sounds in the underbrush behind him—scratchings and scrabblings at first, then a choked-back whisper. His flying brush began to falter.

Mr. Raymond was not one of the fortunate painters able to remain in concentration while sidewalk superintendents breathed down his neck. For that reason, he usually worked in woods or deserted meadows, or found a place along some secret cove, never so near as this to people and houses.

Who could it be?

The Clawsons, he thought suddenly, with a flush of rage starting up the back of his neck.

The horrible Clawsons, with whom he had to eat strained meals each day, while Father Clawson chomped fish and Mother Clawson purled on about depressed classes and minorities, in comparison with whom her opinion of herself did not suffer; and the ineffable Flora made it obvious, in her pretty way, that a pass from Mr. Raymond would not be unacceptable.

A thing, he thought viciously, in which he'd be delighted to co-operate, if the arrangement might be considered a purely temporary one.

He had painted all over the world and had lived in boarding places from Chicago to Tibet; he considered it juvenile to let himself be annoyed by casual table companions. Usually, he let the conversation, of whatever caliber, flow around him, joining it if he wished, making friends if he felt like it. But no man, however thick-skinned, could ignore the threefold assault made on privacy by the organized Clawsons.

He said in a loud voice, "Cattle!"

There was a dead silence in the bushes, whereupon Mr. Raymond rose to his feet and strode to the edge of the beech wood. Behind a tree squatted not the Clawsons, but the two little Ellis girls, the smaller one already scrabbling up to run, the other scared, but standing her ground.

"Oh," said Mr. Raymond flatly. "I didn't know it was you."

"Who did you think it was?" Mertis asked warily.

"I called you what I thought it was. Look here, you're bothering me. Run off, will you?"

Maggie, who had got some distance away, turned around and came back. She said, "That's our aardvark."

"Is it? Who made it?" Mr. Raymond said, with interest.

Neither of the two little girls said anything. They both looked a trifle shocked, he thought.

Finally Mertis said, looking away, "We did."

"Oh, nonsense. You couldn't have."

"Yes, we did."

It wasn't a lie—Mertis had had a share in the aardvark. It had been her idea. And if she said "we" then she didn't have to break the promise to Aunt Evelyn, who had asked them please not to say if people inquired who made any of the animals.

"Yes, we did," Maggie chimed in. "We made it and it's ours and we want to play with it."

"Oh, Lord!" Mr. Raymond said.

To himself, he said, Blast and damnation!

He had only working sketches—he needed three or four sittings with the thing, in different lights, before he could hope to decide on his picture. If these youngsters played with it, moved it . . . *broke* it, he thought with horror, because it would, obviously, crumble at a touch—

"Look," he said. "Please go away. I'll give you each a dime."

Maggie said, "We don't want a dime. We want to play with our aardvark."

Mertis said, "Come on, Maggie. We can use a dime."

Mr. Raymond was acting just the way Aunt Evelyn did when she wanted them to go away. Mertis jerked her head at Maggie, saying, "Well, come on."

"No, I won't," said Maggie.

Mertis looked at Mr. Raymond.

"She's awful stubborn. She wanted to play with it yesterday and it wasn't dry, and last night she couldn't go to sleep, waiting for today to come."

"Oh," Mr. Raymond said. "I see." He hesitated, went on unwillingly, "Well, it's yours. I guess you'll have to have it, won't you?"

He went back to his easel and the two little girls followed him.

"You couldn't leave it long enough for me to paint it?" he asked. "Wouldn't you like to play something else?"

He glanced at Maggie and saw that her eye was glued to his watercolor box, spread open where he had left it.

"Wouldn't you like to play painted Indians?"

"How?" Mertis asked. "We've never played painted Indians."

"Well, come here. I'll show you," he said, desperately, for the morning light was going, changing into the far different light of noon. "First, you paint your noses blue. Like this—"

Mertis's blue nose, from which red, yellow and ocher stripes fanned out, was nothing extraordinary, as blue noses go; but Maggie's tip-tilt, plumb in the middle of her round, uncompromising, pink-cheeked, sober face, was an artistic triumph.

Mertis looked and burst out laughing, and Mr. Raymond looked, and they both laughed until the tears rolled down their cheeks, while Maggie stared at them soberly; then she gave signs of a different kind of tears.

"Oh, hey, there," Mr. Raymond said, stopping at once.

"Maggie," Mertis said. "Stop crying, because *you can't possibly blow your nose.*"

"We only laughed at a blue nose, not at you," Mr. Raymond said. "Only because a blue nose is funny."

But Maggie was crying over the aardvark; not at what they thought, at all.

"Here," Mr. Raymond said, thrusting his brush into her hand. "Paint mine. See if it doesn't look funny."

He sat, quietly desperate, watching the morning light go, while Maggie made tremulous dabs with the brush at his face.

"That's blue enough," he said. He got up. "See, isn't it funny?"

It was. Maggie's efforts were spotty, but she had really let herself go with the colors.

The little girls rolled on the ground, laughing.

"Now," he said, "you take your shoelace out and make bands for your heads and stick them full of ferns for feathers; and then you go a-whooping and a-hollering through the woods. Anybody you see, you catch and tie to a tree and have a war dance around him."

"You, too, Mr. Raymond?" Mertis asked, hiccuping.

Oh, well, the light was gone. Another day was coming and these were nice kids. He hadn't done anything but mope for days.

"Sure," he said.

Seeing their unbelieving eyes, he knelt down and started to unlace his shoe.

"What's to stop me? I could use a good whoop-and-holler. There're ferns over under that tree. Go pick some."

The band of Indian braves went bellowing and yawping through the woods. They debouched in formation along the shore, finding no one to tie to a tree. Then they thudded at a run along the woods path.

"Ah-oo-oo, ah-oo-oo," howled Mertis and Maggie shrilled, "Ah-wee-wee-wee." Mr. Raymond went, "Ah-wha-wha-wha-wah-wah," clapping his open mouth with the palm of his hand, the ferns drooping over his temples from the shoelace tied around his head.

It was thus, in full cry and panoply, that they rounded a turn in the path and ran into Aunt Candace. She had been out early after wild strawberries in Barle's Meadow, and was coming home with a pailful.

She jumped at first and started to run, because the first one around the corner had been Mr. Raymond. Then she saw the girls behind him and she backed up like a thunderstorm.

"What's going on here?" she demanded. "Mr. *Raymond!*"

"It's a game," Mr. Raymond said. "Indians."

He did not seem at all taken aback.

"You paint your nose blue," he said. "Ferns in a shoelace around your head, a war whoop, and there you are. Indians."

He recoiled, sobered by her face of voiceless fury.

"Miss Ellis," he said at once, "let me apologize, please, if I startled you. I was only being silly, trying to entertain the children."

He got down on his knees to pick up a few scattered berries which had spilled from the top of her pail, and held them out to her.

"I'm terribly sorry," he said.

If he had started to spit in the pail, Candace could not have snatched it away more quickly.

"You girls get straight home," she said. "Your mother'll tend to you. Walk yourselves!"

"Oh, no. It's all my fault—" Mr. Raymond began.

Candace said, "You drunken *bum!*"

She stepped around him and marched away down the path, leaving him with the handful of strawberries foolishly extended.

Mertis said, "I wouldn't want to tie her to a tree, Mr. Raymond."

"Mm-no." Mr. Raymond got to his feet thoughtfully. If that pail had been empty, he wouldn't have liked to take odds on her letting him have it in the face. What an old battle-ax!

"Are you drunk, Mr. Raymond?" Maggie said clearly.

"No," he said, looking down at her.

"Our father was drunk and sunk his boat on a ledge and died."

Mertis flushed darkly.

"Maggie, you shut up!"

"Oh, good Lord," Mr. Raymond said, aghast.

No wonder Miss Ellis had behaved the way she had, if she'd thought him drunk. Myrabel Evans had seemed too kindly a person to gossip about his lapse of yesterday—he wouldn't have believed it of her. Yet probably she'd thought it was too good to keep. Now all the Ellises must think he was a lush, and it was too bad, because he liked them.

As a matter of fact, Myrabel hadn't mentioned it; but he only found that out later.

"Here," he said, glancing at the two sobered faces. "Let's eat these strawberries."

They came at once and began picking the berries out of his hand.

185

"Will you get into trouble over this?" he asked.

"Oh, yes," Mertis said. "Aunt Candy'll say we scared her a-purpose, I s'pose."

"In that case, I'll get straight home with you," he said. He stuck out a hand to each. "We'll have the story told just as it happened."

Jen was at the kitchen door when the trio appeared on the path. She stared, startled, in spite of what Candace had told her. At the sight of Mr. Raymond's worried face with the crown of wilted ferns, which he had not thought to remove, she gurgled and almost lost control. But Candace would be listening somewhere, she knew, and she must be sure not to laugh out loud.

"No wonder you scared your aunt," she said, looking at the two little girls.

"I did it," Mr. Raymond said. "I painted them up and invented a game. We were making a racket, but I didn't really suppose we'd meet anyone. Miss Ellis thought I was drunk, and I don't blame her."

"I don't know as I do, either." Jen's jawbones ached with control. "The three of you!"

In spite of herself, she choked and the words ended in a hiccup.

Mr. Raymond, deeply relieved, grinned at her through his war paint.

"Laugh," he invited. "If you'll give me a washcloth and some suds, I'll scrub them. And myself, too."

"C-come in," Jen said, standing aside. "You can do all the scrubbing you want to at the sink, Mr. Raymond."

The kitchen was a hungry man's dream and it smelled like his heaven. Jen and Evelyn had been fixing vegetables for dinner, and in front of Evelyn on the drainboard were piles of bright red radishes, yellow fat carrots, slices of orange turnip. A big browned pot roast, surrounded by pale, translucent baby onions, stood ready to go on the stove. On the side-table were five delicately tanned apple pies.

186

Mr. Raymond, who, after all, had had no breakfast, stopped in his tracks, as if transfixed by an arrow from one of his own Indians.

He breathed hollowly, "Oh, God!"

Jen put her finger on her lips and pointed to one of the pies. "After you're washed up," she said, in a low voice.

Evelyn had stayed back-to at the drainboard, hoping she might be able, in some way, to avoid facing a stranger. But as Mr. Raymond walked over to the sink, she had to move and turn around. She stood for a split second, taking in the sight of him, and then she let go a great shout of laughter.

It was too much for Jen. She gave up, too. They collapsed, each into a chair. The walls of the kitchen shook as Mr. Raymond's deep bellow and the lighter notes of the children joined in.

Myrabel, who had been setting the table in the dining room, heard the racket, and came scurrying in as lightly as a blown feather. She stood in the door, gasping at the sight.

"Well, Mr. Raymond!" she said. "I see you've reelly gone back to your painting."

JUNE went out with a northeast storm of gale force, which blew for two days. For forty-eight hours the wind howled around the house, rattling rain against the eastern windows with a sound almost as sharp as sleet. The rain washed out Grampie's vegetable garden and mashed into green ruin the stalks of the day lilies by the back porch. A wild apple tree which had stood in the shore meadow for years blew down. Even with the doors closed, the house was full of the muttered rumble and roar of the seas on the back-shore ledges, and the eastern windows were streaked with salt spray blown in over the meadows.

Such a storm in June was not unknown, but it was unexpected. June had given forth with some warm, sunny days, as hot as summer; to be house-bound in weather which had gone back to the chill of March was hard to bear. Jen had a day.

Jeb and Grampie were worried about their traps, for with warmer weather and the good fishing in shallow water, they had moved a good many traps inshore. Jen thanked heaven that they had to spend most of their time down at the harbor, making sure the boats and gear were secure; because, with all she had on her mind besides, she didn't know how she could have managed, seeing their long faces and realizing what their glumness meant. No sense to borrow trouble—they might come out of it all right, with only a few traps gone. And she couldn't stop to borrow trouble, anyway. Here she was, stretched right out straight, forty things to think of at once.

The children couldn't go outdoors, and they got tired quickly of everything there was to do in the house. Evelyn finally rigged them up in waterproofs and boots and took them for a walk; but the wind was impossible. It knocked Clay down and rolled him over in a puddle. Everybody came back with drabbled clothes and had to change. Clay had to be washed and dressed from the skin out.

Candace tore into Evelyn for being such a fool as to take children outside in such weather; Evelyn fled—whether back outdoors or into her room, Jen couldn't say.

Mrs. Clawson and Flora complained that the living room was cold; they complained that the dining room was cold. Their bedrooms, they said, were uninhabitable with damp. Fires as big as winter fires had to be started all over the house at a time of year when airtight stoves had, normally, been dismantled for the summer and stowed away in the barn.

Jen thanked her stars that she and Myrabel hadn't yet taken down the stoves in the upstairs rooms. She saw to it that there were good fires everywhere and plenty of wood. The Clawsons' rooms did not seem damp to her when she went up to see, though she did not say so. She merely stoked up fires and opened dampers.

The summer dining room, however, in which just a few days ago she had taken the stove down, had a definite chill. The big, many-windowed old room had never been meant for use in cool weather. Gram Ellis, whose creation it was, had used it mainly for Sunday-night suppers, when the wide doors could be opened out onto the front porch; she had entertained the Ladies' Aid, the Dorcas Society, the Literary Club, the V.I.A., there, on sunny summer afternoons. Its small fireplace was cheerful, for looks, but it could not heat the room, and Jen had solved the heating problem earlier in June by putting up a sheet of zinc over the fireplace and installing a small, wood-burning heater. But in warm weather, the stove overheated the room. The fireplace was enough, and it was much more pleasant to look at. But now, seeing Mrs. Clawson's face of tragedy, Jen wished she had let the stove alone.

"We think it most ill-advised of you to have removed the stove," Mrs. Clawson said dismally.

"I know it was," Jen said. "I'm sorry, Mrs. Clawson. But weather like this at the end of June I couldn't foresee, and a week ago that stove like to roasted you outdoors."

"It's a dreadful climate. I don't know why Floyd insists. Every summer, he *insists!*"

"Well, it's certainly miserable right now," Jen said. "I could give you your dinner by the living-room fire, or in your room, if you'd rather."

"Thank you, no. I don't care to eat off a tray. Haven't you a smaller room with a stove, where you could set a dining table and we might eat in comfort?"

What she wanted, Jen knew, was to go into the room off the kitchen, known to the family as the "winter" dining room. Mrs. Clawson had suggested this before. Her family, she said, was accustomed to a smaller dining room; it was more *intime,* and less draughty; and, of course, when other boarders came, it would be private.

"No," Jen said. "I'm very sorry, Mrs. Clawson, but I haven't."

Actually, the winter dining room would have been more convenient for Myrabel to serve in, since it was so near the kitchen; but it opened also into Candace's bedroom, and in recent weeks Candace had spread her things out into it, calling it her sitting room.

Jen had already explained to Mrs. Clawson that it wasn't available. Up until today, the summer dining room had been pleasant. Jen felt she had no right to disturb Candace; nor did she wish to risk the battle sure to follow if she did.

Mrs. Clawson said, "My husband has to be careful of his sinuses. He *must not catch cold.*"

Considering some of the weather Mr. Clawson had stayed out fishing in, Jen didn't believe that anything in the summer dining room could chill him; but she said, "I've got an oil heater I can put in there, Mrs. Clawson. It will be warm by dinnertime. And the weather'll surely clear off in a day or so."

Mrs. Clawson said, "Really!"

She came down at noon in a heavy topcoat which she had shortly to take off. Jen had a cheerful, blazing fire going in the fireplace, and the oil heater, though old-fashioned, gave off plenty of heat. It gave off, also, a slight keroseny smell, not objectionable unless one did not care for keroseny smells. Mrs. Clawson didn't. She said so.

She said, "Myrabel, this soup is cold. I'd like it hot, on a hot plate, please."

Myrabel said, "Oh, I'm sorry, Mrs. Clawson."

She took the plate to the kitchen, heated another under the hot-water faucet and dried it, filled it with steaming lobster stew from the kettle on the stove and returned it to the dining room.

Mrs. Clawson touched the edge of the plate gingerly with one finger.

"I asked for a hot plate, please, Myrabel. This is cold."

Myrabel forgot herself far enough to say, "Well, I don't see how it can be," but she picked up the plate again and traipsed away with it to the kitchen.

As she went through the door, she heard Mrs. Clawson say, "They really should send things out here by dog team." Flora said, "Let's ask them to, Mummie."

Myrabel thought, That makes me mad. That reely makes me mad.

She said nothing to Jen, who was looking worried enough, now that Jeb and Jebron had come in looking glum as bedposts. Instead of changing the plate this time, Myrabel shoved it, stew and all, into the blazing hot oven and left it there. When she took it out, she had to use a heavy pot-holder in each hand to keep from blistering her fingers. But by the time she got it back into the dining room, her wrath had cooled a little and she relented.

She said, "You be careful of that plate, Mrs. Clawson, because it's hot."

"Lord, I couldn't let the poor old scrawn burn her tongue off," she said, telling Jen about it. "I don't know if she whanged her finger on to it, because I didn't wait to see. But when I went in to clear away for the meat course, she was still haggling at that stew, trying to get it cool enough to eat. That Mr. Raymond, he's a card, he is. He winked at me."

Mr. Raymond, too, had a passage-at-arms that noontime. It was to be concluded that everybody was feeling the tension of the weather.

As soon as the door closed behind Myrabel, Mrs. Clawson said, "Really, this place is too awful. Floyd, we've just got to go somewhere civilized. I can't stand this another minute."

Mr. Clawson said, not looking up from his plate, "You won't get cooking like this in Bellport, at twenty dollars a day."

"I don't know that I want to go to Bellport. It's full of Jews."

"Is that really so?" Mr. Raymond said. "You surprise me."

Mr. Clawson lifted his leonine head.

"Certainly," he said. "Place is cluttered with them. Ruined it. Taken right over. Can't go anywhere without running into a bunch of rich Yids."

"Truly?" Mr. Raymond said. "But how do you tell?"

Flora placed her finger on the tip of her nose, turning it prettily down.

"Der hexcent," she said thickly. "Hunmistekable, Mr. Raymond. Oh, and that reminds me of a story."

She told the story.

"You see? Loud," Mr. Clawson said. "Spot them a mile away."

"Astonishing," Mr. Raymond murmured.

"Nothing astonishing about it. Run into it yourself, haven't you?"

"Well, no. No, I haven't, Mr. Clawson."

"Floyd," Mrs. Clawson said. "How about Nova Scotia?"

"Go there later for the tuna. Nova Scotia's no good now, Emmeline, you know that."

"You don't care for it here, Mrs. Clawson?" Mr. Raymond asked pleasantly.

"I certainly don't. Do you?"

"Oh, yes. Very much."

"Food's good," said Mr. Clawson. "About all you can say for the place. They aren't fitted up to take decent care of paying guests."

"And the company's good, too," Flora said, glancing sidelong with unmistakable intent.

It was the first time Mr. Raymond had taken much part

in table conversation. Usually, he had been silent, though polite when directly addressed.

"I find the food here interesting," he said. "Especially the fish. Not, of course, what I'm accustomed to at home."

"You get so tired, so deadly tired, of seafood," Mrs. Clawson said, with an irritated glance at her husband.

"Rather have it any time than this steak," he said. "Eat fish every day in the week and never get tired of it. Any kind, no matter what."

"Did you ever try gefüllte fish?" asked Mr. Raymond. "My mother's recipe for it is out of this world. No?"

He took a mouthful of steak, chewing it down with relish.

"We Raymonds," he went on serenely, in the teeth of an icy, growing silence, "are a mixed people. From Adam, a Hebrew, who, I understand, was plain dirt. Mrs. Evans, is that apple pie?"

"You can see it is," Myrabel said, setting a succulent wedge in front of him.

It looked like wonderful pie, but he couldn't, Mr. Raymond thought, eat another mouthful if he went to the devil, not with those three pairs of frog eyes avoiding looking at him. He folded his napkin, placing it beside his plate.

"What's the matter?" Mr. Clawson asked, with a rasp in his voice. "Is it some fast-day or other, when you can't eat apple pie?"

"Mm. No." Mr. Raymond pushed back his chair. "If there were a fast-day, I expect we all should've kept it three weeks ago, on the 6th, shouldn't we?"

Mr. Clawson thrust out his jaw. "What was that—Yum Kipper?" he asked offensively.

"V-E Day," Mr. Raymond said.

In his room, where he had been painting all day, roughing out on canvas his ideas from his watercolor studies,

Mr. Raymond put on his raincoat. He had not been able to get the scene at dinner out of his mind, even though for three hours he had been trying to concentrate on his work.

Damn fool, he called himself. What good did you do? It stopped that little tart from making googoo eyes, that's all. Now I'll have to get out of here, or I'll lose Mrs. Ellis the rest of her boarders. If it weren't for that, though, it would have been worth it.

He might as well go out. The light in the room was too gray now to work by. The storm had settled low over the land, the wind coming in black, gusty squalls. The windowpanes were blind with rain. Maybe if he took a good walk, he'd get back his temper, along with his lost appetite.

He cleaned his palette and brushes meditatively, looking at the roughly blocked outline of his painting.

Wouldn't be such a fool as to try to paint moonlight. Early morning was the time; sun coming up; that cold, golden light through the green leaves. The dark footprints across the dew-wet grass.

No job for a dauber; and, Lord, he was a dauber, after half a lifetime of it. But it seemed to be the only thing that could keep him absorbed. Let him give it up, and after a month or so his nose yearned after the smell of paint.

The Airbrush School, that was what he belonged to—pretty reproductions, blue sky, blue water, white seagulls, yellow sand. Look what happened to him when he tried other things; green and purple stwizzles, that "ain't a picture, Mr. Raymond"; two rocks and a cow's skull. A whole month wasted. And a hangover, the like of which he never hoped to see again.

Well, there was nothing realistic, or cubistic, or surrealistic about this—this *Dryad's Room*. It was pure, sentimental romanticism, never to be bathed by the coldly modulated light of a gallery showroom wall.

Unless he could get into it that slightly inhuman touch of malice, which the original artist had put into the anteater.

Not inhuman, he thought. Not malice. What it was, was the secret self-sufficiency of wild animals, inimical to humans. Feral. Like foxes. You saw it sometimes in cats. Humor there, too.

Oh, hell. If he couldn't put his finger on it, how was he to paint it?

Outside the house, he headed into the dripping trees, following the path down Barle's Point to the beech grove, where for the past ten days he had spent so much of his time.

The anteater would be melted to a mush, in this rain, and that was too bad. He was going to miss it. Its creator should have used something more lasting than beach clay.

Even yet he hadn't found out who had done it. Mertis and Maggie, his firm friends now, had several times shown him clay animals—battered fragments, mostly, showing the hard usage of children's toys. There was a squirrel, minus tail and legs; a wonderfully made little cat. The girls were as mum as clams about who had made them. Obviously, someone had told them not to say. To question one of the grown-ups would seem like prying—after all, it wasn't any of his business, if an artist wished to remain anonymous. But the enigma puzzled him.

Damn place was full of enigmas. There was the old battle-ax, who had nearly crowned him with the bucket, who listened at doors—his friend Myrabel Evans had told him that, explaining that she hadn't gossiped about his drinking spree; there was the youngest sister, the pretty one, who flitted about like a grig and chattered like a magpie; there was the sunbonneted virgin who had laughed at him—you saw her face so seldom that you really couldn't say what she looked like. Except you remembered, from that day in the kitchen, that she did have beautiful hair, masses of it, dark-red and shining; only the way she had it wadded up, you'd have to look twice to see.

He didn't think it could be any of them. Nor Jen, nor the old grandfather. Nor Myrabel, he thought, grinning, for Myrabel was proud to show you her art. Might be the boy, though. Jeb. He was a quiet, undemonstrative kind of chap—seemed to have a good deal there, below the surface. If it were the boy, with a talent like that at his fingertips, then his family certainly ought to see that he got some training.

Training? his mind said. What for?

The skill in those small works of art was already finished and supple; the sophistication age-old.

Humph! He could train *them*.

Mr. Raymond stepped off the path into the beech grove. Great gusts of wind lashed its branches, rain ripped among its leaves. The whole wood was full of movement and of the savage smell and thunder of the sea. Somebody in a long yellow oil-coat was trying to anchor a square of flapping canvas over the anteater, having a hard time of it because of the wind.

What-ho, I've caught the dryad, he thought, and then stopped short with a little pucker of disappointment.

It was no dryad. It was one of the Miss Ellises—the sunbonnet one. Only today, she had swapped the stovepipe for a yellow oiled sou'wester. Her face was absorbed and quiet, as she worked weighting the bellying canvas down with stones.

I'll be darned, Mr. Raymond said to himself.

Pink cheeks, streaming with rain, and she had left off her glasses. She was quite young—obviously younger than he was—and that yellow get-up was becoming to her. He stared, astonished. Up to now, if anyone had asked him how old Miss Evelyn Ellis was, he'd have said at least forty.

But then, the only time, actually, he had ever got a good look at her face, it had been wide-open, laughing at him.

After a moment, he grinned to himself, and strode into the grove over the watersoaked soft grass.

"Hi," he said.

She didn't so much as look up.

"Catch hold of that loose corner, will you, Jeb?" she said. "I wouldn't bother with this, but Mr. Raymond's been painting him, and I don't know whether he's finished."

Mr. Raymond laid hold with a will.

"Aren't you a little late?" he asked. "He's surely melted by now, isn't he?"

"I forgot—" The words faltered and died on her lips. She stared at the strong, rain-splashed hand, obviously not Jeb's hand, on the corner of the canvas. The wind had been making such a racket that she had noticed nothing amiss with the voice.

"Oh!" Evelyn spun around, dropping the rock she had been going to lay on the canvas. Then she ran past him and away through the grove.

"Good God!" Mr. Raymond shouted, irritably. "What ails these damned women?"

Well, this one wasn't going to get back first to the house with any tale of drunken Indians.

Mr. Raymond ran after her.

She wasn't headed toward the house, he saw, but down the path toward the end of the point. Somewhere down there, where the narrow headland met the sea, he might be able to corner her and explain that he wasn't a death's head, or any other kind of a wild fright, but only Jeff Raymond, a mild lug, who never, unintentionally, hurt anyone in his life.

He pounded panting through the trees, guided by an occasional flash of yellow slicker. Then he lost it.

Blasted woman could run like a deer.

The path petered out, forked right and left. He stopped. From somewhere on the left, a stick cracked.

Mr. Raymond sprinted left, plunging through a spruce thicket which ripped a hole in his dripping raincoat. He brought up face to face with Grampie and Jeb, who had been down on the end of Barle's Point to salvage any of their traps which might have washed ashore. Jeb, Mr. Raymond noticed, had on a gabardine trench coat, like his own.

The two stared at him.

"Oh, blast and damnation!" Mr. Raymond said. *"Now what will everyone think?"*

"Hi," Grampie said. "You're quite a feller for tarryhooting around the woods."

"Apparently," Mr. Raymond said.

"Was you chasing Evelyn?"

"Yes." Mr. Raymond stuck out his jaw. "Yes, by God, I was."

Grampie grinned.

"Good," he said. "I hope you catch her."

"But you won't," Jeb said. He was starting to grin, too.

"All right," Mr. Raymond said bitterly. "I was only trying to get near enough to apologize. I think I frightened her."

"If you come on her in the woods, quick-like, she'd be apt to run like a rabbit," Grampie said. "No harm done."

"Aunt Evelyn's okay," Jeb said. "She's a little nervous about strangers, though, Mr. Raymond."

"I see. Well, I'm sorry."

Grampie said, "Well, don't worry about it. It's just that she's got her own projects, and people ain't one of them."

"Projects?"

"She makes things," Grampie said.

Mr. Raymond said incredulously, *"She's the one?"*

"She's what one?" Grampie glanced at him, patiently, a puzzled look in his eye.

"Those clay models—she's the one who makes them?"

"Them little clay playthings? She's made them ever since she could walk. Always had kind of a knack."

"Knack?" Mr. Raymond said indignantly. "The woman's a genius."

He saw they were looking at him in a bewildered kind of way.

"Evelyn?" Grampie said. "She's always been a mite odd, kept herself to herself. But them little things, they lay around the house till the kids bust them. I s'pose they're kind of cute."

Jeb said, "If she is, you couldn't make her think so, Mr. Raymond. She's—she's okay, though."

Mr. Raymond said, "Mm, well. Where would she be by now, Mr. Ellis? Would you have any idea?"

"Oh, she's well and gone home by now," Grampie said. "Holed up in her room, if I know Evelyn. She's had that vanishing trick ever since she was small. Done it to me, many a time. Sidesteps into the woods and waits till you've gone by; then after you're done hunting the woods over for her, you find she's home in her room."

He and Jeb started along the path, and Mr. Raymond fell into step with them. He said, "Mind if I walk back with you? You aren't scared of me, are you, Mr. Ellis?"

"Well, just don't take out after me, that's all," Grampie said.

He grinned at Mr. Raymond and Mr. Raymond grinned back.

He said, "My name's Jeff, Mr. Ellis."

Grampie nodded.

"And I guess you think I don't mind my own business."

"I hadn't thought about it that way," Grampie said.

They walked back through the soaking woods together, past the meadow with its flattened grass, past the beech grove, loud with the sound of wind and rain.

As they neared the house, they heard someone scream

1 9 9

and saw a flash of light, like an explosion, on the lawn. Someone in a yellow oil-coat, from which, in the dusk, blossomed an orange petal of fire, stood motionless for a second at the foot of the porch steps and then started to run.

Mr. Raymond took off like a deer, tearing his trench coat off as he ran. He slammed the wet coat around the slight figure, knocked it down and rolled it over and over on the grass.

THE day, having started out like a wave breaking over Jen, continued to work up into climax. It seemed to her, after the noon dishes were cleared away, that she couldn't face one more thing. Clay was fussy—in Myrabel's opinion, he'd eaten something and was working up a blueberry stomachache. Andy and the girls were into everything; whatever room they went through, it seemed as if three pint-sized whirlwinds had struck there; and Neal was glum and brooding, spoiling for trouble.

"My Lord, there's some days when the old Scratcher lays an egg in your pocket," Myrabel said, in exasperation. "Neal, for heb'n sakes, get out from under my feet, before I go over you like a truck."

"Take the orts out to the hens, Neal," Jen said, and she spun on him when he muttered something unpleasant. "Neal! I never in my life saw anyone so crabbed. What's the matter with you?"

She stopped, noticing with compunction that the look on his face was more harassed and worried than anything else. She reached over and ran her fingers through his tousled hair.

"Well, take the orts out, dear," she said. "And then don't worry about any more chores today. I can manage all right."

For a moment he leaned his head hard against her hand;

then he shrugged it off. He picked up the refuse dish and started for the barn.

Something about the half-finished gesture of tenderness touched Jen to the heart.

It ain't right, she told herself, for a woman to be so drove up that she can't take time off to tend to her kids when they need her.

But what could she do? She and Myrabel, especially today, were stretched right out straight.

Neal hadn't been his blustering, hearty self for quite some time now. Jen was puzzled, more worried over him than she would admit. She knew it had something to do with Candace. He was being especially nice to Aunt Candy these days, hanging around the house and her room a lot. More often than not, when Jen needed him, he was busy doing something for Aunt Candy.

Such behavior wasn't normal in Neal, unless Candy was paying him, and Jen was sure she wasn't. Neal was stony broke; he didn't even have movie money. At least, he was always asking Jen for some, or borrowing from Andy. In the summertime, the boys earned their own money baiting trawls down on the wharves; so far, Andy had been doing well. He even had nine dollars saved up for a bike. Neal was a fast baiter and in demand, because he did a good job on a trawl. Last summer, he had made fifty dollars. But this year, he hadn't been near the wharves, so far as Jen knew.

If things went on in this way, she'd have to talk to Neal; Maybe, though her stomach crinkled at the thought of it, she'd have to speak to Candy. It would be an ordeal; Candy hadn't spoken to Jen, more than to say something like "Please pass the salt," for days. She sat at table, moved around the house, with her face set, grim and silent.

That woman is over this place like a tent! Jen told herself. I wish she was in Toko, there!

She realized she was thinking a good deal more viciously

of Candace than was her custom to think of anyone, and she pulled herself up short.

After all, I can't blame her too much. With all of us around and the boarders in her hair, and the kids raising holy mud in the house she's always had to herself. But the first chance I get to get out of here, no one's going to be able to see me and the kids for dust.

Neal took the orts out to the hens and hurled them, dish and all, over the henyard wall. Then he realized his mother would probably send him back for the dish, so he smooched glumly in to retrieve it.

The rooster, big, belligerent, red, with shining green, droopy tail-feathers, took a run at him, and Neal let go with a kick that missed by about two inches, but drove the rooster off his course, so that he slammed with an indignant "Squa-rr-k" up against the henyard wire. Considerably cooled down, he stood eying Neal with a mean, yellow, unfriendly stare.

"You fly at me, you fat lug," Neal told him, hot-eyed, "I'll drive ya so far it'll take a dollar to send a letter to ya."

He hauled back his foot, but the rooster had had enough. He only pursued those who fled—fainthearts, like Russ or Clay.

Neal started back to the house, kicking the orts dish along the gravel walk in front of him.

It was pretty heavy business, being Aunt Candy's heir. It meant she was after you every minute of the day, wanting errands run, little chores done. Half the time, they weren't so little, either; they'd take a whole afternoon. And she never gave you anything—maybe a handful of those screwy dates and nuts that you were so sick of. She never bought chocolates.

Joe Palmer had a new red and yellow sports sweater he'd earned baiting trawls, a stag's head on the front of it whose antlers stretched from the tip of one of Joe's shoulders to the tip of the other one. Boy, was it sharp!

Neal wasn't buying any sweaters. He was losing his whole summer's work. Other boys were getting his regular business; when last summer everyone down at the wharves had tried to get him, and he'd had a darned good trade worked up. You couldn't buy sweaters with a handful of candied orange peel.

Thousands and thousands of dollars in a future impossibly far away didn't seem so much. Not when you compared them with afternoons right here and now. Afternoons you had to spend going around to stores to match a silk thread, for creep's sake. Roosting on a chair holding thousands and thousands of little skeins of yarn for Aunt Candy to wind into balls.

But the worst was, when you really thought about it, that to get all that money you had to wait for someone to die. The idea made his stomach flop right over, with an all-gone feeling, as if he were going to vomit.

Aunt Candy might live for thirty years yet; thirty, added to thirteen, was forty-three. Forty-three years of orange peel. Neal himself would be an old, old man.

You could learn to fly an airplane, play ball with the Red Sox, join the Marines. All those things to take your pick of. And you'd chosen to sit around and wait for somebody to die.

Like the crows around Byde Palmer's sick cow that died when Neal was a kid. He'd never forgotten how he and Joe went up to the meadow, all agog to see Joe's father's sick cow; and there was the cow on her knees in the daisies, with her head stretched out in front and great big tears, it looked like, running out of her eyes, and the trees around the meadow all full of crows. He and Joe had thrown rocks till their arms were lame, but the crows just flew up and came back; and after a while, Joe had said, "Oh, to heck with it"; but Neal had wanted to be sick.

Shoot, Aunt Candy wasn't like a sick cow, of course. She liked you, and you'd just be getting to like her when she'd do something so darned mean, you wanted to . . . But the feeling was the same. Sick as a dog.

Neal slammed the tin dish into a corner of the L-kitchen, a place approximately ten feet from where it belonged, and Myrabel eyed him as he came through the door.

"It's about time you movie actors had some of the shine took off of you," she said.

Neal liked Myrabel, but he couldn't even grin at her.

"Between you," Myrabel said, "you kids have about pooped your mother out. Jen, you take Clay upstairs for his nap and lay down on the bed till time to start supper. Jebron wouldn't have no objection if the kids and I cleaned out the barn chamber, would he?"

"Why, no," Jen said. "But it's an awful job, Myrabel. I've meant to get to it, but I haven't had time. You don't want to do it, do you?"

"I don't intend to do it," Myrabel said. "I'm bossing. Come on, the whole of you, get rigged up. Time I get through with you, folks won't know you from a cobweb."

The little kids pricked up their ears, and even Neal came to life. They had no objection to working under Myrabel's direction, which, like a military dictatorship, was apt to pay off in dividends of entertainment for the immature. They got into their oldest dungarees without a murmur, while Myrabel exploded into half a dozen plans.

"We get that mess out of there and some space clear, it would be a lovely place to set up a pingpong table," she said. "You can find some smooth boards—or the storm doors, that's it—for a table. Knit a net out of twine and whittle out some bats. It ain't no trick at all to whittle out them little flat bats. My Randall and my George and my Timmy made a lovely pingpong set once. All they had to buy was the balls. You build the rest of it and I'll bring you some of them little light white balls. There's a whole box of them home in my shed. Only we've got to clean out the space first."

The five of them left for the barn discussing earnestly how a pingpong table could be made out of storm doors, and quiet settled over the house.

Before she lay down to rest, Jen put some wood in the summer dining-room fireplace and checked the oil heater, which she had decided to leave on for the comfort of the Clawsons, until suppertime.

She didn't quite trust an old-fashioned oil heater, she thought, peering down through the air vents in its top, at the steady flame. But, there, people in the old days had used them all the time, leaving them on all night sometimes when everyone was asleep. The only time you had trouble with one was when it was dirty or out of repair, and this one was neither. Grampie used it in his shop all winter; Jen herself had given it a good scrubbing this morning, putting in a new wick, making sure the wick was tight so it couldn't work itself up or down.

As she went back down the hall toward the kitchen, she met Lynnie coming out of Candy's room. Lynnie was all dressed up in a new white transparent raincoat, with peaked matching hood over a bright blue dress. She looked very pretty. She also looked unhappy.

"What a nice get-up, Lynnie," Jen said, stopping. "You look swell."

"A man bought it for me," Lynnie said, giving her a brittle glance. "Or so I'm told. I won't be back for supper, Jen."

She went on and out into the rain, slamming the front door behind her.

Oh, dear, Jen thought. Another row with Candy.

She had heard voices coming out of Candy's room, a little while ago. She couldn't help but know it was about the same old subject—money.

Jen still paid Lynnie for helping around the house, but

only by the hour now—for the actual time she worked. With Myrabel's steady wages coming out each week, Jen couldn't afford to do more. Lynnie would work for a few days until she had a little money ahead; then she wouldn't be seen around the house for a week, except at odd meals, coming home late at night, sleeping until noon, starting out again in the afternoon. Up until today she had seemed about the same as ever—gay, undependable, without a serious thought in her head. Jen didn't believe she was letting any man buy clothes for her; that was one of Candy's daydreams. Lynnie could have saved her wages and bought them. They weren't expensive, only well-chosen, for Lynnie had taste.

That woman, Jen thought indignantly. She takes the life right out of everyone. Or tries to.

She thought at once of Neal. She was thinking of Neal when she went by Candy's door and it snapped open and Candy put out her head.

"Did Lynnie go out? Where's she gone?"

"I don't know," Jen said. "Yes, she went out."

What came over her she didn't know, except she was tired and mad and her resistance was down. She certainly hadn't intended to bring up the matter of Neal with Candace today.

She said, "I want to speak to you, Candy."

Candace shut the door in her face. There was a brief silence; then she opened it again. A crack only.

"What about?" she asked harshly.

"About Neal. He's tired and off his feed, and I'm worried about him."

"What's that got to do with me?"

"A lot," Jen said. "As you very well know. I don't know what you've promised him, but I can guess. I'm sorry, Candy, any of the other children will be glad to do errands for you, and I'll do anything I can. But I've got to ask you to let Neal alone. At least till I can find out what ails him." ˙

The crack vanished and the door shut with a click.

Jen went on into the kitchen.

"I'll be some glad when this day is over," she told the bellowing Clay, who was convinced that the whole world had gone away forever and left him strapped in his high chair. "Come on, honey. You and Mama'll go have ourselves a nice nap."

He settled cozily in his crib. He wasn't hot; he didn't have a fever, Jen saw, with relief. He was just contrary, today, like everybody else.

She lay down on her bed with the uneasy feeling that she'd said too much—as she always did, if she spoke out when she was mad. But she was so tired that every bone in her body seemed instantly to unshackle itself and go floating off on cushions of cloud, each one in a different direction.

When she woke up, she thought with a start that she'd slept too long. It was beginning to get dark. Then she saw by her alarm clock that it was only five. The storm was bringing an early dusk. She didn't need to hurry.

Rain was falling around the house with a steady roar, out of clouds that looked like the wool off a black sheep. What an awful storm—disastrous in June, when so many lobstermen had brought their traps inshore. Jen didn't dare to estimate how many Jeb and Grampie might lose. Poor Jeb, if he lost those traps, after he'd worked so hard—

You stop it, she told herself firmly. You stop worrying. What happens will happen.

Jeb and Grampie had gone mum as clams about what they were planning to do. She suspected that Grampie had gone right ahead and mortgaged the house, using the money to pay Guy's bills. She'd find out, of course, when she sent in her next payments. But Grampie said, when she asked him, "Never you mind, Jen. You just keep right on running the house."

Well, she would. No woman could do more than she

could do, and she'd certainly done everything to keep him from it.

She got up, with a sudden return of energy. It was wonderful to feel rested and herself again.

She washed in her commode basin—the bathroom, of course, was downstairs, in the aunts' part of the house—combed her hair and put on a crisp housedress which still smelled fresh from the iron. Over it she tied a white apron, sprigged with tiny blue flowers.

She left Clay in his crib. He was asleep, his damp, curly red mop nuzzled comfortably into the pillow. He'd feel himself when he waked up, too.

Jen bustled downstairs into the kitchen.

Let's see. Baked lobster and popovers for supper. Asparagus from the garden, if there was any left. If not, green salad, with River dressing. Strawberries and cream for dessert. Jerry had sent up some lovely ones. Maybe a fresh cake, with chocolate frosting.

Myrabel must still be out in the barn with the kids. Get things started in good shape, then call them, so they'd have time to get cleaned up for supper.

The kitchen had a soot-and-hot-metal smell, and she pulled her attention away from her planning, sniffing anxiously. A chimney fire? No, the range was barely warm, the fire low. Besides, it didn't smell like that . . . more like overheated tin, or something.

She heard someone cry out, frantically, from the front part of the house, and, suddenly, she knew. The day when the old Scratcher laid an egg in your pocket wasn't yet over.

Jen flew down the long hall to the summer dining room and flung open the door. The air was heavy with a blistering, metallic, keroseny smell. Smoke and soot were pouring out of the air vents of the heater; its metal was red-hot. Evelyn, in her oilskin coat and sou'wester was kneeling beside it, trying to twist the hot wick-screw to *Out*. Her coat was streaming water; apparently, she had just come in.

"Don't touch it!" Jen said. "Get away from it!"

Evelyn said with a gasp, "You can't turn it down. It's been turned up as high as it will go. We've got to throw it outdoors. . . ."

The flame flared higher; points of it came up through the air vents in the top of the heater. Jen had ripped off her apron to use for a holder. With horror, she saw Evelyn grab the heater, barehanded, by its blistering handle. Using the apron, Jen grabbed the other side herself. Even through the cloth, she could feel the flesh shrivel on her palm and fingers, and the apron caught fire. Flame shot up her arm in a searing flash.

But they got the deadly thing out through the screen door and onto the front steps, swung it and let it go, as far as they could heave. It landed on the wet lawn, rolled over and exploded with a flash and a muffled *woosh*.

Jen realized that the sleeve and shoulder of her housedress were ablaze and she fell on to the couch hammock, thrusting down into the cushions and rolling on the flames until they were out. She remembered Evelyn stumbling down the steps into the rain; a confused sound of men's voices shouting. Then she was lying on the living-room couch, with Grampie bending over her.

"Jen, my dear Jen," he was saying in a shaken voice. "No, keep your head down. Just lay still."

"Someone ought to tend to that thing before it sets something afire," Jen said muzzily.

"It's all right," Grampie said. "It's out, Jen."

The rain had damped down the flames considerably, but Mr. Raymond was still out there, playing the stream from the garden hose on to the smoldering debris.

Jeb came tearing down the hall from the kitchen, where he had telephoned the doctor.

"Richards won't come," he said frantically. "He says to bring them down to his office."

"What's the matter with him—he busy?" Grampie said, getting to his feet.

"He says it's not his office hours, but he'll see them if we bring them down," Jeb said. "Ma. Oh, Ma, are you okay?"

"I'll talk to Richards," Grampie said. "Set here with your mother, Jebby."

"I don't see how it got turned up," Jen said. "It couldn't have turned itself up. It was all right when I left it."

"Just lie still, Jen," Grampie said. "We'll get the doctor and get something for that hand."

Jen's brain cleared with a rush.

"Where's Evelyn? Jeb, where's Evelyn?"

"She's in her room. Myrabel's in there. Don't get up, Ma. Please lie still."

He put a shaking hand on her shoulder, and Jen, feeling dizzy again, lay back on the pillow.

Grampie strode into the kitchen to the phone. He saw that Mr. Raymond was there, talking into the phone, pleasantly, but with a note in his voice that stopped Grampie in his tracks.

"Listen, you damned medical-school pill-pounder," Mr. Raymond was saying. "We've had a bad accident here. Do people have to wait to get hurt till you have your office hours? You seem to be the only doctor available. If we have to take two injured women out into this storm, I'll guarantee there won't be enough left of you to box up and mail to the Medical Association. How about it?"

He listened briefly.

"All right. What do we do for burns, till you get here?"

"Oh, dear," Myrabel said, at Grampie's shoulder. "I wish we had one of them good old doctors who'd always come when you needed him, to someone besides the summer people. I wish Dr. Eben hadn't died. I wouldn't have Richards, personally, to a sick lizard, but—"

"Shut up, Myrabel," Grampie said. "He's a fine doctor,

knows his stuff. Probably been run ragged today. What's he say?" he asked, as Mr. Raymond put down the phone. "He'll be right up. Hot blankets, hot water bottles, keep them quiet. Keep them warm," Mr. Raymond said.

He swung around on Myrabel. "How is she?" he demanded.

"Oh, I don't know," Myrabel said wildly. "She won't say a word. She just lays there hanging on to her hand."

Dr. Richards came. He was modern, efficient, and, as Grampie had said, he knew his stuff. He treated Jen for shock, eased her pain and dressed the superficial burns on her hand, arm and shoulder. He said she'd be all right, but to stay a day or two in bed. But Evelyn would have to be hospitalized, he thought. The flesh of her palm and fingers was all but cooked where she had grasped the handle of the heater. It was too soon to say what might happen to the hand; she wouldn't be able to use it for a long time.

JEN lay in her bed in the room over the kitchen, thinking impatiently, There's no reason in the world why I shouldn't get up.

Only ten in the morning, and she had waked up at five, the way she always did when the sunlight began streaming in through the window. Mortal flesh couldn't stand lying in bed another whole, livelong day with nothing to do. Yesterday she had slept, helped out by Dr. Richards's pills, which had eased the pain in her hand and arm. Today she felt fine. The pain was almost gone. Her arm and hand felt stiff—hurt if she moved around much—but that was all. Whoever heard of an able-bodied woman's staying in bed for a little thing like a burnt hand? She couldn't remember a time since the children were born when she'd spent a day in bed.

Myrabel came briskly through the door with a glass of orange juice.

"Well, I see you're awake at last," she said. "How do you feel now, Jen?"

"Awake! I've been awake five mortal hours."

"Oh, no, you haven't," Myrabel said serenely. "I've had this juice up here three times this morning. Here, you drink it. You've got to keep your juices flowing."

"How's Evelyn?" Jen asked anxiously.

"She's got an awful bad burn," Myrabel said briefly. "Dr. Richards took her to the hospital over to Bellport."

"How bad?"

"It's just on her hand," Myrabel said. "Jebron says if her oil-coat hadn't been wet, she might have been—well, it might've been—"

She stopped.

Jen felt sick, thinking of how terrible the burn on Evelyn's hand must be. That oil heater had been red-hot; its handle as nearly so as made no difference. Evelyn had grabbed it barehanded.

"What does Richards say?" she asked.

"He says he doesn't know. He says that plastical surgery, that's wonderful, he says. But he can't say how much good to her that hand'll ever be."

"Oh, Myrabel," Jen said.

"Mm," Myrabel said. She looked sick, too, Jen saw.

"I didn't tell you yesterday, you was too sick yourself, and groggy from them red pills. Don't they make you feel funny, though? I had some of them, when I had my gall bladder out, after my operation, that time, so's I could sleep. Red bullets, the nurses used to call them; mix you all up, like. The first day, all day, I thought Bert was Santy Claus, I don't know why, he never had no whiskers."

She was talking fast, Jen could tell, so that she could keep from crying. Well, that wasn't to be wondered at; Jen wasn't so far from it herself.

"I'll go get you some breakfast," Myrabel said. "Oh," she went on, stopping on the way to the door, "Evelyn said would you keep this for her till she gets home again."

She pulled out of her pocket a small, old-fashioned key on a slender silver chain, and handed it to Jen.

"It's the key to that black cupboard in her room," Myrabel said. "The doctor made her take it off her neck. I s'pose he thought she'd be under ether, and the Lord knows what anybody'd do under ether. Anyway, she says please keep it and not let anyone have it."

"Put it in my top bureau drawer, will you, Myrabel?" Jen said, holding it out with her good hand.

"You better put it under lock and key," Myrabel said grimly. "And you know why, Jen. I take it Evelyn don't want her things rummaged through."

Jen nodded. "My tin cash box is in the drawer. That's got a combination lock, Myrabel. If you'll give it to me, I think I can work it with one hand."

Myrabel stood by while Jen opened the box, put in the key and chain and set the lock again.

Something about her silence made Jen look up at her curiously, as she handed the box back. Myrabel was looking very queer indeed.

"I ain't saying a word about who turned up that heater, Jen. But I know what I think."

"Myrabel!" Jen said, horrified. "Oh, no. Oh, surely not!"

Myrabel said nothing.

"It was a narrow escape the house didn't catch fire," Jen said. "You know what Candy thinks of this house. It ain't possible she'd ever have done such a thing. It was an accident—it must have been. The wick overheated and expanded, or something."

"You fixed that wick yourself," Myrabel said. "You know as well as I do that them things don't titrivate themselves up and down."

"It would have been insane," Jen said, looking at her. "She ain't crazy, Myrabel."

"Candy's had spells when she's been crazy-mad," Myrabel said. "All her life. She's got the worst temper I ever saw on mortal woman, once she's sulled to a point where it blows off on her. Well, Jen, I wouldn't have mentioned it, and you sick, but I can't get my mind off it. If it's so, it's something you ought to know and maybe tell Jebron."

"It isn't so," Jen said forthrightly. "I may as well say I've been lying here thinking I might've put it together wrong, or left the wick a little bit loose. Whoever's fault it is, it's mine, Myrabel."

It wasn't, she knew. She could have put one of those heaters together with her eyes shut. But she had to get the idea out of Myrabel's head. Anyway, there must be some other explanation that would be clear enough, once she got over feeling groggy, and could think.

"Evelyn must have been mistaken about it's being turned up," Jen said. "She was pretty excited, Myrabel."

"No, Jen." Myrabel shook her head slowly. "I went out and looked, yesterday morning. You could tell, from what was left of it. That wick was turned up as far as it would go."

"Maybe it exploded up," Jen said stubbornly.

There was a brief silence in the room.

Myrabel said, "You'd be the one to know about it, Jen. But I went to school with Candy Ellis."

She smiled down at Jen and there was understanding and affection in the smile.

"I'm nothing but a Calamity Jane," she said briskly. "You forget it, Jen. I'll go get your breakfast."

After she had gone, Jen lay thinking.

Myrabel was right—the heater couldn't have got turned up without hands. Clay, she thought. A job like that would be right down his alley. But she'd looked at the heater, and then gone and taken Clay out of his chair and put him to bed. Not Clay. The other children had all been out with Myrabel.

Maybe Mrs. Clawson had come down to make sure the room would be warm for her to eat supper in. No. The Clawsons always took naps after dinner, come hell or high water. Besides, none of them would have touched it—they were all scared to death of it. They'd said so.

Who else? Nobody.

Candy had been mad, no doubt of that. Jen recalled the glimpse she'd got of Candy's face, just before she'd clapped to that crack in the door.

No, Jen told herself. It's not possible. No one could do a thing like that.

She thought, with a chill creeping along her spine, of what might have happened. Of what had happened. Evelyn, in the hospital, with a hand that might be crippled for life. Her nice, supple hands, with the strong fingers.

Oh, poor Evelyn. It would be so awful for her at the hospital among strangers. She'd be in a ward. . . .

Oh, no! She mustn't be, Jen thought, and then, with a sinking at her heart, but what could any of us do about that?

Her mind, slipping sideways as it seemed to be doing today, presented her with a sudden picture of Evelyn, surrounded by the strangers who terrified her so—a picture of Evelyn lying in the high ward bed, in a sunbonnet.

Oh, stop it, Jen told herself. Don't be such a fool.

It was only Dr. Richards's pills, making her head fuzzy.

Evelyn would have to manage. She would manage, too, something told Jen. She would close herself away there as successfully as she did at home, shutting the door of herself with the same finality in all their faces.

To think of it, she lives among us, as familiar as a chair or a table we see every day, or our own faces in the looking glass. And no one of us knows her at all. How can she get along not loving anybody, not letting anybody love her?

Jen remembered night before last—Jeb, Grampie, Myrabel, the white, terrified faces of the children.

All of them schooling around me, worried to death over me. When Evelyn was hurt so much worse, and she all but alone in her room. Myrabel saying, "She won't say a word. She just lays there hanging on to her hand."

After a moment, Jen pulled out her handkerchief and wiped away the tears.

If Evelyn needs money, at the hospital, then Candy would just have to come across with it, that was all. It was time that nonsense stopped.

I'll butt in on it, I'll talk to Grampie, that's all. Candy—

Thinking of Candy, she felt suddenly as if she were freezing over.

She couldn't have done it, in a house with people sleeping, a baby asleep in his crib. If she did, then she isn't right. It's not safe here for the children.

The thing was, you never would be sure, now, whether she had done it or not.

Myrabel came bustling back upstairs with a tray.

"I called Richards," she said. "He said to, if you showed any signs of life. He says you can get up for supper."

"Good," Jen said listlessly.

"I ought to be ashamed," Myrabel said. "Letting my nerves run away with my tongue. I ain't a mite of good in an emergency, that's all. Never was. A bag and a bundle of nerves. Now, you eat every mite of that, Miss Jen Ellis, and take that gloomy look off your face."

Myrabel must have noticed traces of the tears. Jen wondered if she thought she were fooling anybody.

"You want something to read while you eat?"

"I couldn't keep my mind on reading. I'm too worried, Myrabel, and that's a fact."

"Why? We're all right. My land, Jen, if you've got one chance to rest, take it, for the Lord's sake."

Well, if Myrabel could snap back to a normal way of thinking, so could she. Anyway, it was only those pills . . .

"Rest?" she said. "And you down there going crazy, with all there is to do!"

She wouldn't have used the words "going crazy," if she could have stopped them in time. She could feel her own mind flinch away from the sound of them. Myrabel, apparently, didn't notice.

Down in the kitchen, fixing Jen's tray, Myrabel had got herself in hand.

"If it's the boarders you're worrying about, don't worry," she said. "Them Clawsons is gone."

"No!" Jen said, staring. "When?"

"Yesterday morning. I was some glad to see the last of them. I told that Flora so."

"Myrabel, you didn't!"

"Didn't I, though!"

"Oh, Myrabel!"

"Now, Jen." Myrabel plumped Jen's pillows with an expert hand, settling them more stiffly behind her back. "You want me to cut that meat up finer?" she asked.

"Darn it, no! I didn't burn my teeth out," Jen said crossly.

"All right. I put in a pan of cookies before I come up, and I've got just time to tell you while they bake. I wasn't going to tell you till you felt better, but— Well, Jen, I'd say it was worth it, if you asked me, just to get them Clawsons out of the house. Lord knows, there's plenty of summer people to board, you can fill up the house again tomorrow. Only, I thought maybe you'd want to wait a day or two. You know what *she* done, the night you girls was hurt? Old Mis Clawson?"

Myrabel settled herself comfortably in the chair by the side of the bed, her hands wrapped in her apron.

"She come down, feather-white, when she heard that explosion go off, and Jeb saw her on the stairs and told her what had happened. All she said was, 'Oh, dear. What about our supper?' and if it'd been me, I'd of give her a mouthful right then and there. But Jeb, poor lamb, he was so tore out about you that he never said nothing. Then, later on, when we had you all settled away, and I was cooking supper fast's I could, in she come, right into the kitchen.

" 'Myrabel,' she says, 'we can't be expected, surely, to eat in that *place,* tonight.'

"I says, 'No more you are, Mis Clawson. It's covered an eighth of an inch deep with soot, added *to* which, it stinks.'

"She hauled up her nose and says, 'It *what?'*

"I says, 'It smells.'

"She says, 'Oh.' "

Myrabel's imitation was quite good and Jen giggled in spite of herself.

"I says, 'I'll have you some supper in about fifteen minutes, Mis Clawson, upstairs in your room on a tray.'

"I thought that was best, Jen, seeing the living room was such a mess, them bandages, and all."

Jen nodded.

"Well, I had the trays all set, right that very minute. That Mr. Raymond, he set them for me."

"Mr. Raymond?" Jen said.

"Oh, that Mr. Raymond, he was wonderful, all through it. Jeb and Jebron, they was out trying to get some decency back into the summer dining room, you know, smooching the dirt around from one place to another, the way men will with a rag, and Candy—" Myrabel stopped.

"Candy wasn't no help," she went on shortly. "She was in her room with the door shut. So, that Mr. Raymond, he took a-hold like a Trojan. He washed the kids—tch, was they dirty, Jen, after the time we had cleaning up the barn chamber, and I wish you could see that barn chamber, it looks lovely; and then he took them out in the L-kitchen and they built a fire out there and he fried a whole mess of bacon and eggs and started them in on their supper, whilst I was cooking the Clawsons'. Oh, they had a high old time out there. Of course, the kids all think he's lovely, and my land, I do, too. But I was telling you about Mis Clawson and the trays.

"She says, 'No, thank you. I've already expressed my preference for not eating off a tray.'

"I says, 'Mis Clawson, you are good and goddam lucky you arun't eating off the floor, the way things is in this house tonight.' I was just as *nice* as she was. I never raised my voice."

Jen said, "Oh, Myrabel!" beginning to laugh weakly, and Myrabel went on with the tale.

"It rolled off of her like oleo off a hot flapjack, you'd think I hadn't said a word.

" 'You'll set the table in the winter dining room, please,' she says. 'I *prefer* to eat there. And don't keep us waiting any longer than necess'ry, because I don't wish my husband to get past his appetite.'

"Well, I was so mad I opened my mouth three times before a word come out, and meanwhiles, Mis Clawson she turns round and starts to sweep out of the room. Well—" Myrabel choked with laughter, and it was a second or two before she could go on—"she swep' right into the face and eyes of Candy. Seems Candy was right inside the door, hearing every word that was said, and out *she* come.

"Well, you know how Candy looks when she's mad, like death, them black eyes and her noseholes thin. They stood there, fronted up, and then Candy says, 'Missis Clawson,' she says, 'I have not invited anyone to eat meals in my private sitting room.'

"And Mis Clawson says, 'Miss Ellis, we are leaving here in the morning,' and her voice sounds like goat tracks on a tin roof.

"So Candy she never bats an eye, she just turns around and goes into the winter dining room and shuts the door and locks it. Mis Clawson, she corsets up the stairs. It was

2 1 9

right after that that Mr. Raymond come in from the L-kitchen, where he'd been feeding the kids, and asked what else he could do. So he set the trays.

"And it was truly a beautiful supper that we sent up, Jen, it truly was. Them baked lobsters looked lovely, and there was enough asparagus from Grampie's patch—though I guess that's the last mess we'll get, it's by—and I didn't make popovers because I can't make them pop the way you do, but I did make Queen of Muffins. There was that nice crisp head-lettuce, and I made French dressing, and strawberries and cream; and we got down them little individual silver coffeepots out of the cupboard that belonged to old Gram Ellis, and polished, and we put the coffee in them, good coffee, Jen, Mr. Raymond made it, he can make awful good coffee for a man. And when the trays was all ready, I says to him, I says, 'Well, there's their supper, and you know what I'd like to do, I'd like to spit in each and every one of them little coffeepots,' and he says, 'Oh, no, Mis Evans, don't do that. Let's reelly be subtle,' and he went out and picked three sprigs of that mock orange blossom, pretty it was, too, with the rain on it, and he put one sprig on each tray. And then he carried up the trays."

"*Mr. Raymond?*" Jen said, shocked. "Couldn't you have got Jeb?"

"Mr. Raymond wanted to. And when he come downstairs after the last one, I says, 'There, Mr. Raymond, for one of the few times in my whole life,' I says, 'I feel reelly and truly like a pure Christian, don't you?' And he busted out laughing and hooted and hollered his head off, and he says, 'Mis Evans, if this is the way a pure Christian feels, I reelly and truly do.'

"My Lord," Myrabel went on. "Jeb and Grampie and I and Mr. Raymond, we set down to that supper, and we *cleaned it*. And darned if they didn't all get acquainted, and they spent yesterday scrubbing soot together out in the summer dining room jabbering away ten to the dozen. That Mr. Raymond, he beats all!"

Between spells of chuckling, Jen had finished her breakfast. She felt energy pouring back into her. She wouldn't have known she was the same person.

"Was the dining room a terrible mess, Myrabel?" she asked.

"I never saw worse," Myrabel said cheerfully. "You ought to seen them white curtains, hung and *festooned* with soot! My land, every single thing in that room, pictures and all, had to be scrubbed. It was God's living mercy that the doors was shut, or we'd have had that greasy soot all over the house. But we ain't, have we? Now, you take it easy, Jen, and stop your worrying. We've got three whole days before any more boarders come, and the Clawsons is gone for good. Oh, but I started to tell you about the Clawsons."

She had begun to get up, but now, with a windy moan, she let herself sag back into the chair.

"That palavering Flora, she come downstairs yesterday morning with a handful of dollar bills to settle up their board and room. *Dollar* bills, mind you! Well, I says to myself, likely that's all they *have* got. So she says they was leaving earlier than the time they'd engaged the rooms for, and they'd decided not to pay for their last day, it had been so uncomfortable for them and they reelly felt it wasn't due us. So I just said, polite-like, for her to please pay what she thought she owed us, because I had a great deal to do clearing up after the tragedy. That's what I said, '*tragedy*,' just to remind her of who it was who was truly uncomfortable.

"So that rolled off of her and she says, another thing, she and Daddy and Mummie never stayed in any place where there was Jews, and I said, 'Didn't they?' And she said she supposed of course we didn't know Mr. Raymond was a Jew, and I said it was nice that such a pleasant man should be religious as well, and me, myself, I was brought up a Baptist.

"So she paid, and she miscounted and give me an extra dollar bill, and I *give* it back to her for fear she might need it. And then she said Mummie was all to pieces and they were going right now as soon as Daddy could get the Cadillac sent up from the garage, and I said something I heard on the radio once that I've been saving for five years to get the chance to use it. I says to her when she went through the door, 'Don't think it hasn't been lovely,' I says, 'because it hasn't.' "

She sniffed loudly in the direction of the kitchen.

"Oh, my God, I forgot my cookies!"

IN a room at the Bellport Hospital, Evelyn awakened slowly. Her head felt thick and muzzy, and for a while she lay with her eyes closed, listening to a muted bustle which seemed to be coming vaguely from somewhere far off. It sounded like exactly what it was— feet, in a hurry, going up and down a corridor.

Oh, yes, I'm in the hospital, she thought. I got burned. My hand.

She could feel now the bulk of the enormous wrapping that immobilized her hand and arm.

The hand didn't hurt any.

She felt quite well. It was silly to be in a hospital.

The hand merely felt numb. It felt, she thought, suddenly turning cold, as if it weren't there.

For a moment, she lay fighting down the icy wave of fear and nausea.

My hand. Why couldn't it have been my foot? Or best of all, my head, for what am I, what can I do, without my hand?

She tried to move the unwieldy white mass, but she could not stir it. Inside it was no sensation whatever.

But I *live* through my hands.

The iced silk of snow, the cat's back warmed by the sun.

New green leaves, the cold veins running through them. Dry herd's-grass, the delicate seeds; the yellow wax bean's smooth pod. Old driftwood, wonderfully shaped by sea-worms; the kitten's foot, soft-padded and light-boned. Shapes to touch, to feel flow through the fingertips, fluid, electric, like another kind of blood.

Evelyn lifted her other hand and laid it on the bandages. It curved easily over the bulky contours, brown against white, strong, flexible, the nails trimmed close to fit the shape of the fingers.

Rough texture of gauze, like buckram; hard, unyielding . . . a cast or a splint. Her hand was there. Hurt. But it was there.

I've studied out how to meet other things; I can study out how to meet this. I've always wondered what would happen to me if I were sick. There'll be people invading; they'll come like an army through a broken wall. Give people a chance, ever, and they'll burst in, with their talk and their curious eyes. I must study out how to meet it; the best would be to wait till it is over, and they have gone away again.

With some kind of a vise to hold material steady, you would be able to learn to work again, with one hand. Not shore clay, that would be too soft. Modeling clay. Now you would have to bother to get some modeling clay. It could be done.

I've got one hand, maybe the other one, someday. And my eyes. Thank God, it wasn't my eyes.

The vise could be simple—two flat surfaces, upright, parallel, with a screw to tighten them together. Jeb could make it for her; he was so handy with tools, and he wouldn't ask questions. Fasten it, somehow, to the worktable . . .

A large warm hand came firmly down on her forehead, and she thought, with a shrinking inside herself, Now it begins.

This was the human touch. Except for children, no one had touched her for years. It was as she remembered it—pleasant-textured, oddly comforting and . . . meddlesome.

"I think she's awake. Open your eyes, if you are, Miss Ellis."

A large man stood there, wide, with a suggestion of potbelly. Dark-blue suit, soft cloth worn smooth, smelling of tobacco and ether. Round moon-face, sober, concerned, interested, confident.

I'm taking care of you, the expression on it said. You've nothing to worry about now.

Like God, Evelyn thought. Like God and somebody's soul.

"I'm Dr. Wright. I fixed up your hand. How's it feel?"

Evelyn said, "Well enough."

"Good. Pain you?"

"No."

"Good again. It's going to be all right, you know. Matter of time. Takes time for a deep burn like that to heal. But you'll use it again. How's that sound, eh?"

She managed a small smile.

Now he could go away. He's told me and that's all that's needed, and I'm grateful to him—oh, how grateful I am to him. He won't go away, she thought ruefully. People aren't built so that they ever go away.

He said, "They tell me you're a sculptor, that you'll be worried to death over your hand. . . ." He was smiling. "Well, we couldn't allow anything to happen to a sculptor's hands."

Who could have told him that? Not any of her own family, certainly, she thought, in suddenly rising amazement. Who?

She said, quite forcibly, "Nonsense!"

"Eh? Oh, still groggy, I guess. Well, you understand about your hand, don't you?"

She nodded and said, "Thank you."

"Not at all. It's what I'm here for. Good night, now, and get a good night's sleep. Miss O'Halloran, if that hand gets to paining her, see that she gets—"

Evelyn heard his voice fade away down the corridor.

She breathed out relief in a long sigh.

Two flat surfaces joined by a screw that you can tighten, she thought, and—

A nurse bustled in, her arms full of things.

"I'm Miss O'Halloran. Hello."

"Hello."

"The nicest-looking man and two little girls have just left you these, m'm, look, Miss Ellis, aren't they nice? Little tiny yellow roses and—"

The nurse was looking doubtfully at the round, small, tightly wadded bunch of white wildflowers.

Bunchberries, Evelyn thought. Maggie. One of Maggie's very bouquets. Already beginning to wilt from the squeezing they'd got in her hand.

The nurse said, "And the other little girl, the older one, sent you up this."

She handed over a tiny, round, water-polished pebble.

Mertis.

Evelyn smiled.

"That's what we like to see—a smile or two," Miss O'Halloran said. "My, I'd laugh out loud if I had a handsome beau like that."

Beau?

"My father," Evelyn said.

Miss O'Halloran stared. "Father, nothing! He'd be quite a boy if he'd had you. At his age, Miss Ellis." She smiled archly. "Well, all we know is what we guess at."

She went flying out the door, closing it softly behind her.

Jeb, then, and the nurse was being facetious, Evelyn thought.

She stared in puzzlement at the roses. They were subtle

and delicate, with a faint, vanishing fragrance. Jeb was a dear, but his choice would have been carnations. The Ellises didn't send flowers except to funerals, and then it was always carnations. Jen? No, not Jen. Who?

Her head was muzzy, and she'd better go to sleep while the door was closed. Before someone else came bustling in. What a place for people to come bustling in!

She realized, with gratitude, the blessed fact of the closed door.

Yet how could that be? What am I doing in a private room—a nice one, too, she thought, glancing around at the room's antiseptic but pleasant crispness. We surely can't afford it. Pa can't, I know.

Candy? Candy never spent money.

Unless . . .

The only time Candy ever spent money was when she had done something so outrageous that her own terrible conscience made her take the worst punishment it could devise; and, Evelyn thought, her mind working clearly and coldly, to divert attention from herself and reinstate her with other people. For Candy, God help her, cared what other people thought.

Evelyn lay thinking bleakly of another time, long ago, when Grammie's nice house had been filled with smoke and soot from kitchen to attic; day before yesterday, the remembered smell had come back to her, as she stepped in off the front porch and saw the heater ablaze in the summer dining room.

It could be Candy who was paying for the room. It could be she who had sent the roses.

PART FIVE
Candace

LYNNIE opened the door to Evelyn's hospital room and peered wonderingly around it. She saw Evelyn was indeed there and she came in, cautiously closing the door behind her.

"Well, here you are," she said. "I tried to tell them downstairs that you were in a ward, but she said no, Room Four."

Evelyn smiled and said, "Hello, Lynnie," but she looked hunched-up and beleaguered, as if she were huddling into the pillow for protection.

Lynnie stopped dead in her tracks.

"What have you done to your hair? You look different."

"I don't know. The nurse fixes it."

"Oh. Well, she's made you look like a million, I'll say."

The dark-red mass was in two heavy braids, but Miss O'Halloran had let it fall loosely around Evelyn's face, in certain wide natural waves and tendrils.

"Somebody's sent you some pretty nice flowers, too. Yellow roses. And what's that? Bunchberries! Who thought of that, Ev? Some of the kids?"

"Maggie," Evelyn said briefly.

"I could've picked some daisies and buttercups, I suppose," Lynnie said, a note of bitterness in her voice.

Evelyn said, "Never mind, Lynnie."

"I do mind. I haven't got a red cent, Ev. How do you feel?"

"Well enough."

"Oh, shoo, Ev! How do you *feel?*"

Evelyn sighed. She might have known Lynnie would want full details.

She said succinctly, "All right, so long as I keep still. If I move, my hand hurts like the devil."

"I should think it might. You had a close shave, you know it?"

Evelyn nodded.

"Everyone's talking about it around town. You're quite the little heroine. A woman was even out from the Bellport *News*. Now, don't look as if somebody'd hit you with a dead fish. Of course they'd want the story. I think it's something, myself. She wanted a photo of you, but there wasn't any—"

"No," Evelyn said shortly. "There wasn't."

Wait. Wait, she was telling herself. In a week, in a couple of weeks it will all be over. I can go back to myself again, not feel like a ballroom full of people.

"They got one of Jen, though. Jen said she gave it to her to get rid of her."

"How is Jen?"

"She's okay. She had a burn on her palm, and some blisters up her arm. She just had to rest a day in bed. How come the private room, Ev?"

"I don't know. Don't you?"

"Nobody's mentioned it at home. Pa, I suppose. He hadn't ought to afford it."

"No," Evelyn said quietly.

"Ev, I don't suppose you feel like it, or it's the time to, but I've got to talk to you."

"It's all right, Lynnie."

"Candy hasn't been to see you, has she?"

"No."

"Our high-and-mighty sister. She's lying low in her room. You know why?"

"No."

Oh, Candy. Poor Candy.   ⅄

"She was the one who turned that heater up, Ev."

"No one turned it up," Evelyn said sharply. "It's old. The heat might have melted the wick."

"Melted the wick! You're the great mechanical mind, aren't you, Ev?" Lynnie looked at her. "You know you haven't forgotten that she did the same thing once before to Grammie."

Evelyn stared at the white lumpy bulk of her bandage, not saying anything.

"Ev, don't you dare get that blank look on your face. You remember. The time she wanted to have electricity put in the house and Pa wouldn't. Only that time it was an old Rayo parlor lamp turned too high and no one got hurt. All it did was soot up the house. Well, this time it was different."

This was what it was like when you couldn't run away. If you didn't get out of their way, they entangled you in their emotions, their fights, their everlasting inner compulsions to get back at each other.

Evelyn said, "Nothing's been done that can't be fixed, Lynnie."

"You and I were hiding in the closet," Lynnie said in a flat voice. "She'd been mad as a hornet for days and we thought she was looking for us. We saw her turn it up— we thought she was turning it down."

"I remember. I don't think she knew the heater would explode."

"I don't think she even thought," Lynnie said. "Our Candy gets mad, she can't think. The way she always gets her own way!" Lynnie's voice shook, so that she stopped. Then she went furiously on. "Years ago, she wanted Pa to put in electricity. This time she wanted the boarders out of the house. So she waits around like an old bat in a bush, and the first thing we know, the house is made so uncomfortable that she gets what she wants. *Both* times, Ev, and God knows how many countless times in between. That lamp, all the harm it did, Jossie had a big cleaning job scrubbing soot out of almost every room in the house, and Pa was so mad at the lamp he went down and ordered the wiring done. Mad at the *lamp,* mind you! Well, this time—the boarders are gone, okay; but Jen was laid up and you almost crippled for life. That was running it close."

"I know. Candy didn't—"

"Look, Ev. I won't stand for it. You and I are the only ones who ever knew she turned up the lamp. Well, I'm going to tell about it. And I'm going to tell about the heater. I want to try to get her put away."

"Put away?" Evelyn said.

"Don't be stupid. Committed. To an asylum, where she can't do any more harm."

"No, Lynnie."

"Why not, for heaven's sake? No sane woman would turn up a heater like that and prance off and leave it. Not in a houseful of people. I'm going to, and you've got to back me up."

"No."

"Why?"

"Because Candy's not crazy, Lynnie."

"Then she's so sane she scares me to death."

Evelyn nodded. That was a very penetrating thing for Lynnie to say.

Lynnie, she saw, didn't even know she had said it.

"It's the first time I've ever got a handle on her, and, believe me, I'm going to twist it. A handle that I ever dared to use, I mean."

Lynnie thrust both hands into her soft mass of amber-colored curls and pushed them upward and back from her face. It was an old mannerism, one she had had as a child, and Evelyn suddenly remembered what a lovely little girl Lynnie had been.

Now . . . If Candy were put away, declared incompetent, someone else, of course, would handle her money. Lynnie would get her share of it, without doubt.

"What are you thinking of?" Lynnie said fiercely.

"I was woolgathering," Evelyn said gently. "I think I was seeing you as a little girl, wishing on dandelion fluffs."

Lynnie stared at her. Her face flushed darkly.

"My God! Dandelion fluffs! Ev, if you only could know, just once in your life, how exasperating you are to people!"

"You never wished for money. Or dresses, or things. You wished not to hurt anyone."

At the word "money," Lynnie's face flushed a darker red.

The word hung in the air between them, with a sound inexpressibly ugly.

Lynnie said, "Oh, *nuts!* I had a crush on Miss Gorham, the Sunday School teacher. It's a long way between me and Sunday School. You might at least listen to me, Ev, not go off a million miles away!"

"All right," Evelyn said. "Things have got to be kept bearable between people, if they're going to live together. Candy mustn't know we've known about that lamp all these years. Pa or Jen mustn't know she turned up that heater. You can't tell it, Lynnie."

"Oh, yes, I can. I hate her. I'm going to use it to pry that money out of her. Maybe she'll fork over, rather than have people know. What do you think Pa would do, with all he thinks of Jen, if he knew?"

She might have added "and of you," but Evelyn didn't notice.

She said quietly, "How do you think he'd *feel?*"

"I can't help that. All these years, and now I've got a chance."

"No, Lynnie."

"Yes, Ev!"

"I won't back you up in it," Evelyn said.

"Oh, Ev."

Tears came into Lynnie's eyes, dropped slowly and unchecked on to the spotless front of her blouse. "Please help me get my money. I need it so. I've got to have some decent clothes to get married in."

"Married, Lynnie? You and Russ?"

"Oh, Lord, no, of course not Russ. Ev, you just don't live in the world, do you? This is Ralph Strong. He's a lawyer, from away. You wouldn't know him."

"Why, Lynnie. He's nice?"

"He's awful nice. He says never mind, get married in any old rag, it's all the same to him. He says after we're married, if I want to, then, we can sue Candy. But I want my money now. I think of all our folks, they had nice weddings. I want some new clothes and a—a nice wedding."

"So you should have."

"So I'm going to tell Candy we'll yell what we know on the housetops. If she doesn't fork over. And if she won't, then—"

"Wait," Evelyn said. "Let me think."

"All you say is, Candy wouldn't be able to bear it," Lynnie sobbed. "Well, I—I'm not able to bear it. I don't care about her. Or anyone but Ralph. I want my money and to go away from here."

"I'll talk to Candy."

"*You'll* talk to her!"

"I can."

"You're scared to death of her. You always cry—"

"I do, don't I? Lynnie, go and ask her to come and see

me. Tell her I've got something important to talk over with her."

"She won't come. Just for that."

"She'll come."

"But—"

"Lynnie, go away. See Candy and then go talk to your Ralph. Don't talk to anyone else, don't mention anything. Promise?"

"Well, all right, but I don't see it. Ev, what are you going to do? Oh, Ev, don't get that blank look, now! I need help. I—"

"Yes, you do. I'll help, I promise it. Come back this evening, Lynnie."

After Lynnie had gone, she lay quietly, her hand resting on the bulky, angularly shaped bandages.

No, she thought, Candy wouldn't be able to bear it. Knowing that anyone knew such things of her, taking such a blow in the face of her pride, Candy might well step over the line, wherever it was, that marked the sane from the insane. Some might think she had already stepped over it; and perhaps so strong an obsession as Candy's might be a kind of insanity.

Yet to Evelyn, who knew her so well, the pattern seemed simple. Keep the Ellis house as a mausoleum for the Ellis pride, with nothing changed from the days when the young Candy, eldest daughter of a town's first family, lived there; so that now, in changed and changing times, she might walk from room to room, knowing that Grammie's table was here, as always; that Grammie's chair was there; and Candy—Candy stood the same as she had been when she was important to someone, when she was loved.

Oh, Candy, poor Candy! When I have so much and you have so little, that I should be the one to take your nothing, any part of it, away! You and Chris and Guy and Lynnie—you were all so beautiful when you began, before the world and your lives flowed up over you like a sea. And I was the useless, the homely, the unwanted one, and I still am so. But when it flowed up over me, I breathed it, lived on it, I didn't drown. Oh, poor Candy!

The door opened cautiously, and Mr. Raymond, bearing his hat in one hand and some parcels in the other, stepped tentatively over the threshold.

Evelyn, not having heard anyone come in, looked up and saw him. She started violently.

Mr. Raymond promptly put his hat over his face.

"I'm sorry," he said, from behind it. "I know people are tramping over you, and I won't stay. I just wanted to leave you these things. I'm not really anyone to be afraid of, Miss Ellis."

"You chased me," Evelyn said, "and then, when you finally caught me, you knocked me down."

In utter amazement, Mr. Raymond removed the hat and stared at her. He saw that she was smiling.

She said, "Thank you."

He had meant to leave his things and go away, not wishing to be one of those who took advantage of her helplessness to impose himself and his affairs. But now he came over and laid the parcels down on the edge of the bed.

"I've brought you a likeness of your aardvark," he said. "I'm a dauber, so a likeness is the most you can say for it. And these other odds and ends, you might like to open when you're by yourself. Can I get you anything? How about a big ugly bulldog with an underslung jaw to sit outside the door and keep people away?"

She nodded. "It would help."

"I'll go," he said soberly. "What I've got to say is here." He touched the parcels with the tip of his finger, and stood for a moment, looking at them.

"I've no right," he said. "You'll think me a plain, nosy fool. And please don't think I feel any sort of right of eminent domain, because I'm a dub at painting and always will be. I'd better cut the wrappings."

He pulled out his pocket knife, slit the tape on the larger parcels, cut the strings on the smaller ones.

"You see?" he said. "The best I could do, my anteater has no secret. My gargoyle was born yesterday. Corny, isn't it?"

She said nothing, looking at the watercolor sketch he had placed in her hand.

"Never mind," Mr. Raymond said. "I'll take it when I go. It's—"

"No," Evelyn said. "Please leave it."

Mr. Raymond flushed a little. He looked completely delighted. He said, "I'll go, now," and didn't go, standing by the bed beaming down at her with such a look of pleasure that Evelyn began to chuckle, and then to laugh; and they laughed together in appreciation and enjoyment.

He said, "I know you. I've known you for a very long time," and at her startled glance he made a quick gesture with his hand. "No. Skip it. Presumptuous. Nosy. It's in the book I brought you. Are you as comfortable as you can be? The room's very warm. Scorching outside in the street."

"I think I'm just not used to the way the air smells in a town," she said.

It seemed, suddenly, natural to speak what you were thinking, simply, not be on guard.

"They must have a fan they could put in here," he said. "I'll ask them. Those heavy braids of hair . . . they make you hot and uncomfortable, too. Impractical, for lying in bed. Wouldn't you like them whacked off?"

Evelyn thought, Oh, the lightness, the freedom! And it would mean at least fifteen minutes less of Miss O'Halloran's fussing over her, fixing the great unwieldy head of hair.

She said, "It would be heaven."

"There's probably a hairdresser close by. I'll ask the nurse," he said, and turned to go. At the door, he asked, "Did you like the roses?" and went away, not waiting for her nod.

Evelyn lay looking at the big box of modeling clay, the container of plaster of Paris, the smooth, blond, shining sticks of bronze. She read Mr. Raymond's card:

"Please make another aardvark that will last forever. Please need help, melting the bronze. I know how."

In the second parcel was a book of poems, titled *The Poetry of Freedom.* Turning it in her hands, she saw he had dog-eared a page.

"I think continually of those who were truly great,"

she read, in bewilderment, and looked down the lines to the ones he had marked, with a hard stab of thick-leaded pencil:

*"Never to allow gradually the traffic to smother
With noise and fog the flowering of the spirit."*

CANDACE stopped dead in her tracks in the door.

"Evelyn Ellis! You've cut off your hair!"

"Yes," Evelyn said, fibbing composedly. "The doctor thought it best. It was so hot and heavy."

"He's a fool," Candace said. "I'll have something to say to him. You look like a fright."

She came into the room, her face reflecting the unpleasantness of the shock.

"Set yourself up here in grand style, haven't you? A private room and hothouse flowers! Who sent you that trash?"

Evelyn glanced at Mr. Raymond's box. She said, "Well, it's a mystery."

She waited until Candy's hard little black eyes stopped circling the room, because until Candy had seen everything she would not listen.

She braced herself for the next question and it came.

"Who's going to pay for all this?"

Evelyn asked, "Don't you know?" and bit her lip, for the look of outrage on Candy's face was evidence enough that *she* wasn't paying. Candy said, "Certainly not."

Well, I was wrong about that, Evelyn thought, startled. Pa, then. But Lynnie had said Pa didn't know about it. Who, then? Nonsense, it must be Pa. Well, he mustn't.

Candy sat down by the window, as far away from Evelyn as she could get. She opened her bag, pulled out some lavender wool and started to knit, working the needles with sharp jabs.

"I don't know what you want," she said. "I suppose you think I ought to come to see you without your driving me to it. Just now, I'm very busy."

"I know," Evelyn said. "I'll get it over, Candy. Lynnie's been talking to me."

"What about?" Candy's hands, moving the needles, became motionless.

"She's going to get married. She needs her money."

"She's needed it twice a week for the last ten years. Where would it be now, if I'd listened to her?"

"Let her have it, Candy."

"Russ has got plenty. We need it more than he does. You stay out of it, Evelyn."

"No," Evelyn said. "I can't stay out of it, now, Candy."

"What do you mean, you can't stay out of it *now?*"

"It's gone on long enough. Perhaps, as you say, it was a good thing for you to take care of Lynnie's share, so that now she needs it, she has it. But the time's come to turn it over to her, Candy. It's only just and fair."

But Candy wasn't listening. She said, "What are you mixing in for? Something new, this is."

She stared at Evelyn, in her eyes a dark, congested look which Evelyn knew and recognized.

Fear. Candace was frightened.

She did turn up the heater, then, Evelyn thought. Now she thinks I know she did. Well, I suppose I knew it all along.

For Candy was no fool. In this unheard-of situation of Evelyn's standing up to her, telling her in that inexorable voice that there was something she must do, Candy indeed saw something new and supplied her own reason for it.

Her hands moved stiffly, starting to work the knitting needles again; but the movement was automatic, awkward, as if her fingers, suddenly, were lame.

"There's nothing new," Evelyn said, gently. "I promised Lynnie, that's all. Her marriage is all that's new."

Ordinarily, Candy would have given her a blast, refused to discuss the matter. But now, after a second or two, she only turned and looked out the window.

Oh, poor Candy. Sitting alone in her room for hours on end, while the wild, passionate coil of anger and jealousy untangled itself, leaving her sick at heart over what she had done. For you could not have lived with Candy all those years without knowing that, now, she was sick at heart. This was the face which, years ago, she would have taken to Grammie's blue-gingham-covered bosom, to cry her eyes out there and be comforted.

"Oh, Grammie, I don't know what got into me—I can help it, but I don't want to, not until it's over. Oh, Grammie, someday I'll hurt someone, and not be sorry till afterwards. Oh, Grammie . . ."

And the old voice, soft as oblivion, covering all evil with the mother-bird down of comfort.

"There, little Candy, Grammie's little Candy, of course she gets mad if they plague her, there, there, it's all over

*and nobody hurt after all, and see now, here's a new dime
with the President's mark on it. . . . Put it in our bank,
Candy."*

Candy, at sixteen!

Old crooning voice, old hands, clawlike yet seeming
boneless, busy building their impregnable fortress of
bright new coins and puddled love around the adolescent,
sharp, bitter, defenseless pride.

Oh, Candy, safe within the walls until death tore them
down. With your brains and your courage and your wit
laid waste under the piles of useless rubble.

When what you should have had, Evelyn thought, look-
ing at her with the clear, quiet gray eyes, was a couple of
sound smacks on the elegant little lace drawers Grammie
made you, and your nose rubbed hard into the trouble
you caused, before it was too late.

"Candy," she said, "Lynnie really means to get her
money now. She's not marrying Russ Allen. She's going
to marry Ralph Strong, a lawyer."

"Why? Because she's got to? Who's Ralph Strong—one
of the barroom crowd?"

But the look on her face was dark, unmistakable, ugly.
It was the word "lawyer" which had done that, as Evelyn
had known it would.

"I think she'll sue you, if you don't let her have it. Even
if she didn't win, it would cost you a lot to hire a lawyer
to defend."

"She's got no money for lawyers."

"She's marrying one," Evelyn pointed out.

She watched the rising tide of Candy's anger and spoke
steadily against it, for almost the first time in her life.

"If you'll give Lynnie a check for her share," she said,
"I'll make mine over to you legally, Candy. In writing.
There'll never be any more claims on you as long as you
live."

This way was better than the one Lynnie had wanted to

take. Because if you destroyed Candy's pride, there'd be nothing of her left now but ruins.

"Claims on me!" Candy said. "I'll have to support you and you know it. Give me a release from that in writing, if you can."

"All right. I'll do that, too."

She saw the anger in Candy's face replaced by astonishment, then by a blank, bewildered consternation.

She didn't expect that, Evelyn thought.

"What will you do? How will you live, Evelyn?"

"Freely," Evelyn said. "And peaceably, Candy."

"What a feather-headed fool you are! You know you'll heir the house with me and have to live in it. And who'll have to pay the bills, I ask you that?"

"You can have any claim of mine on the house. Legally. Forever. A quitclaim, I think it's called. Will you give Lynnie her money?"

"She'll only get what Grammie left her," Candy said. "If she gets anything. The interest on it belongs to me for my trouble in handling it all these years. She'll have to agree to that. In writing."

Interest? Evelyn had no idea what the interest might amount to. The income on $15,000 for seventeen years, she thought, watching Candy's face.

"I'll buy Lynnie's equity in the house for five thousand dollars," Candy said suddenly. "That's every penny she'll ever get out of me. Otherwise, let her sue. I wish you'd both get it through your heads that I don't have to give either of you anything. That's my last word. I don't wish to discuss it, Evelyn."

She thrust her knitting into the bag, gripped it firmly in her hand and rose to her feet. The light from the window struck her glasses, making her eyes look curiously groping and blind.

God help you, Evelyn thought.

The house and Grammie's $15,000. Of course the interest must amount to more than five thousand dollars. For if Candy had had to face "giving away" any of the original legacy, she could not have done it.

SEATED at the old-fashioned desk which had been her grandmother's, Candace wrote two letters in her beautiful, flowing hand. In the days when handwriting was considered one of the arts and children had been taught really to write in school, Candace had learned the Palmer method. She had spent hours, both at school and at home, making long lines of ups-and-downs and blended circles, until her hand, balanced from the muscle of her forearm, perfectly controlled the pen. Grammie, with great pride, had always referred to her as the best writer in the family.

Lynnie, last Christmas, had given Candy a ball-point pen, which Candy had considered a waste of money, and had said so. Driven into a corner about it, Lynnie at last retorted that since the pen had cost eighty-seven cents, perhaps it was extravagant, when you considered the few stinking pennies she had had to stretch out, buying presents for everyone. If Candy didn't care for it, she could take it back to the drugstore; which Candy had done, quietly keeping the eighty-seven cents.

Now, her old-fashioned steel nib, dipped into a ten-cent bottle of ink, moved soft as down over the handsome, heavily coated paper, her effortless writing as clear and legible and as unrevealing as printer's script.

Her first letter was to George Begley, the town lawyer, asking him for an appointment at his office; the second was to Mr. Ebbets at the bank. She sat for a long time over the second one, her lips compressed. It informed Mr. Ebbets briefly that, within a few days, she wished to withdraw five thousand dollars. After a while, she sealed and addressed the letter; then she stuck it into one of the pigeonholes of the desk. No need to send it until she found out from Begley just what Lynnie's scrub lawyer could do to her. Coming from a place as far away as Wisconsin, he very likely didn't amount to much. A New England-trained man like Begley could probably tie him into double knots. She hated to get involved with Begley; you couldn't trust a lawyer. But he was Pa's lawyer. He would send the bill to Pa. In any case, there were a few matters she would need to know; and she meant to find out, too, whether that quitclaim business was legal.

She had trouble stuffing the letter into the pigeonhole, which was already full of Grammie's things. All the pigeonholes and drawers of the desk were crammed with Grammie's correspondence, papers and possessions. Candace had never been able to bear the idea of throwing them away. It comforted her, even now, to take out old letters and read them . . . brought back the days, when, as a special treat, she had been allowed to sit at this desk and rearrange Grammie's papers.

They had seemed like such important papers then. And in a way they still did, being symbols of the many things that, when she was young, she had learned from Grammie.

Oh, the days when the maxims in the copybook were true and you lived your life by them! Like law and poetry they had seemed when Grammie said them. She could hear the old voice now:

"Neither a borrower nor a lender be . . ."

"A stitch in time saves nine."

"Take care of the pennies and the pounds will take care of themselves."

"Do unto others . . ."

It wasn't the maxims which had changed. It was the times. You could not live your life by them now.

"Always keep a receipted bill, Candy, love. You never know when some dishonest person's going to try to collect twice."

Right here was the package of receipted bills, tied with red ribbon—a thin package, because Pa took care of most bills, turning over to Grammie only the ones that pertained especially to her. On top was a bill, dated 1912, for a new bobbin-holder on her Wheeler and Wilson sewing machine.

Red ribbon for bills, blue for personal letters, pink for lodge and organization correspondence. Green for recipes, purple for poetry clippings, kept until she and Grammie could paste them in the scrapbook. What fun, when Grammie had let little Candy sort new papers, retie the colored ribbons, making meticulous double bows. How pretty they had all looked!

The ribbons were faded now. Perhaps, sometime, it would be nice to buy new ribbons and put them on, in the same colors. But Grammie would understand if money wasn't spent for that. She would know that the colors of your memories stayed fresh and bright.

Strange, how the memory of Mama had faded, until you could call up only the pattern of some dress she wore. You would need a photograph, now, to remember how Mama looked. But Mama had died when her children all were small, while Grammie, who had taken her place, seemed always to have been a part of life. She had lived until you were twenty-eight years old. And perhaps it wasn't so strange that Mama was so completely gone. Grammie hadn't liked her much. She hadn't been an Ellis.

Candace fingered the letters, pulling out a bundle here and there. How many times Grammie had been Noble Grand of the Lodge, President of the V.I.A., the Women's Club, the Ladies' Aid. She, Candace, had never been. She did as much work—more, perhaps, than Grammie had, and she was always on committees. But they didn't elect her to offices, the way they had Grammie. They wanted the flashy, gabby ones now, the women who went in for canasta and the New Look, the ones who could suck up to the summer people. Presidents and Vice Presidents, they felt, should be the ones who could most easily approach the summer people when it came to soliciting funds. Candace wasn't one of those.

She recalled, grimly, how she had lost her chance to be President of the V.I.A. at the business meeting this spring. She'd really thought she might be nominated this time; some of the ladies had been talking it over. But at that same meeting, the matter of raising funds for repairs on the Town Hall had come up, before the election. The Treasurer, at once, had produced a list of summer residents. The question had been, How much money could the V.I.A. reasonably ask each one to donate?

"I think we might ask Mr. Finch for a hundred dollars," someone said. "He gave a hundred to the Fire Department last year."

"I'll put him down for that. Maybe we'll get fifty," the Treasurer said.

After a little bit of that, the bile had come right up into Candace's throat. She got to her feet.

"I would like to suggest," she said crisply, "that if we need to raise money, we do it by giving baked-bean suppers and entertainments, the way our people have always done in this town. Repairs on the Hall mean nothing to the summer people. They are not residents of the town, and I can see no reason for asking them for hand-outs. We have always been an independent town, standing on our own two feet, with no need to depend upon begging-letters or charity. I would like to put that to a vote."

Claudie Allen had seconded the motion; but it hadn't passed. And Nell Palmer had been elected President in the voting which immediately followed. Nell Palmer, whom Mrs. Finch had once invited to afternoon tea.

Well, times had changed. Even Grammie couldn't have stopped changing times.

Letters from cousins, long dead, addresses lost by the

way. Grammie used to write everyone; she would have nine or ten letters a day. She was the kingpin, the center around whom all the relatives, near and distant, revolved. Little Candy tripped out of the house in her white picoted dress worn over a blue slip, and her wide-brimmed straw hat with the two long tails of watered ribbon. Her black patent leather pumps clicked on the sidewalk, going for the mail. Going for Grammie's mail.

But whom could you write to now? Cousin Etta, in California, didn't answer letters. She might be married or dead. And she was all there was left. How the Ellis family had died out, come apart at the seams. And the Federated Women's Clubs never wrote asking Candace to preside at annual county meetings.

She pulled down the bundle of poems, flicking through them without untying the ribbon. This was the last batch Grammie had clipped before she had died. She had never had time to put them in her scrapbook with all the other poems she had saved and her favorite on the front page, surrounded by yellow roses cut out of that lovely old wallpaper and pasted on.

What a beautiful poem it was!

"Let me live in my house by the side of the road,
And be a friend to man."

That was Grammie for you. A beautiful spirit, gone forever.

In a way, it was too bad Grammie's scrapbook had been buried with her, for it would have been a comfort to have now to read. But when you were grief-stricken, you didn't stop to think of the hollow times to come.

Candace had taken the scrapbook out of the desk and gone through the house to the front parlor, where Grammie lay. She had thrust it down, past the peacefully folded hands, out of sight, so that no one would know it was in the casket. At the time, she felt that something Grammie

2 4 5

had set so much store by should go with her. Afterwards, she wished she hadn't done it. The idea had given her the horrors. She would wake up nights, cold and sick, dreaming of the scrapbook sinking into a mass of corruption. Then she had got over that.

No matter where you looked, you couldn't find any poetry like that now. Once it was all over the papers and magazines. Now it wasn't being written. Times had changed.

Candace put back the bundle of clippings. She picked up her letter to Lawyer Begley and closed the desk. Then she put on her knitted coat sweater and went out of doors, marching purposefully around the place. She peered through the orchard, the lilac bushes, into the clump of birches by the brook. Her avid face cocked sideways as she heard children's voices in the playhouse; she moved up on it quietly to hear what they were saying.

Mertis and Maggie and Andy were in the playhouse. Not Neal. It was Neal she was looking for. Nonetheless, she stood still, listening.

She heard Maggie say, " 'n Russ'll be the best man and Mama'll be the best woman, and Mertis 'n I'll be flower girls and throw flowers for Aunt Lynnie to walk on. I don't know what you'll be, Andy."

Candace's lips tightened.

So the Keppels were already talking wedding, were they? Behind her back. Candace and Evelyn Ellis should be bridesmaids at Marilyn Ellis's wedding. No Keppel should stand up with any sister of theirs.

Andy said, "I won't be in any old wedding. Heave around a lot of old flowers, for Pete's sake! Feel like a fool. Besides, you don't say 'best woman.' You say 'bridesmaid.' I never saw anyone as ign'runt as you are, Maggie."

"I'm not, either," Maggie said, hurt. "If it's 'best man' of course it's 'best woman.' Isun't it, Mert?"

"No, it's really not," Mertis said.

"Wull, I don't care, then. Let's play wedding."

Andy said, "Oh, poo!"

"Let's play the rhyme game," Mertis said.

"Sure. The rhyme game."

"You two only want to play the rhyme game because you can make up rhymes and I can't," Maggie said.

"Wull, I want to play wedding."

"Once around apiece," Mertis said. "Please, Mag. Then I'll tell you a truly awful secret."

"Truly awful?"

"Mm-hm. I know the worst thing you ever heard."

"I'll bet you don't," Maggie said darkly. "Okay, then. But I can't make up a rhyme."

Mertis said, "You first, Andy. I'm thinking of the best, the nicest, the loveliest one of all. Who is it?"

Andy said, "Mama."

"Oh, Mama's too easy to guess," Maggie said. "Of course she's the loveliest. 'T isun't fair."

"All right. Leave out Mama, then, and Grampie and Aunt Evelyn. All them. Who's the loveliest?"

"Mr. Raymond," Andy said.

"Okay, that's right. Now make up the rhyme."

There was a silence.

In the branches over Candace's head, a white-throated sparrow let go with his three or four heartbreaking, clear notes. The birch leaves rustled; a small wind poured through them, and the brook, over its pebbles, made a quiet sound.

Andy said gloomily, "There's no rhyme for Geoffrey and there's no rhyme for Raymond."

"There is for Jeff. He said to call him Jeff."

Maggie yelled, "I got one, I got one! Jeff, Jeff, couldn't get his breaff."

Mertis said, disapprovingly, "Maggie, it isn't your turn."

"But it's the only one I ever thought of, Mert. I never thought of one before!"

2 4 7

"Hey, wait," Andy said. "How's this? Jeff, Jeff, couldn't get his breaff. Cause he loved Aunt Evelyn most to deaff. How's that, hanh?" He whooped. "I win the game!"

"No, you don't," Mertis said coldly. "Maggie gets five for that. She thought of part of it. You only get five, Andy."

"Now my turn," Maggie said. "Ask me one, Mert."

In the bushes outside, Candace had stiffened all over.

Evelyn and that—that Jewish dauber! Impossible. Children's nonsense. No man had ever looked at Evelyn. No man ever would.

You heard about those people, though, changing their names, insinuating themselves, trying to marry into the best families. Could it be that this one was up to something like that? If so, he'd be told a few needful things.

"Wull, *ask* me one," Maggie said.

"Shut up. I have to think. Who's the worst, meanest, ugliest, nastiest, that nobody loves and never will?"

"I don't know," Maggie said, in a shocked voice.

"Well, think."

"I can't. Nobody's so awful as that."

"Give up?"

"Wull, nobody *is*, Mert."

"Aunt Candy," Mertis said.

Jen Keppel's kids. What could you expect? There were some things that even the Ellis blood couldn't overcome.

Well, she felt the same way about them, the whole kit and boodle of them, if they only knew it. Except Neal.

"Candy, Candy, she's a dandy," Andy said, heady with former success.

"Shut up, Andy. It's my turn to make it up, now Maggie's give up," Mertis said.

Andy chanted, "Aunt Can*dace*, rubbed her face, up and down a pillowcase. How's that, hanh?"

Mertis said, in measured tones, "Aunt Can*dace*. Homely in the face. The awfulest thing in this whole place."

"She isun't as awful as that, Mert," Maggie said stubbornly.

"I guess you'd think she was, if you knew what I know. If you knew what she did."

A paralyzed look came into Candace's face. After a moment, she put up her open hands and pressed the palms against her cheeks. She leaned forward, but the children were whispering now. She couldn't hear a word.

What did that horrible child know?

No one had been around on that rainy afternoon. Candace had made sure. She had checked, carefully, the whereabouts of everyone. No one could have seen her leave her room and go into the summer dining room. It couldn't be that, they were whispering over. What was it?

She had had her punishment, surely, in the hours she had spent horror-stricken over the dreadful thing which had nearly happened, for which she was responsible.

Though, later, when she'd been able to think more clearly, she had realized that she needn't shoulder the entire blame. She hadn't realized that the heater would set itself on fire—all she'd meant to do was to smoke those awful people out of the house. Evelyn—Evelyn had been to blame. Grabbing the thing in her hand, like that, and running with it! Any sensible woman would have smothered it out with a rug.

I have already atoned for Evelyn's injury by refusing to accept her share of the house. I shall go on atoning for the rest of my life, because I am going to support Evelyn as long as she lives.

I'm wrong, of course—that child doesn't know anything.

Who would credit a tale involving Candace in an action which might have destroyed Grammie's house? Three-fourths of her horror, afterwards, had centered in the thought, chilling her heart, what if I had burned the house down? No one would believe such a story. Of course.

Jen must know somebody had fooled with the heater. It could have been the baby. Jen had talked it over in front of the children; and Mertis, now, was merely making up lies about Aunt Candy, whom she didn't like. But . . .

I'd better go back to my room and think this over, she told herself, wildly.

She was beginning to get stirred up again, and when she was stirred up, she couldn't think.

Oh, Grammie. There's no one to help me now, and I mustn't get into trouble over this foolish thing.

She went away from the playhouse as noiselessly as she had come.

Back in her room, she sat down stiffly, in Grammie's Boston rocker by the window. The old chair seemed to fold comforting arms around her. She closed her eyes, rocking to and fro for a long time.

If they would go away and leave me here, I could live my life. I could keep this house as Grammie kept it. I could keep the land. With my own money, I could be peaceful and happy here; not nagged forever by them and their everlasting change, change, change.

I must not think of violent things. There is no question of violence. I must think quietly, of shrewd and peaceable ways to make them want to go. Because if I let myself think of violence, I may do someone a harm.

For she knew, now, that she was really letting herself think about it. She had meant to burn the house down. She had come to a place where she could no longer bear to do nothing. Her anger had got away from her, and that was what she had done.

How could I? How could I bear to live without this house?

If I gave Lynnie that money, without strings, now that everyone is slopping sentimentality over her wedding, they would all think so highly of Aunt Candy that even if some child's poppycock story did cast suspicion, no one would give it a second thought. I had better give Lynnie the money.

But, oh, dear God.

Five thousand dollars!

She felt the perspiration come out on her forehead.

Oh, Grammie, it's my punishment for giving way to wickedness. Oh, Grammie, your lovely house!

It wasn't wickedness, little Candy, little dove. You did it for me, to cleanse it of those people. Give Lynnie the money. Punishment will make you feel better, and you know I never could bear to see you cry. It's not my money, it's the bank's that they paid you for interest. You don't have to touch mine. That's for you, Candy, little dove. It was always meant for you.

Candace pulled the letter to Begley out of her pocket and tore it to shreds, dropping the pieces neatly into her wastepaper basket. She got out the letter to Mr. Ebbets, at the bank, and put it into her sweater pocket.

Then she went with a firm step into the bathroom to wash her face in the icy water from Grandfather Malcolm's artesian well, that came up two hundred feet out of the deep ground. There had always seemed something secret and dark and clean about that water. She let it run for a long time over her hands and the hot, throbbing arteries of her wrists, until she felt fresh and cool, herself again, her face not showing anything.

Now she had better go find Neal. He might as well run the letter downtown to Ebbets. It would save three cents' postage and cost him nothing but his time. Certainly, a twelve-year-old had plenty of time to give away. The children in the playhouse, no doubt, could tell her where Neal was. As a matter of fact, she rather relished the idea of going down there now, coolly, and walking in on them. It would cause a flurry.

But the children were gone from the playhouse. There was nothing but a curled feather blowing in the draught on the playhouse floor.

She found them all in the workshop in the barn.

Neal, up to a few minutes ago, had been blissfully alone

in the shop, planing a block of wood which he hoped would sometime be a play-boat's hull. Now Mertis and Maggie and Andy sat in an unrelenting row, looking at him. He was flustered and angry, blurting out something which he cut off short when Aunt Candy appeared in the door.

"Neal," she said, "I want you to take a letter down to Mr. Ebbets at the bank."

Neal turned red. He stared blankly and mumbled something.

"What's that?" she said, briskly. "Well, here's the letter. Come and take it."

Neal hunched his shoulders.

"The trouble is, Aunt Candy—" he began.

"What trouble? What trouble? I haven't got all day, Neal."

"I—I haven't got much time to finish this boat."

"Nonsense! Since when has your time been so valuable?"

"Well, it is right now. I want to get this boat done to sail tomorrow. I promised Joe Palmer."

Candace gave him a long look.

"A promise to one of your playmates is more important to you than . . . other things?"

Neal wavered, but he stuck to his guns.

He said, "Well, the thing is, Aunt Candy—" He stopped. "Yes," he said. "Yes, it is."

"You're tossing away a good deal, Neal, but that's your business. If you were older, you'd realize where your interests are. Take this letter, Neal."

Neal had had all he could take.

"I guess if I was to take my time to go clear downtown this afternoon, Aunt Candy, you'd have to pay me. I've run an awful lot of errands for nothing."

She spun on her heel and walked out of the barn.

Neal took a hesitant step after her. He brought up short

against an almost tangible wall of cold stares from three pairs of eyes.

He shrugged. "Aw, the heck with her. Go on, you kids. I got to get my boat done."

To do Neal justice, he was nervous and jumpy, having been run ragged for weeks. If the other kids hadn't been sitting there, he would have been more polite, remembered his manners. As it was, now he'd have to take a going-over from Jen for sassing Aunt Candy. But it would be worth it. This afternoon, tomorrow, all the days to come, he'd be free. To play ball, to go round shore beach-combing with the boys, to get jobs baiting trawl, to be in and out of boats. Not be sticking around until he was miserable and sick to his stomach, being somebody's damn heir.

Mertis slid down to her feet and sidled toward the door. She didn't look shamefaced—Mertis never did, no matter how much she got caught out. But she did say, "I take it back, Neal," which was going some, for Mertis.

Maggie said, "Wull, that wasn't much of an awful secret. It was only a big fib."

"If it was so, it'd have been awful awful," Andy said. "Sucking up to Aunt Candy, so's she'd leave you her sticky old money."

"And her giving you dates and candy in her room, so's none of us other kids could get any," Maggie said.

Neal let out a bellow. He let go a good crack at the seat of Mertis's dungarees, but for once, she didn't fight back. She ran.

"And the rest of you little stinks, shut up, too!" Neal said furiously. "Gwan, get out of here!"

He ran at them and they fled. For quite a long time they hunted for Mertis, meaning to work her over for telling them such a fib. At least, Neal had proved to their satisfaction that it was a fib.

But Mertis was nowhere to be found. She was lying

doggo in the only place they wouldn't think to look for her —in Aunt Evelyn's room.

For once, Neal had taken the wind right out of her sails, lost her just about all the edge on him she'd had. And she had to admire him, sneakingly, too. Because she could read Neal like a book, and she knew what she knew about him and Aunt Candy.

In her room, Candace dressed to go downtown.

Let him go with the Keppels, she thought. He's one of them and I don't know how I could ever have thought different. I'm better off without him.

PART SIX

J EB stood up in his skiff and looked anxiously down on the rippled water, where it made in shallow around Chandler's Ledge. The day was fine and blue with a high sky and a puff of morning wind which would probably work up later into a mild southwesterly. The sun was making a white glare on the Bay to the east; but here by Chandler's the water was a dark, silky green. On the ledge, a lazy swell moved up and down—all that was left of the big storm. It had been fine weather for nearly a week, but the sea had taken an unusually long time to go down; he and Grampie had had to wait, fidgeting, until the big combers stopped rolling on the ledges, before they could even find out how many traps they had lost. Jeb had had fourteen set here, by Chandler's. So far, he had found only three.

And it looked as if three would be all he was going to find, he told himself glumly. The water here had been swept bare. Not another buoy in sight.

Then he caught sight of one, so close in on the ledge that the swell, sucking back, left it rolling on the rockweed. He edged the skiff in as close as he dared, and managed just to reach the buoy with his long-handled gaff. It was his buoy . . . scraped and furred up from the mauling it had taken on the rocks, but the warp was still on it.

Jeb hauled it in. All that was left of the green glass-bottle toggle was its neck, with the white rubber stopper, wrapped with the two turns of manila which had fastened it to the warp. The trap came, crabwise, up through the water—smashed flat, as if somebody had let it have a dozen wallops with a sledge-hammer. Laths were splintered, even the bows were broken. He might be able to use the heads and sills again, but the rest of it was a goner.

Disgustedly, Jeb dumped the remains amidships in the skiff. He got out an oar, paddled the skiff's bow around so that she headed away from the ledge and started his out-board.

Another one like this and I'll be out of business, he thought, as he headed out toward Grindstone to join Grampie.

Let's see. Eleven lost here. Four on Little Nubble Shoals. Two on Grindstone. Twenty traps left out of thirty-seven.

That was a hundred and nineteen dollars' worth of gear.

Well, Grampie'd warned him he was setting in too close to the rocks. But the way Jeb figured it, Grampie was trying to make him be careful, not get too close in, him-self, in the skiff. It was a temptation, because the skiff was shallow-draught and steady. She'd go anywhere. And right now, there were a lot of lobsters in around the ledges. Trap for trap, Jeb had been catching as many as Grampie had. But now Jeb wished he'd listened to him.

Wonder how he made out, Jeb thought. He must've lost some. He had traps fairly close in, on Grindstone, himself.

Grampie had finished hauling and was hove to, washing up, when Jeb came alongside. The old man was pretty mad, Jeb could tell, by the way he jabbed the whiskery old stub of broom down into the water and slammed the mess from the day's hauling off the boat's washboards. Old pieces of rockweed, starfish, sea cucumbers, whore's eggs were flying off over the stern in a cloud of slimy water.

Grampie was apparently dissatisfied, among other

things, with his broom, for as Jeb clambered aboard, he muttered something, whirled the broom around his head and let it go, off over the water as far as he could heave.

"Well," he said, glancing at Jeb's smashed trap in the skiff, "I see you've got our trademark aboard."

Jeb said nothing, making the skiff's painter fast to the stern cleat.

"About time I had a new broom," Grampie said. "If I was ever going lobstering again, which I ain't. How many'd *you* lose?"

"Seventeen," Jeb said.

Grampie had been hauling off his soaked work gloves, wringing out the salt water. Now he balled up the gloves and heaved them after the broom.

"Of all the grunt-headed ways for a man to make a living," Grampie said, "this beats all. This beats the hoary-headed, red-tailed, pink-whiskered old all. I'm going to drive this goddam floating Ouija board up to the shallowest end of the muddiest salt pond I can find, till the clam-flats come in over her cheeserind. Then I'm going to take out and start walking."

"Me, too," Jeb said. "Ulysses."

"Hanh?" Grampie rounded on him.

"Ulysses, I said."

"Ulysses who?"

"Ulysses the Greek."

"Oh. Him. Well, you can tell Ulysses there's eighty traps out there he can have free and for nothing. I wouldn't haul 'em again if the buoys waterlogged and sunk."

Jeb made a quick calculation. Grampie had had a hundred traps. If he had eighty now, that meant he had lost twenty. A hundred and nineteen dollars plus a hundred and forty . . . He tried to add it in his head, then realized he was too tired and too disgusted to care.

Heck, let it go. The traps were gone. Over a third of their whole string.

2 5 7

Grampie started his engine. He headed along the shore of Grindstone Island, muttering and mumbling like a safety valve under too heavy a head of steam. As they coasted along, fairly close in, he scanned the shore.

"I wouldn't haul them cuss-fired traps again if they filled up with the old solid-gold king-lobsters of all time, weighing fifty pounds apiece and ready-boiled on a mother-of-pearl plate. Jebby, is that a trap washed up on them ledges, or a stump?"

"Where? Oh. A stump, looks like, Grampie," Jeb said, and they went along.

"Not if they filled up and busted the laths off. You can tell Ulysses that, by God!"

Jeb said, "I will, Grampie."

"What's *he* got to do with it, anyway?"

"Ulysses got sick of going on the water," Jeb said. "So he said he was going to take an oar over his shoulder and start walking till he came to some place where they asked him what the oar was. Then he was going to stay there."

"Well, he was a smart man. Knew when to stop. There never was an Ellis yet knew enough to stop going on the water for a living and went and got himself a job in a factory, cutting up dead horses for glue. Jebby, what's that up there on Grindstone beach?"

"That's a trap, Grampie. Looks as if the buoy and warp were still on it."

"Well, let it lay there and rot. Here's one Ellis, by the living, jumped-up Jesus, that's through."

When they came to the Mussel Cove, on Grindstone Island, Grampie headed the boat into it. Without a word, he dropped a killick overboard and anchored the boat. Then he hauled in on the skiff by its painter and got into it, throwing down the painter and settling himself on the middle thwart with a cracking of his rheumaticky knees.

"Hand me that bucket of lobsters, Jebby," he said. "Them's the last lobsters I'm ever going to catch. I'm going ashore and boil 'em and eat 'em."

Gosh, I've never seen him so sore, Jeb thought.

There must be seven or eight dollars' worth of lobsters in that bucket.

But to heck with it. If he's going to cut up dead horses for glue, I might as well.

They built a fire out of driftwood sticks, on the small, smooth beach, and stretched out in the sun while the lobsters boiled to a fine, even red. Grampie ate five. Then he wiped the tomalley off his jackknife, got out his tobacco and filled his pipe.

"You suppose that castaway trap we saw's any good?" he asked.

"Doubt it."

"Well, if it is, some poor fool'll find it and fix it up and set it to fishing again," Grampie said. He let out a prolonged, peaceful cloud of smoke. "I'm some glad it won't be me."

Jeb felt too low to talk. His cap was over his eyes and he could feel the hot sun burning through his damp dungarees. In a little while, after that feed of lobster had settled down, he would go swimming in the cove. That would help. But right now, he wanted to lie still, maybe think through some of the worry in his mind.

With over a third of their gear gone, he and Grampie were in a spot. It would take time to replace thirty-seven traps—why, that was all he'd been able to build all winter. And they needed every trap they had. Lobstering wasn't any too good for part of the summer, when the lobsters crawled away to shed their shells and grow new, bigger ones; but he and Grampie had planned to fish their full string right through till fall, picking up what they could. They planned on hauling once every three or four days, and on the days between hauls, going handlining or trawling. By keeping at it good and hard, they could just about meet payments at the bank. If nothing went wrong, that is. Now, things had gone good and wrong.

In spite of Ma and Aunt Candace, who still didn't know what Grampie'd done, he'd gone ahead and mortgaged the house. He had taken the money and paid Guy's bills, and of course Ma'd not be long finding that out. It wasn't a case, now, of just paying some dealer when you had the money. Now you had a definite commitment at the bank.

They had enough and some to spare to make the first payment. But how about the next one, and the one after that? And now, of course, there'd be Aunt Evelyn's hospital bills—

Jeb flopped over on the hot sand and laid his forehead on his crossed arms. Fishing was the heck of a business to be in, anyway. One day you were a going concern, the next you were bankrupt. Maybe his mother was right. Maybe he ought to get his diploma and go somewhere and train.

Train for what? An engineer? A mechanic? Spend his time crawling around on a garage floor, or at some airport, up to his elbows in airplane engine grease? It wouldn't be bad, at that, if he could get a job working on turbo-jet engines.

Take Grampie, sitting there. Take Gramp Malcolm. If you put end to end the gear they'd lost in their lifetimes, it would reach from here to Bellport. And they had both been experts. It wasn't as if losing gear were any fault of their own. What they'd done, they'd set themselves up against something that was too strong for any man, no matter how good he was. The sea, itself. Wind squalls and tide rips. Treacherous, muddy, sandy, ledgy bottom. Storms no one could foresee.

You realized now, all right, what the remarks on Gramp Malcolm's chart meant. Without much thinking, right now, you could add some of your own.

"Muddy bottom, God Blaft!"

"Hell in a Notheaft Snowftorm."

"An old baftard of a tide rip . . ."

The silky sand under his bare forearms reminded him of the soft texture of the chart, and he saw it suddenly in his mind's eye, hanging where he had thumbtacked it on the fishhouse wall, with its new notation written in Grampie's hand and a different color ink: *"Guy drowned, Sept. 1947."*

CANDLEMAS BAY.

Lovely as some place you might have made up in a daydream. Green, sleepy islands; little wooded coves, trees down to the water's edge; high, granite bluffs; black, bullbacked ledges where the surf washed over; water stretching away forever, blue, white-capped, shining in the sun.

Water, cold-green, treacherous; no man's friend.

Grampie said, "They still learning the school kids about Ulysses? They was, when I went to school."

"Hanh?" Jeb said, his grunt muffled in his sleeve.

"I said, I learnt about Ulysses when I went to school," Grampie said. "I never heard that one about the oar, though. That must've been kind of a freak he took he got over, because according to some poem that four-eyed schoolmarm made me learn, Ulysses took out and went a voyage when he was a pretty old man."

"That so?"

"Ayup," Grampie said. "Turned everything over to his boy, and a lot of them old codgers, they lit out." He went on, conversationally, " 'There lies the port; the vessel puffs her sail; There gloom the broad dark seas. My mariners . . . you and I are old; Old age hath yet his honor and his toil; Death closes all. But something ere the end, Some work of noble note may yet be done, Not unbecoming men that strove with gods.' "

Jeb rolled over and stared at him, astonished.

Grampie grinned, a little sheepishly. He puffed on his pipe.

"What's that?" Jeb asked. "There any more of it?"

"There's a lot I can't recall. 'It may be that the gulfs will wash us down. . . .' Didn't mind taking a chance on that, seems so. 'Though much is taken, much abides; and though We are not now that strength which in old days Moved earth and heaven, that which we are, we are; One equal temper of heroic hearts, Made weak by time and fate, but strong in will To strive, to seek, to find and not to yield.' H'm. Time was, I used to read everything I could get my hands on about seafaring men."

Jeb sat up, his hands clasped around his knees, looking off over the water. Not so much the words as Grampie saying them had moved him in a curious way. He suddenly saw Grampie as a young man, starting in, before he and Gramp Malcolm had ever lost enough gear to stretch from here to Bellport. "Time was," he said now. Never "in time to come."

Sometimes, something almost made you hear time, as if it went by overhead on rustling wings, dropping everyone away into the years. Nathan had been nineteen. Nathan, Daniel, James. Malcolm, Jebron, Guy. Jeb. Jebron Malcolm Ellis, seventeen. Here and now.

"I even used to know a feller named Ulysses," Grampie said. "Ulysses Lunt. Born at the time when everyone was naming their kids after Ulysses S. Grant. Uley, they called him, Uley Lunt; owned a herring weir down off Gimbal Head when I was a boy. I recall the time he tried to fertilize Cow Island, little dump of rocks he owned, nothing ever growed there but puckerbrush, but Uley figured if he could get some grass to grow, he could raise him some sheep. One fall, he had a glist of herring he couldn't sell; kind of a poor fall for the herring business.

"He took about five hundred bushels out in dories and wheeled them up and dumped them on Cow Island. Helmonious job, he had; liked to killed himself, wheeling a wheelbarrow up over them rocks and into the middle of the island. His feet fell flatter'n flounders. He come in to Candlemas afterwards, and I recall him limping around upwards of all winter.

"Well, say. The gulls had a regular heathen holiday. They hung in a cloud over Cow Island for months and they et every one of them herring. Pa said it was the first time in his life he ever knew of a flock of gulls to winter-through fat. Come spring, there wasn't no more grass growed on Cow Island than there ever was. Goosed up the puckerbrush a mite, maybe, but that was all. When Uley went out there in June, with five-six sheep, he was some surprised."

Grampie stretched out his legs. He burrowed his lean rump comfortably into the round hollow he had dug for it in the sand.

He said, "There's always something to snap back in a man's eye. He gets mad, he's apt to cut off his nose to spite his face. Like Uley, throwed them sheep overboard. You going swimming?"

"Ayeh," Jeb said.

"Well, go ahead."

He watched benignly, while Jeb plunged around the placid green water of the cove, and came ashore to dry off in the sun.

"How much of that trap stuff of your father's did you have left?" Grampie asked.

"Laths and nails for fifty," Jeb said. "I cut the bows for that many. There aren't sills and crosspieces, though."

"I've got some," Grampie said. "Enough, I guess. See, we lost thirty-seven, we build fifty, we'll be better off 'n when we started."

Jeb grinned at him.

"We would if we weren't out of lobstering for good," he said.

Grampie said, "Hanh?"

He went down the beach to the skiff.

"Well, the day's young yet," he said. "Le's take the skiff and go get that castaway trap. Might be some sills in it we could use. Lord God, Jebby, look at your painter. Don't *never* heave down a piece of rope aboard a boat without coiling it up. Times a man's life depends on a piece of rope, for God's sakes."

RUSS said, "It's a thin man's pickings, anyway, lobstering in the summertime. Time you get your string fixed up again, you won't get your seed back, Jebron. Oh, sure, I know you can handline or trawl, in between hauls, but that's tough, too, with ground fish at a cent a hundredweight."

"That's so," Grampie said.

Russ cleared his throat.

"You hear about Johnny's new seiner?"

Jeb sat up in his chair. A seiner?

Grampie said, "Johnny having a new seiner, is he?"

"Ayeh. She's building, now—boatyard down Rhode Island way. Sixty-five feet."

"That's a good-sized boat, Russ."

"Ayeh. Well, look, Johnny wants to go seining. He's got a hunch might be good money in it. So he and I ordered the boat built from this Rhode Island place, but we thought we'd kind of cut our teeth this summer. Go in my boat till the big one's done. We're rigging up for it right now, and we're going to need a crew. So far, we've only got Warren Palmer."

Grampie grinned. "He and Johnny don't jibe any too well, do they?"

"Oh, Warren's poor bait, but he's all we can find, and anyway, we can't get anyone else, and Warren can cook. Why don't you and Jeb come with us?"

They were sitting on the screened back porch in the warm July evening. Jeb had been fooling with the radio, but there was nothing of interest on the short wave, and he had switched it over to some dance music, which was coming in low. Russ had arrived soon after supper, all dressed up in his Sunday suit. He had not said why he was dressed up, or whether he planned to go somewhere. A few months ago, everyone would have taken it for granted that he had come to beau Aunt Lynnie out to a dance; but now she was married to Ralph Strong and gone away. They had gone right after the wedding, for Ralph's vacation was over and he had had to go. He had taken Aunt Lynnie to Wisconsin.

Russ had been best man; he didn't seem at all concerned over Aunt Lynnie's marrying somebody else. As a matter of fact, Aunt Candy was the only one who seemed at all dissatisfied. She was still having it over about how Lynnie had pulled the wool over everyone's eyes. To everyone's amazement, she had given Aunt Lynnie five thousand dollars, calling it a wedding present, which fooled no one. Talk was that Aunt Lynnie would never have seen the five thousand, if the man she'd married hadn't been a lawyer. Now, to hear Aunt Candy, anyone would think that Aunt Lynnie's quiet marriage had something about it not quite respectable; and Jeb noticed, with some amusement, that Russ was managing to avoid being in the same room with Aunt Candy whenever he could. He dropped by every few evenings to talk fishing or listen to the radio, as he had always done; but his coming tonight, all togged out, was something of a mystery.

"Johnny's had this bug in his hat ever since last winter when he got a pretty good buy on a purse seine," Russ was going on. "You know Johnny's hunches. Don't amount to a damn, unless you happen to agree with them yourself."

To hear Russ and Johnny talk about each other, no one would suspect that they worked together like a right and a left hand, and undertook no new project unless it had been thoroughly gone into by both of them. If Russ reported that Johnny thought seining might be profitable this summer, it was a foregone conclusion that Russ thought so, too.

Gee, it would be fun to go seining with them, Jeb thought. Seiners, if they ran into any fish at all, usually made good money.

But he wasn't sure how Grampie would feel about it. If Grampie was going to keep on lobstering, Jeb was going to stick with him.

"We figure the way fishing is now," Russ said, "you've got to fit up to do any kind, if you want to make money. Dragging isn't what it was, you have to go too far offshore now. You can drag all over the Bay, not get a damn thing in the cod end of your net but somebody's old boot."

"That's what I've always said," Grampie said. "Used to be the best kind of fishing all over Candlemas Bay."

Russ said, "Ayeh. Johnny took a trip down to the Jersey coast this spring, Jebron. Wanted to learn about that drift-net method they use down there, with mackerel. Seems they set a long line of nets, parallel to the coast, off a ways, hitch one end to their boat and let the whole outfit drift all night. When the big schools of mackerel start coming in from deep water, they hit the nets. Some of them boats gross five thousand a week."

Grampie nodded. "I heard about that method," he said. "That's good fishing, Russ."

Watching him, Jeb could see that such talk was like a battle flag to an old fighter. Grampie was sitting forward in his chair, his eyes bright, his fingers rubbing his chin. The hard old thumb and fingers made a rasping sound, moving up and down the tough whiskers.

"You only get big market mackerel that way," Russ said. "Because the mesh of the net's big enough to let the small ones through. That way, you don't wipe out the whole school, and you don't have any trash-fish problem on your hands."

"Pity the draggers don't get the same idea," Grampie said.

"Well, they better get some sense about it before long,"

Russ said. "Or there won't be any ground fish left to drag. But the fishing business is screwball, anyway, Jebron. Used to be, a man could bring in a couple of thousand pounds and call it a good day's work. Now, at a cent or maybe two cents a pound, two thousand won't pay for his gas. He has to load down his boat or he can't meet expenses. The way he feels, he scrapes up everything going, even if he has to heave the little ones overboard."

Grampie said, "I was pricing salt codfish down to Coleman's the other day. Fancy grade, packed in them little wooden boxes. They was Candlemas Bay fish, shipped out of here from one of our fish wharves, to a buyer in Boston. Wholesaler in Boston shipped them back here to Jerry Coleman, Jerry he offers to sell them to me at sixty-nine cents a pound. I says, 'Jerry, I probably sold them same fish for two cents a pound. My stomach wouldn't digest 'em.' "

Russ grinned. "What do you want? Them was traveled fish. Been on a trip to Boston, you couldn't touch them with a ten-foot pole. Well, a lot of people get their living out of it, Jebron. The best you can say for it, it's the way things are."

He shifted a little in his chair, and the wicker creaked under his solid weight. "That's good dance music, Jeb. Where's it coming from?"

"Boston," Jeb said, grinning.

"Well, turn it off, or you'll get a bill for it. What I was saying, Jebron, Johnny wanted me to see if you'd go seining with us in my boat for the rest of the summer. Said if we could get you, we'd be as far ahead of the game as if we ran an extra boat."

"Well, I don't know," Grampie said. But he was pleased, you could tell that.

"We thought we'd go after pollock first. Then big mackerel, when they start running. Gear'll be ready Tuesday. We didn't know but we'd take a run out to Seal Island, first."

"Better try Gimbal Head, this time of year, hadn't we?" Russ winked jubilantly at Jeb.

"Okay. I'll tell Johnny you'll go, Jebron. Jeb, that skiff of yours'll come in handy."

"That drift-net rig you was telling about," Grampie said. "That wouldn't work in Candlemas Bay."

"I know it. Lord, you drift five minutes in the Bay, you'd be ka-whango onto a ledge or an island. Johnny had a notion about next spring, Jebron. Say we do pretty well purse-seining this season, we could get a bunch of them gill nets and go down off the Jersey coast in the new seiner—she'll be a big, seagoing boat. Follow the mackerel north."

"Gorry!" Grampie said. "By Jesus, Russ, I'll go along with you."

"Fellow Johnny talked with," Russ went on, "his outfit followed the mackerel clear to Cape Elizabeth, last year. Coined the money."

Grampie's fingers rasped furiously at his chin.

"You mull it over," Russ said. "We'd like to be able to count on you. Jeb, where's your ma?"

"Why, in the kitchen, I guess. I don't know."

"Well, go in and tell her to hustle up and show, or we'll be late for the movies."

Jeb blinked. "She going to the show with you?"

"She might be. If I can pry her loose. Or find her, even. I thought she'd be around."

"I wondered why you were all dolled up," Jeb said disgustedly.

It would be a lot more fun to have Russ sit here and talk seining, especially about the new project down the New Jersey coast. So far, nothing had been said about Jeb's going along, and he was dying to know. Now Russ was planning to go off to the movies with Jen.

"The show's no good tonight," Jeb said, with authority. "Some darn title like 'Love's Dream,' or something."

2 6 8

Russ eyed him.

"I wouldn't want to come between a mother and her children," he said, raising an eyebrow. "Why don't you go see where she is?"

Jeb started off in a disgruntled fashion, letting the inside door bang behind him.

"The new seiner's going to be diesel-powered," Russ said. "I was kind of figuring if we could get Jeb to diesel school this fall, he might cram in enough by spring so's he could help out running the engines. Wanted to talk it over with Jen before I mentioned it to him, though. What's your idea of it, Jebron?"

"I'm for it," Grampie said shortly. "If you can convince Jen, Russ."

Russ grinned.

He said, "That's the sixty-four-dollar question."

Jeb found his mother in the kitchen, dispiritedly trying to help Myrabel shell a big basketful of green peas for tomorrow's dinner.

Jen's hand was healing well, but it was still stiff, in a light bandage, and in the fortnight since the accident, she had come to realize how few things you could do with one hand. Never having had a disability of any kind, she was taking it hard. She could do the planning and look after the children; but when it came to sweeping, or washing floors or dishes, or, she thought in a kind of fury of frustration, shelling peas, she had to let Myrabel take over.

During the first week in July, six new boarders had come, so that the establishment now numbered eighteen people. Jen told herself it was no use to worry, even though she lay awake nights worrying. Since Lynnie's wedding, Candace had seemed her normal self—no easier to get along with, sharp, nosy and acid; but her black, brooding mood was gone. At least, she was speaking again. Jen had come to the conclusion that she and Myrabel had been mistaken about Candy's turning up the heater. Everybody had got excited and scared, that was all; at such a time, it was natural to want to blame someone. Jen still meant to move out of the house, with the children, as soon as she could; in the meantime, the thing to do seemed to be to finish out the summer. Her main worry, now, was that Myrabel would be worn out; but Myrabel was a woman of affairs, never so happy as when she had many things to attend to all at once.

"Oh, shoot," she told Jen, when Jen suggested they'd better write the next batch of boarders not to come. "Cook for five, cook for twenty-five, what's the difference? All you do is dump an extra bucket of water in the stew. Besides, all them people, them teachers, they've planned their vacation, it ain't likely they could get rooms any other place, now. Besides, I like it and it comes easy to me, Jen, and I need the money."

So six quiet, pleasant schoolteachers had taken the place of the late, unlamented Clawsons. Mr. Raymond, at meal-times, was surrounded by a gaggle of ladies; but he seemed to be enjoying himself very much, and he told Jen, calmly, that he was still planning to stay forever.

He was, Jen saw to her astonishment, tremendously taken with Evelyn. She thought, privately, that it would do him little good, until she saw them one day in the orchard, Mr. Raymond talking ten to the dozen, Evelyn listening in her remote way. But at least she was listening.

She had come home from the hospital with her hair cut short in a style that was really becoming to her; it turned out to be naturally curly hair, which no one could have suspected. When she was indoors, it waved around her head in a gleaming, soft cloud. Myrabel was delighted with it. So, apparently, was Mr. Raymond. But outdoors, Evelyn still wore her sunbonnet.

Her hand was immobilized, in a sling. It would be a long time before she could use it. Evelyn did not seem concerned. If anyone asked her, she said it was doing well enough; otherwise, she never mentioned it.

"I'd give up now, if I were you," Jen told Mr. Raymond.

"No," he said, dolefully. "I'm a stubborn man, Mrs. Ellis."

"Well, it'll be a long time," Jen said. "But you're welcome here, Mr. Raymond."

He was, too. Jen couldn't think of anyone she had come, in such a short time, to like better. It was too bad Evelyn was such a fool about people. Jen was thinking about Evelyn, as she sat at the kitchen table, haggling open the pea pods with her thumbnail, and making an awkward job of it.

"Ma," Jeb said, behind her. "Russ's out here. He wants you to go to the movies."

"Tell him I can't," Jen said automatically, without looking up. "I'm too busy."

Jeb reported, with alacrity, to the porch.

"She can't, she's busy," he said, sitting down in his chair again.

"You don't say," Russ said laconically. He got up. "Where is she—in the kitchen?"

In the kitchen, Myrabel was saying, "I don't see how you figure that what peas you can shell with one thumb makes any percentage to me. Why don't you go with him? It'd do you good."

"Atta girl!" Russ said from the doorway. "You talked her into it, Myrabel."

"My soul!" Myrabel said, blinking at his finery. "You look some elegant. I wouldn't go to the movies to look at no movie star, Jen, I'd make him take me parking, if I was you. If she won't go, I'll go with you myself, Russ."

"No, you don't!" Russ said firmly. "I ain't going to have Amos Coughlin knocking the living pickle out of me."

Myrabel produced one of her famous blushes.

"What you know about Amos Coughlin won't jiddle your pendulum," she said. "Get him out of here, Jen, before I can't resist getting my hands into that yeller marcel wave."

"There you go," Russ said. "Womenfolks either want to pat my wave, or they want to pull it. Jealousy's all it is. 'Look at that lovely wave,' they say, 'wasted on a man!' I always say, 'Babe, there's never been a hair of it wasted yet—' "

"You shut up," Myrabel said. "Don't go out with him, Jen. You'll put your head right into the lyron's mouth."

Russ grinned. "That's what we want, all right. How about it, Jen? You like a ride with a nice lyron?"

Jen laughed.

"I'll have to fix up a little, Russ. I can't go anywhere in this old housedress. I hadn't ought to . . . there's still so much to do."

"Jeb," Russ bawled, at the door, "come in here a minute."

His bellow echoed through the house, and Jeb came on the double. Neal and Andy, who had been using the last of the daylight by passing a ball on the lawn, came loping in to see what was up, and from the backstairs, the two little girls pattered down, agog. Anything with Russ was exciting.

"That's what we like," Russ said, approvingly. "Everybody jumping. You kids hop to and shell your mother's peas for her. She and I's going out on the town."

"My Lord," Myrabel said disgustedly. "I can do it twice as quick if I don't have this crew to tumble over. All right, the lot of you. Settle down. I'll whack up the peas, and whoever gets through first gets a prize."

Russ grinned at Jeb, who was glaring at him sourly.

"Bet you don't win the prize," he said.

He helped shell peas, himself, until Jen came downstairs, ready to go.

"Movies?" he said. "Or a ride?"

He stopped the car at the driveway entrance, waiting to see whether he should turn right or left down the highway.

"A ride, I guess," Jen said. "Unless the movie's something you really want to see, Russ."

" 'Love's Dream,' " he said. "I'd like a ride, myself."

He swung right, in the direction away from town.

It would be heaven, Jen thought, just to sit here relaxed for weeks, watching the road, fawn-colored in the dusk, roll backward under the car's hood, feeling the July breeze warm on her face from the open window. Russ's Chevvy might be old, but he took care of the engine himself, and it ran like a watch. He was heading inland along the highway that led north toward the woods and lakes. Where was it, up this way somewhere, that she and Guy used to go, years back? Brant Lake. A lovely place. In the days when she and Guy were in love with each other.

She felt her tired back molding itself into the well-worn, comfortable cushions. Other cars, coming toward them, passed with a blare of bright light and a sleepy *shush* of tires. She could see Russ's hand on the wheel, picked out in light and shadow.

She thought, hazily, what a good hand it was, strong-boned, the fingers blunt and capable. How long it was she had known Russ. Ever since Guy had brought her here to Candlemas to live, eighteen years ago. Russ had always been in the background, somewhere, big, light-hearted, kindly; the only friend Guy had seemed able to keep, as through the years all others had dropped away. Except for the war years, Russ had always been around; she remembered how much she had missed him while he had been away.

Oh, this was heaven. She hadn't realized she was so tired. The motion of the car and the humming engine were making her let go.

"I'm terrible company, Russ," she said sleepily. "I seem to be so tired I can't see."

"Well, rest," he said. "That's the idea. Partly," he added, under his breath.

She let her head tilt back; and all at once the jangle, the commotion, the grinding responsibilities fell plunging out of consciousness. Jen slept, leaning a little toward Russ, as the car rolled silkily down the concrete.

She awakened to a lightly colored darkness and a sense of warmth and comfort; and, coming to slowly, as she always did, she realized that her head was pillowed soundly on Russ's shoulder. His arm was around her and he had tucked his auto robe snugly about her feet, for the crisp, night air was cold. The car radio was on, turned down low. Its light was the soft glowing spot of color on the dash. The car was parked close to a glimmering sheet of water, whose whiteness she could make out through the windscreen. It was full dark, now. Late, she thought, with a little flurried movement. My soul, I feel as if I'd been asleep for hours.

As if to answer her, the cottony baritone coming in over the radio said, "The time is now eleven-thirty."

Jen said, "My goodness, Russ!"

Russ tightened his arm.

"I was afraid you'd hurt your sore hand, flopping on it," he said. "So I made you comfortable. Fine one you are!"

In the darkness, she could see the flash of his grin.

"Come out with a man and sleep the entire evening," he said.

"I'm sorry as I can be," she said. "I seem always to go to sleep, these days, if anyone gives me half a chance."

"You're worn out, that's why," he said indignantly. "I've been sitting here for two hours, getting mad about it."

"Two hours?"

"Well," he said sheepishly. "I slept, myself, for a while."

"I should think you might. My soul, Russ, your arm must be paralyzed."

"Does it feel like it?" he asked. "It doesn't to me."

No, it didn't. she thought. It felt strong and vibrant and tingling.

"I'm a lump," she said, startled. "I'm sorry, Russ. I'll sit up and be company for a while."

Russ put his other arm about her and held her lightly against him.

"You're the best company I ever saw, asleep," he said. "Makes me wonder what you'll be like awake."

For a moment, she felt the pressure of his cheek against hers, warm and male, smelling cleanly of shave lotion.

"Russ . . . ?" she began. "You—"

"Talk, talk, talk," he said shakily, under his breath, and his mouth on hers muffled the words and stopped them. He kissed her tentatively at first, then with a passion that left her breathless.

"Jen," he said softly, "you always wondered why I never married, and I did, too. Now I know."

The car moved quietly up the driveway and stopped outside the L-kitchen door. The house was dark, every light out.

"The respectable Ellises have all gone to bed," Russ said. "It's only you fly-by-night Keppels that's out and around at this hour. Funny Myrabel didn't leave a light for you."

"She probably did," Jen said. "Candy always turns the lights off, after just so long."

"I better go in with you, see you get a light on," he said. "You don't want to risk a tumble, hurt that hand."

"Oh, you're an old woman—"

"Uh-huh. You ought to know."

Jen said, "Sh-h."

"Who's to hear us?"

He helped her solicitously up the steps and opened the door for her. "It's about time somebody took a little care of you."

He caught her good hand, as she fumbled for the light switch in the kitchen, and drew her to him.

"Sh-h," Jen said again. "You mustn't—"

"Who's got a better right? I don't care if somebody does hear us. Besides, I'm not making any noise."

He kissed her soundly. "M'm," he said.

The light came on behind them with a businesslike click.

Candy stood in the door, her hand still on the switch. She was a curious sight, with her scanty hair braided into two skinny pigtails, and her brown bathrobe held tight across her front with one hand. But there was nothing funny about her, standing there.

"Hello, Candy," Russ said, not turning a hair. "I was kissing Jen."

"So I see. It's three o'clock."

"Is it?"

Candy stared at them, her eyes gleaming under the bright overhead light.

"Just what do you think you're up to, Jen?"

"Myrabel would say she was putting her head right into the lyron's mouth," Russ said.

"You know I won't put up with it. Not in this house," Candy said.

Russ said, "You're not putting up with a thing for very long, Candy. Jen and I are getting married, as soon as the law'll allow."

He heard the sharp intake of Jen's breath and pressed her hand warningly.

"It looks to me as though the law had better allow it pretty soon, then," Candy said acidly.

"I agree with you," Russ said.

"I should have thought you'd feel more at home down around Boxtown," Candy said, staring at him. "Or hasn't Henriette Murphy got a younger sister?"

"All right, Candy," Russ said. "I used to go with Henriette. She's a married woman now, with four children. Lives in Providence. I don't think she's likely to come between Jen and me, at my age. I knew if you ever unloaded on me, Henriette would come walking right up out of Boxtown. Now you've got it off your chest. Jen and I are going to get married. It'd be nice if we was all of us friends."

"A woman with six children!" Candy said. "You're doing well for yourself."

"I figure I'm doing damn well."

"You planning to move in here, too? Some of our own family can always sleep out in the barn."

"Oh, shoot, Candy," Russ said, good-naturedly.

He was holding on to himself, Jen saw, and she admired him for it. She herself, she thought, would be tearing mad by now.

"I've got a house," Russ went on. "As soon as we're married, I'll move my family into it. Let's just skip the rest of it, Candy."

A look of such relief and pleasure came over Candy's face that Jen was appalled. She opened her mouth to say something, but Candy spun on her heel and went away, shutting the door behind her with a snap.

"Phew!" Russ said. "I've been dreading that for quite a while. I guess it would've been considerably worse if I hadn't told her I was taking you and the kids away from here, Jen. Now, you can give me hell, if you want to. I was going to propose, all neat and aboveboard on my knees, maybe; not rush you into anything."

"How she must hate us all," Jen said.

"She just wants Grammie's house," Russ said. "To heck with it, Jen. Will you marry me?"

"Six children, Russ—?"

Russ grinned, looking at her face, which told him what he wanted to know.

"Well, they all like me," he said, putting his arms around her.

"I can see you, proposing on your knees," Jen said, and she turned her face up to his.

A FEW hundred yards outside Sheepskin Rock, Russ's boat circled, rising and falling to a slow, lazy ocean swell. Twenty miles away, the Candlemas Bay islands looked low and hazy, above them the puffy, cumulus clouds of August. To the east, the ocean stretched to the horizon.

It was a fine, calm day for seining mackerel, if you could find any mackerel to seine. So far, through July and the first three weeks in August, Russ's crew had done well, first with sea pollock, then with mackerel. It had been a phenomenal herring season in Candlemas Bay. Weirs were packed full along the coast; the herring seiners hit a bonanza. Russ and Johnny were glum, wishing they had rigged up for herring-seining with a small-meshed net. Then the sea-going schools of mackerel followed the herring in.

The first big schools were reported at Crow Island, twenty-five miles to the westward. Amos Coughlin, Myrabel's friend, let out the news over the radiotelephone, one evening at dusk; and every seiner in Candlemas Bay went racing west into the darkness; for the first boat back with a load would be likely to receive a top market price. Russ's boat went tearing along with the rest. But as they were passing Gimbal Head, Grampie, who had been staring ahead thoughtfully at the calm, dusky-colored water, said to Russ, "Mackerel ain't going to take long to get up here from Crow Island, Russ."

Russ said, "No?" glancing around at him from the wheel.

Grampie said, "If we was to lay to, under Gimbal Head, tonight, and keep our eyes peeled tomorrow morning, we might not have to lug a trip of fish so far as some of these fellers will."

Russ said, "You think so, hanh?"

He reached out and slowed the engine imperceptibly; the nearest seiner behind them, who was skippered by Elwell Palmer, began rapidly to overhaul.

Johnny said, "Well, I'd be glad enough to be out of this rat race. Every boat from here to Nova Scotia'll be down Crow Island way tomorrow. Set around a school there, all you'll be liable to get would be somebody else's goddam finger."

Elwell slowed down, too, as he came abreast, and leaned out to hail. "What's trouble, Russ? Ain't you going? What's Cap'n Jebron say?"

"Little engine trouble," Russ said, fibbing with a bland face. " 's all right. Water pump, I think, El."

Elwell waved jubilantly. "See ya down there. Next week," he called, and went roaring away.

One boat less, all the more fish for him.

Warren Palmer, the fifth member of Russ's crew and, also, Elwell's brother, looked after him glumly.

"I d'no why we hang around here on just one man's say so," he grumbled. "Ain't no signs of fish here. Won't be none, neither. If El gets in before I do with a trip of mackerel, I ain't never going to hear the last of it."

"That's all right, Warren," Johnny said. "You'll feel better after a good night's sleep."

The next morning, a mile off Gimbal Head, they laid the seine around eight thousand pounds of big market mackerel, which they sold at the Candlemas fish wharf for twenty cents a pound. Jeb and Grampie shared $512 for that first trip.

Afterwards, as the market glutted, the price went down—to eighteen, to twelve, to ten cents a pound. Now, with the first big schools thinning out a little, it was back at twelve, and there was still something over a month of the season left.

Jeb had pooled his money with Grampie's to help him meet the mortgage payments on the house. This morning, sitting up on the stern, while the boat circled for another school to seine, he figured up in his head that they had about eight hundred dollars left to pay. Which was going some, he told himself. They might be able to pay the whole thing this summer, if the mackerel, now, hadn't gone for good.

For the last four days, the outfit had cruised without sighting a fin. At Gimbal Head, where they'd seined a good many schools this summer, there was nothing. They went from Seal Island to Iron Island, up Nathan's Reach to Duck Cove, to Green Island; nothing. On the fourth day, Russ headed the boat for the open sea.

"We'll go out to the Rock and set around a whale," he said disgustedly. "Might be a few mackerel in his poke."

Grampie didn't seem to think the fish had gone. If they had, it would be the first time in the history of the mackerel runs that they'd petered out before fall. They'd be back, he said.

For a long time, Jeb had been sitting up on the stern, idly trailing a pollock drail behind the boat. He didn't expect to catch anything—there wasn't a sign of a pollock, and he had to be careful his line didn't foul the tows— the seine boat and his skiff—which was hard on the arm muscles. But fishing was something to do. Life was pretty easy aboard a seiner when you were cruising for fish. You sat and kept your eyes peeled for a school; or you rested and trailed a pollock drail. There was always a chance something might latch on which would go good in Warren's frying pan; and anyway, you had the alive, vibrating pull of the line against your hand.

It was wonderful, this far out from land. Jeb, being an inshore fisherman, hadn't often got off to the Rock, and it seemed like a different world to him. Inside the Bay, some island or ledge was always within jumping distance, so that, looking up from hauling traps or trawls, a man saw land and woods and bluffs, or the white buildings of the towns on shore. Off here, no land broke the sweep of the ocean to the east. Two tiny specks away out were sea-going draggers, which must have gear overside, they were moving so slowly. If he turned around, he could see the low, black bluffs of the Rock, with the wide, tan patch across them, from which the Rock got its name, and the businesslike white shaft of its lighthouse thrusting up out of the granite. But that was all. Astern, where he was looking now, the great, empty, blue platter of water went to the horizon. Even the horizon didn't seem to limit it much.

What he noticed most, when he had time to sit still and lazy, like this, was the feeling of quiet which seemed to be here, no matter what sounds were being made. Behind him, the boat's big engine rolled over with a slow, powerful rumble; Johnny had the radiotelephone on, which exploded every few seconds into a cackle of voices; Grampie and Russ were yarning with each other, a foot or two behind and below him. The seine boat and the skiff towed with a swish and gurgle of water at their bows. Yet what you noticed was *stillness*.

Maybe it's a case of hearing what you see, he told himself, lazily trying to figure it out. Your eyes take in all this space of sky and water, and so your ears register some of it. Or maybe space like this does make a sound, and all you know how to call it is stillness.

This is all I ever want to do, he thought. This is for me.

He stretched out his legs, feeling warm content go down

into the tips of his toes. Later on, when the boat was fishing, he'd have to wear rubber boots to protect his feet, but now they were bare. He was bare and brown from the waist up and from mid-thigh down, clad only in shorts. The hard, outdoor work this summer had toughened his muscles and added an inch to his height—six feet now, taller than Guy had been, broader across the shoulders; and the other day in a wrestling match, he had put Russ flat on his back on the ground.

The sun was hot on his skin, cooled by the light breeze of the boat's passage. The water was clear green, sparkling. What he'd like to do was take a header off the stern, have himself a good swim; but Russ had put his foot down about that.

"There's all kinds of sharks out here," he said. "Once in a while you see a killer whale. Water's too cold. Damn it, no, Jeb."

Jeb grinned to himself. It seemed pretty queer to have Russ making a noise like a father, but he guessed he could put up with it. He guessed he'd have to. At first, he hadn't known just how he felt about sharing his mother with Russ, or Russ with his mother. Now he was used to it, everything was okay. Russ and Jen were getting married on Labor Day, and they were all going to move into the big old house Russ had bought down in the town. That is, all of them but Jeb. As soon after Labor Day as makes no matter, Jeb was going to Providence, Rhode Island, to diesel school. And in the spring, when the new seiner was done, Russ and Johnny and Grampie were coming down to Providence, and they were all going to take the boat south to the mackerel-fishing off the coast of New Jersey.

Things were turning out pretty good for him. No wonder he felt good down to the ends of his toes.

Deep inside him a warning sounded, and Jeb pulled himself up short.

Don't ever so much as admit to yourself that things look

good. Like Grampie says: "The prettier she looks, the sharper you want to watch her. Because when things look smooth, that's the time when a man's apt to be careless."

I suppose if I live to be a hundred, I'll never forget the things Grampie's taught me. I wish I'd ever live long enough to know as much about this job as he does.

He glanced around at Grampie, sitting just behind him, with Russ. The old man had his short-stemmed pipe shoved into his mouth, right up under his nose. His shapeless black felt hat, spattered with dried mackerel scales, was squashed down over his ears. He was relaxed, yet there was still something alert and tense about him, his eyes searching the long plain of water, even while his deep bass voice rumbled casually on, yarning with Russ.

If there were fish out here, Grampie would find them.

Jeb heard him say, "I wouldn't wonder'n we found a few pollock today, maybe."

"Pollock!" Russ said. "What's the use of them—a cent a pound."

"Get enough, might make a day's pay out of it," Grampie said. "There's some around."

"You think so?"

"Well," Grampie said.

They followed his glance off over the water. Everything seemed the same as it had been all morning. Blue, lightly crinkled water, flat, lazy ocean swell. There were no pollock signs, no gulls flying; nothing on the surface to show a school of fish; but Grampie seemed to stiffen a little, and Russ let out a delighted guffaw.

"I swear to God, Jebron, I saw your nose grow a quarter of an inch longer," he said.

"Maybe it did. How about heading her up to the west'ard a mile or so, Johnny?"

Johnny spun the wheel and they went up past the Rock toward the wide expanse of Candlemas Bay.

Warren Palmer, the cook and the fifth member of the

crew, came up from below where he had been getting everything ready in case Jeb caught a fresh fish that would go in a chowder. Warren was a lanky young man of thirty or so, with a hatchet face and a big bony nose that seemed to dwarf the rest of his face. Grampie once said that the most you could say for Warren's nose was that he could smell with it; he also said that you wanted to look out or it would be right into the middle of your business. There was no great harm in Warren; he was a fine cook and a capable fisherman, but no bluejay was ever more of a busybody. Once having found out your affairs, he would oblige with his ideas on how to run them.

He climbed up and sat down beside Jeb, hauling up his knees and folding his arms around his knifelike shins.

"For creep's sake, Jeb," he said, "why don't you put some clothes on? I sh'd think you'd freeze to death, up here stark, raving nekkid."

Jeb shrugged. He didn't dislike Warren, but it had been kind of nice, here alone on the stern, trailing the pollock drail. His cruising in shorts, whenever he got a chance, was an old worry to Warren. Not for any reason, except that Warren himself generally had on rubber boots, wool pants, shirt and sweater over his underclothes, and a hat; and his way seemed the best to him.

"You ain't caught nothing, Jeb," he went on glumly, after a silence. "Nor won't, neither. Nothing to catch. What you using for bait?"

"Feathers," Jeb said.

"Them damn Japanese feathers? They ain't no good."

Anything Japanese, to Warren, should automatically be preceded by "damn." He hadn't gone to the war because of his flat feet; but no one had spouted war talk more ferociously than he, and it seemed to have given him a permanent fix. He had no use for anyone in the world except the citizens of the United States of America, and very little for them, outside of his own state and town. As a matter of fact, he had been known to refer to the citizens of Rocktown, three miles from his home, as "them damn Rocktowners."

"I was using nylon for a while," Jeb said. "No bites on that, either."

"Nylon!" Warren said. "That ain't no good, for God's sake. If you was a pollock, tell me, would you bite down onto a goddam great junk of yarn?"

"They've been known to."

Jeb grinned to himself. Whatever he was using, the argument would have been the same.

"Oh, when they're biting, they'll hit anything, a cow's tit, put it on there. Them feathers going through the water, they look *something like* a squid, I don't deny, but they *ain't* a squid, and old pollock knows it. Take old pollock, lazing along, with a gutsful of something a pollock'd want to eat, he sees them goddam plastic baits, he won't turn his head. No more'n you would nor I would. What you want's a flounder's belly, the white meat. A natural bait."

"Find me a flounder, I'll put it on the hook," Jeb said, nagged into speech.

"Chrise, we ain't got no flounder, never had the forethought to bring one. That's the trouble with you kids, you don't none of you have no forethought."

"Okay. Then I'll use feathers."

"But, goddammit, ain't I been telling ya them feathers ain't no good? Would *you* bite onto it? Damn right, you wouldn't. But spos'n it was a flapjack with maple syrup on it?"

Warren opened his mouth and snapped at the air, his teeth coming together with a clack.

" 'n there!" he said. "You got him!"

"Why don't you make him a flapjack with syrup on it and let him bait up with it, Warren?" Johnny said, grinning around from the wheel.

"Oh, for creep's sake, Johnny! Wouldn't be no use to bait with a flapjack. I was talking about him, or me, what we'd bite onto, drawing a kind of a parallel there, see?"

"Well, make a flapjack and bait the hook with it and he'll jump overboard and bite it."

"Hanh!" Warren grunted. "All right, eat canned beans for dinner, see if I care a cuss, won't take a man's well-meant advice."

He stretched out disgustedly on the stern and was silent for nearly a minute. Then he stuck up his head like a turtle.

"Honest to God, Jeb, haul it in. It's a waste of time. Them damn feathers—"

The line in Jeb's hand straightened out with a yank that almost took his arm out of the socket. He let out a startled yell and scrambled to his feet, his hands clawing wildly at the line, in his excitement not gaining an inch. Astern of the skiff and the seine boat, there was a sizable flurry in the water; then Johnny swung the boat in a wide arc, so that the line tailed away from the tows without fouling them, and Jeb hauled in his fish. It was a pollock, nearly three feet long, spectacular in black and silver. Jeb got it alongside, and Russ yanked it in with the gaff.

"Hah!" Grampie said. "Hark to the minute gun at sea!"

"Well, for Chrissake!" Warren said.

He eyed the fish as if it had dealt him a personal, intended insult. "Must be a sick one. Sometimes them sick fish'll bite anything."

Russ winked at Jeb.

"Got stomach ulcers, worrying over where the rest of his kin are," he said. "Hustle up and get him into the chowder, Warren."

"Now, I ain't going to cook no sick fish, Russ," Warren said querulously. "I'll open up the beans."

"Oh, cook it, for godsakes, Warren!" Johnny exploded. He could take just so much of Warren.

Warren picked up the fish and started to dress it, affront sticking out all over him. Feathers were new-fangled—not what the old-timers who knew how to fish had used, and he considered himself an authority, not only on fishing, but on most things.

"Hah!" he said suddenly, triumphantly spinning around from the cheeserind, where he had been dressing the pollock into the water. "Look-a there! Told ya. Sicker'n a dog. Lead poisoning!"

He held out three bright pellets that he had cut out of the pollock's poke.

"I be damned!" Russ said, staring. "Machine-gun bullets!" He took one, turning it over in his fingers. "Been quite a while," he said.

Johnny said, "The draggers were saying over the radio that planes from the base were practicing target shooting outside of here, yesterday. Them bullets are bright; I suppose they float down through the water and the pollock grab 'em."

"Them cussid jets!" Warren said. "Cooking up another war. They'll be at it, again, see if they ain't. Well, I'm some glad they can't call on me for this one. That's your kittle of fish, Jeb, not mine, by God!"

He fetched Jeb a hearty slap on the bare shoulders, took the dressed fish and went below to his chowder.

Grampie said soberly, "Better get your pants and shirt on, Jebby." He glanced off over the water, standing silent, his eyes shadowed by the battered brim of his hat.

"That damn chaw-mouth," Johnny grunted under his breath.

"Well, take things one at a time," Grampie said. "Right now, it means that a pollock that was ten-twenty miles outside of here, yesterday, headed inshore today. Maybe he's brought his folks along."

Jeb, dressing below, as far up as he could get into the boat's forepeak to be out of Warren's elbowroom, heard Grampie give out with the time-honored bawl:

"Fish! Off to the south'ard! Get a-going!"

Jeb bounced out on deck, buttoning his last buttons as he ran.

Off to the south, a few minutes ago, the sea had lain blue and empty, lightly rippled by the breeze. Now, out of nowhere, a flock of plunging gulls had appeared on the horizon, white flecks that shone and vanished as they turned in the air and the sun caught their wings.

Johnny rolled the wheel. "How they heading, Jebron?"

"Can't tell yet. Straight for us. No. Two points east, Johnny."

The boat shot across the calm sea toward the distant flock of gulls, her crew strained out like pointers. Warren had simply picked his chowder off the stove and set it on the floor. He was there at the seine boat's painter, ready to haul her in when the time came. The seine boat and the skiff laid back on their tails, their bows towed high. Foaming wake shot out on either side, two crested waves fanning out astern.

"Boy!" Russ said, as they came nearer to the gulls and Johnny slowed down. "Look at those buggers plug!"

The gulls, thousands of them, were plugging over an area of some three hundred feet, plummeting into the water and flying up again, gobbling the shrimp the pollock were chasing. The rusty, raucous squalling carried far over the water; the air was full of wings. Below them, here and there the surface showed dark, curdled whirlpools.

Johnny stopped the engine.

Warren yanked the seine boat up alongside and he and Russ and Jeb piled into her. Russ slid open the hatch, amidships, and tried her motor; the motor, which was tuned like a watch, flipped over and caught at a touch of the starter button.

Johnny came aft and cast off the seine boat.

"Okay, Russ," he said. "Take her. She's all yours."

A few hundred feet off the bow, the school of pollock

suddenly boiled to the surface. The long, racing backs, the heads all pointed toward the center of a circle where they had surrounded their shrimp. Spray shot sparkling into the air. For an instant, the flashing top layer of big fish were thrust entirely out of water by the massive push of the school beneath them, making a tremendous, black-and-silver rosette.

"Oh, baby!" Russ said, prayerfully.

The seine boat took off, the purse seine paying out over her stern.

The seine was a hundred and fifty fathoms long, of mesh-twine, eight fathoms deep. Cork floats buoyed its upper edge at the surface; lead weights on the bottom sank it, so that, as it payed out, it stood perpendicular in the water. Between the lead weights, a stout purse line ran through bridle rings. When the seine boat had made a wide circle around the school, the two ends of the seine would be brought together and the purse line tightened, closing the bottom of the net. It was to be hoped that the pollock would be inside, but anything could happen.

It took quite a lot to scare pollock when they were feeding like this; the big fish seemed, at such a time, to go crazy, piled up in a frenzy of gobbling. But they could be scared. A shark blundering in might do it, or a school of tuna. Or the shrimp might go shooting off somewhere, with the fish after them, before the net was closed. There were a dozen ways to lose pollock. Many a seiner's crew has sat back cursing, with a hundred fathoms of net out and their fish sunk like rocks.

Jeb sat sweating with tenseness and excitement, watching the big seine slide out over the stern and sink downwards in the green water. It was his job, with Warren, to see that it payed out smoothly; a kink or a tangle now could lose the school.

The bobbing line of floats lengthened behind the seine boat in a big arc.

2 8 9

He thought, That's one of the best things I'll ever see, that curve of a line of floats across the water.

They hove alongside Russ's boat at last; the big net was all out. They began closing up, hauling in the purse line. It seemed to come in forever, fathom after wet fathom. Then they had it in and made fast. The net was closed.

Grampie sat down, wiping his streaming forehead.

"What's the matter, Jebron?" Warren asked. "Ain't winded, are you?"

He was obviously winded himself—they all were, for the action had been fast for the past fifteen minutes.

Grampie said nothing, and something about his silence made Jeb glance quickly over at him. His face looked about as usual under the battered black hatbrim—a little tired, Jeb thought, but it was no use to try to get him to take it easy. He made up his mind to get next to Grampie, when they hauled the fish into the bag end of the net, and see if he could take some of the strain off him. They were all pretty tired now, and hungry; they couldn't even think of stopping to eat till the fish were aboard. If the wind breezed up, you'd very likely lose your haul; you might even lose your seine.

But he ought to have some coffee, Jeb thought.

Grampie looked up, catching the worried eyes on him, and grinned.

He's all right, then. Maybe he's just sick of Warren's clack. Lord knows, we've heard enough of it in the last six weeks—

"Blast!" Grampie said suddenly, in the bass tones of disgust. "I thought things had been going too goddam smooth to be true!"

A thirty-foot section of cork toggles suddenly vanished, yanked under water. A thousand or so big pollock surfaced frantically; some fifty of them went shooting out over the side of the sagging seine.

"Shark, or something, out there," Grampie said. "Nudging the net, blast him! Look, there he is!"

The toggles came floating slowly back to the surface of the water, and just beyond them, a big dorsal fin cut a smooth V, jigging up and down.

"Well," he went on, "somebody'll have to go out there, or he'll have the works over."

Russ and Jeb were already moving, hauling in the skiff and casting it off, and Warren jumped, agile as a cat, into her bow. He unslung the harpoon from the leather thongs which held it snugly under the skiff's gunnel.

"Gi'me one progue at him," he said. "Just one progue, Lord God, that's all I ask. You put me over him, Russ, I'll do the rest."

Jeb had been dying to get his hands on the harpoon; but with Russ rowing and Warren in the bow, someone would have to get into the stern to trim the skiff; he sat down on the stern seat without comment.

Russ rowed slowly along the seine, a few feet outside 'the circle of floats. Warren stood in the bow, his legs spraddled, holding the harpoon over his head with both hands. He peered down into the sun-streaked depths, watching.

Looking down over the stern, Jeb could see nothing on the starboard side but the wavering squares of the seine dropping out of sight; on the port side, the deep, motionless green. The shark had gone; or he had withdrawn temporarily to think over the stout twine-mesh between him and his dinner.

"You ain't giving up so soon?" Warren said, glancing around anxiously, as Russ swung the boat about.

"We've got to get the fish aboard," Russ said impatiently. "Can't fool around out here all day."

But, with Warren, the hunt was up. He had his mouth all puckered up to kill something.

"Swing round again, can't ya?" he demanded. "Them damn things always come back."

Then, as they turned, they saw the shark come floating

leisurely upward at them out of the water. At first a huge, wavering shadow, it took slow shape under the boat, and Warren let out a strangled squawk. He froze to a statue of a man holding a harpoon over his head with both hands.

"Well, Warren," Russ said, "you're over him. Progue him, why don't you?"

He glanced overside again, and he himself gulped a little.

"Holy Christmas!" Jeb said, softly, under his breath.

He could feel the hairs on the back of his neck crinkle as he looked down at the thing. It was passing about three feet under the keel, from stern to bow. It was somewhat longer than the skiff, which was fourteen feet, and looked to be some three feet thick where its ugly, underslung head merged with its body.

"I ain't going to stir up no critter like that," Warren said. "That thing could swaller this skiff and not know it. You get us back aboard the big boat, Russ, for the sweet loving Jesus's sake."

"Well, get down out of that, then," Russ said sharply.

Warren had forgotten to move. He was still standing with the harpoon poised over his head. He spun around, dropped the harpoon and sat down limply on the bow thwart.

Russ waited until the monster's massive tail had moved a fathom or so beyond the boat's bow. Then he smacked his oar smartly down on the surface of the water. The shark vanished with a flirt of his tail.

Russ glanced around, dead-pan, at Warren.

"Scares easy," he said. "You ought to have given him just one little progue, Warren. Now he'll be back to frig us up again."

"Ayeh," Warren grunted. "Progue up a man-eater, I guess not!"

His face was brownish green.

Without comment, Russ rowed them back to the boat.

"Well, what was the matter, Warren?" Johnny demanded. "What'd you see? Old Horny?"

"Nothing but a cussid great man-eating shark, that was all," Warren said. He climbed back aboard with evident relief.

Grampie asked, "A man-eater?"

"Well, I guess I know sharks. I been out on Georges, by God, when they was schooling. I used to practice tolling them damn great tiger sharks right up alongside the dory."

It occurred to Grampie that a man out on Georges wouldn't have much reason for tolling sharks, of any breed, up alongside his dory. He gave Warren a skeptical glance.

Pricked, Warren burst out, "Well, it was a man-eater, too. You all think I ought to have let him have it, well, go out and progue him yourselves. I know sharks, by cream, out on Georges I got so I could call—"

"You can call devils from the vasty deep," Grampie said shortly. "Come on, boys, le's get these fish aboard."

If the job of running a purse seine around a school of fish was ticklish, unloading them from the seine into the boat was no less so, and it was back-breaking. The seine had to be hauled, little by little, and piled into the seine boat, until the fish were driven into the small-meshed bag-end of the net, from which they could be bailed out. Sharks and tuna might be a nuisance; but the real menace was weather—a quick squall, or any breezing-on of wind.

The gleaming wet seine piled up in the seine boat, the circle of floats grew steadily smaller. The crew heaved and strained, sweat pouring down. Hauling next to Grampie, Jeb couldn't feel he was taking any of the weight off the old man's arms; sometimes, he was pretty sure Grampie's heft was taking the weight off of *his;* Jeb was working too hard, himself, to be quite sure. He was concerned about Grampie, as he had been all day, now that he thought back over it.

The fish, moving around in the net, tolled back the shark. Warren spotted the big fin, circling, and let out a yell.

"'n there! I told ya. There's that cussid thing back again."

"Oh, hell!" Russ said disgustedly. He began hauling up the skiff.

"Wait a minute," Johnny said. "He's sheering off. Maybe he's changed his mind."

The fin described a circle away from the net; then it turned and came back. The shark passed so close to the boat they could see his dark, tremendous shadow through the water.

Grampie suddenly let out a snort. He climbed into the bow of the skiff. "Come on, Jebby. We'll fix that feller."

Russ watched him with concern. "Well, hold on, Jebron. I better come, too, hadn't I?"

"No need us all quitting work," Grampie said. "Jebby can set in the stern and shove on the oars. That'll trim her all right. You fellers go on hauling, Russ."

"That's a pretty big fish, Jebron."

The old man was looking over the harpoon, testing its edge on his thumb. He hefted it, tried it out for balance and made a couple of jabs with it, flexing his forearm.

"Where'd you get this, Russ? Ain't much of a harpoon. Well, come on, Jebby. Shove me out there."

"Okay, Grampie," Jeb said.

His voice, he realized, made a kind of croak, which he hoped nobody noticed.

He thought, I guess I'm just about as scared as Warren was.

Grampie was checking the twenty-fathom coil of six-thread in the bow, making sure it ran smooth from the harpoon iron to the watertight keg rove to its other end.

"Warp ain't long enough," he said. "Likely we'll lose Russ's harpoon for him. No great loss."

Jeb sat in the stern, shoving the skiff as silently as he could with the oars. It was an awkward place to sit, rowing, and he found that he was inclined to catch a crab. The boat crept closer to the leisurely circling fin.

Grampie said, "Now, Jebby, when I put the harpoon to him, you back water like hell. Then ship your oars, because if I don't hit him right on the cracker, he may yank us round some."

He saw Grampie rise to his feet and his arm come up and back, and the harpoon shoot out, all in one smooth, continuous movement.

Grampie yelled, "Straighten her up, bow on to him! Ship oars," and Jeb straightened her up and brought in his oars, laying them, dripping, along the thwarts to his hand.

The skiff lay bow on to a great, streaked red stain in the water. The six-thread was flashing out over the bow, and Grampie was sitting down on the thwart watching the rope snake past him. Once, it slowed to an aimless jerking, then began paying out again, more slowly.

"Right in the gizzard!" Grampie said. "He won't go far."

He picked up the keg, gingerly, watching as the coil of rope payed out to nothing, and put a little weight against it, giving it a heave overboard as the skiff began to surge through the water.

"That's an old mud shark," he said. "Mud shark, nurse shark, there's different names for him. They grow big and logy, but they scare easy. It's just a butcher's job, killing one. Kind of scared, was you? Well, he was horrible-looking."

Jeb said, "I sure was. I was about as scared as Warren was, I guess."

Grampie said, "Oh, him. He goes to the movies too much. He's just on the water for the money he gets out of it, he don't try to learn nothing."

2 9 5

He was watching the keg, which was plunging along now above the surface, now below it, a hundred yards away. "Better leave that, pick it up later. Ain't much juice left in that old pig, but no sense fooling with him. Le's go back and help bail fish, Jebby. I'll swap thwarts with you, so's she'll trim better, now."

He climbed over Jeb's legs into the stern and Jeb took the forward thwart, sending the skiff sweetly through the water.

He had just seen a beautifully precise and skillful job done, he realized, a harpoon used with the accuracy, almost, of a machine tool. Only, with a machine tool, in a shop somewhere, you'd be likely to know pretty well what was going to happen next—not have to wait five minutes or so for your innards to settle back into place. It made a difference.

He thought, It's what makes all the difference to me.

Grampie said, "A man's scared of what he don't know about, Jebby, what he ain't seen." He faced around, letting out a long breath as if he were tired, and then, seeing Jeb's concerned eyes, he grinned. "I like to climbed the main truck, first one of them things I ever see."

Jeb stopped rowing.

"Grampie, you sure you feel okay, today?"

"I'm kind of tired. We all are, and we could use some dinner. You better keep pulling or you'll lose your advantage. Ebb-tide current's strong, here by the Rock. Be a good thing if we had that outboard, now, wouldn't it?"

Russ's boat was three hundred yards away, and Jeb realized suddenly that he hadn't been making much headway toward her. He put his shoulders into his stroke.

Grampie said, "We ain't ever had the skiff this far out together, have we? Nice, ain't it? Still."

They had had her all over Candlemas Bay, in and out of coves and harbors, taking busman's holiday on Sundays, which Grampie said were days to enjoy—the Lord had enjoyed the first one and it was a good example to follow. Evenings before dark, too, going down around the calm harbor for a spin, trying out the outboard, seeing what she would do.

Neither he nor I, Jeb thought, can stay off the water to save our lives.

Out here, away from the clatter on the big boat, stillness pressed against the ears almost as a great sound would have done, a gale-wind or a prolonged roll of drums. Their voices and the splash of the oars seemed quiet, far away. To touch the water, you had only to put out your hand over the skiff's low gunnel. You realized the strength of the ebb tide, the silent, sunlit current setting away from the land.

Grampie said, "It's been a good summer. About the best time I ever had in my life. But I don't doubt it's made a sucker out of you for going on the water, Jebby, same as, time was, was made out of me."

"Not only this summer, Grampie."

"That's right. I guess it would be a good many summers, not only yours and mine."

He means Gramp Malcolm, Jeb thought. And the others, back along.

Against the stillness, he heard his mind say their names.

But why was Grampie talking like this, sounding as if the summer were over, something to look back on? It was only August.

Grampie said, "Put your back into it, Jebby. You ain't making a mite of headway."

He's all right. I must have the jitters.

Grampie said, "It's a pull for you, Jebby. But it comes in handy for a man to know how strong the tide is."

Russ reached out and caught the painter as they came alongside. He said, "That was neat, Jebron."

"Happened to hit him just right," Grampie said, climbing aboard.

They bailed out pollock until the boat's kids were loaded; they filled the skiff; they put as many as they dared into the seine boat, leaving barely room for the net. At sunset, they started the long run back to Candlemas, with the boats loaded so deep that none of them had more than two inches of freeboard. It made no great matter. The afternoon breeze went down with the sun and the sea was like a vast pond over which the deeply laden boats made a curling, fan-shaped wake.

Warren brought up his chowder, but they were all too tired to eat much. Jeb felt as if it would be too much of an effort to bite down on even a piece of bread. Grampie, he saw, ate nothing. When they were under way, Grampie went down below and stretched out on one of the bunks. They would be nearly three hours running in; then, when they got there, they'd have another heavy job unloading. Johnny, without a word, went down and rolled into the other bunk.

Warren climbed along the washboard to the stern and stretched out, grumbling at the hardness of the deck, an oil-jacket wadded under his head for a pillow.

Russ said, "Go on back and lie down there, too, Jeb. I'll take her in."

Jeb said, "No, I'll spell you steering."

He didn't know why he didn't go back there with Warren and rest, seeing he was so tired and the job wasn't yet done. But he went on leaning against the coop, beside Russ, looking out through the windscreen at the distant islands, now fading into a soft haze with coming night.

"Okay, Jeb?" Russ said, glancing at him.

"Ayeh, sure."

There wasn't any way to communicate this vague uneasiness, this feeling that something was wrong.

Russ said, "Good thing there isn't any wind. This rig steers like a bagful of hammers."

He glanced suddenly, sharply, toward the cabin.

What he heard, Jeb didn't know; he himself had noticed nothing above the thrumming roar of the engine.

Then Johnny put his head out of the companionway hatch. He said, "Russ, come down, will you?"

Russ said, "Take her a minute, Jeb."

He handed over the wheel and went below.

Jeb noted automatically that Russ had been right—the logy boats handled like a bagful of hammers. The silence from the cabin prolonged itself, as Russ did not come back. He said, over his shoulder, "Warren?" and heard Warren's startled "Ayeh?" as Warren came quickly forward along the washboard, jumping to the platform beside him.

"Steer, will you, Warren?"

"Sure. What's matter?"

"I don't know."

But he did know.

In the cabin, Johnny was leaning over Grampie, with Russ holding a flashlight.

He didn't need to have Russ say, "Something's wrong, Jeb," or to feel the strong, steady grip, when Russ's hand came out and held his shoulder.

This was what it was; this was what had been trying to get to him all day; and the summer was over.

IN the late afternoon the sun slanted through the beech grove, golden flakes on the June-grass gone heavily to seed. A light wind, smelling of salt from the ocean, moved through the grove. It flickered the beech leaves and stirred the bent grass from which the small seeds fell, imperceptibly. The anteater was gone; the rains had melted him and the quick grass had grown through the smooth pile of clay. But the beech stump with its riven fork, like a heavy, brooding head, had taken no change from the summer weather—only a few new lichens, a few spreading patches of moss.

On the shore, by Barle's Cove, the four youngest Ellis children raced on the sand and shouted, playing Indian.

They sounded as if a flock of gulls had come into the cove, Evelyn thought. Poor lambs, they had been bewildered and miserable. Now they were letting go.

A time of death was hardest on the children—not only the death itself, which they comprehended as well as anyone, though nobody thought they did; but the lost security in grown-ups made strange by grief; and the horrible ceremonies and trappings. No one had a right to make small adults out of children, forcing them, even for a few days, into a world where they were smothered and terrified.

Death in itself was simple, dignified; it was no occasion for a gruesome public festival held over the pathetic remnant of a man.

Evelyn sighed, thinking of Candace, in her element, taking over; grief-stricken, and knowing it; knowing that everyone knew it; yet able to go ahead with a fierce, juggernaut determination that every grisly detail should be completed, from the crepe on the door to the shovelful of earth on the coffin.

Oh, I am as prejudiced in my way as she in hers, I would have a man after his death taken away in secret, so that no one would see him again, and perhaps that would not be good for the living, either, people being what they are; but it was not fair to my father nor to the ones who loved him to be forced to hear the sound of those stones on the lid of his coffin.

The lines of granite markers in the cemetery, blown over by the peaceful sea wind; the group of people standing heavily by the grave; the voice of the inexperienced, young minister stumbling over the poetry of the Bible; Candace, in her sober, proper, exactly "right" mourning, stepping forward with her handful of stones. From the eldest Ellis daughter, a handful of stones.

Jeb, chalk-faced, to carry that sound in his sore, young heart; and Jen . . .

Looking away from their faces, Evelyn herself had felt as if she were bleeding inwardly. Unable to bear it, she had come away and, gathering up the children, had brought them down here to the cove to play.

He would have loved the poetry, she thought. "Man goeth to his long home." What else had he loved?

Jeb. And Jen. The children, too, but Jeb above all.

Not Candace. Nor Lynnie. Nor me.

He began by loving us, but there was Grammie, like a wall, in between. As a child, I loved him and spoke his language; when I grew up, it was as if I lost my tongue; I had no language to speak to anyone.

A light step behind her made her start and turn; it was Geoffrey Raymond, who came into the grove and sat down on the grass beside her.

She said, "Geoffrey."

"Yes," he said. "I saw you at the funeral. I've been hunting for you since then."

The silence prolonged itself. Once, silence would have stood like fog between her and anyone except children; once, after a few seconds of it, she would have got up and gone away. She had not learned a new language and neither had he. It had been only a matter of finding out, with a few fumbles, that they spoke the same.

He said, "I'm sorry for your sister."

"I am, too. I always have been."

"The house's no place for you, now."

"No."

He said, "It never was."

"No. I know."

He said, "I'm going away soon. My picture's done, and Jen's closing out the boarders. There's no place for me here, either. Will you come with me, Evelyn?"

"When are you going?"

"Today."

He sat quietly on the grass beside her, making no movement, his voice as casual as if it said, "Let's take a walk together." But the look in his eyes was not casual.

Mertis came up the sloping bank into the grove, walking purposefully, a gleam of outrage in her eyes.

"Aunt Evelyn, I don't think it's nice to race around and yell so, not today. But the kids won't keep still. They just mock me when I try to make 'em."

Evelyn said, "Well, never mind, dear."

Jeff said, "Look, Mert, Grampie liked you to have a good time, remember? The most respectful thing you can do is what he'd have liked you to, not what you think somebody else wants. Why don't you play 'Ringgold the Pirate'? He'd have liked that."

"Well," Mertis said doubtfully. Then her face cleared. "Okay, Jeff," she said, and went tearing back down the bank.

Evelyn said, "I don't know how I could leave the children."

"They're leaving you," he said. "They're growing up. Besides, they're Jen's children, Evelyn, and you could have children of your own. You could have mine," he said simply, "if you love me."

He waited, wishing she would say she did. After a pause, he went on.

"We'll go first to New York, to a specialist I know who can tell us whether everything possible has been done for your hand. Then I want to show you the world. It's a beautiful world, a good deal of it. There are places I've seen that I want to see again with you. Paris, and the Mediterranean and the Mau Escarpment; and a village near Nairobi. And I want you to see a Colobus monkey, if we can find one, and to make a small bronze copy of him. I want to take you to a place I know about in some high hills, and build a workshop for us there. But mostly I want you to go with me because I love you, and I don't think I can stand it to go away alone."

"No," she said. "I couldn't stand it if you did."

"Thank God!" he said fervently. "Will you go now? To-day? Now?"

"I—yes, I will."

"I'll pack my things," he said, "and call a taxi. We'll take the train this afternoon from Bellport."

"Jeff, I haven't anything to wear on a train—nor a penny to buy anything. I—"

He got to his feet and helped her up, being careful of the bandaged hand.

"I'll get you what you need. Not a hat—if I have my way, you'll never wear anything over that hair again. Will you get your things?"

She smiled. "Yes," she said, "I'll get my things."

He bellowed suddenly down the bank, "Hey, we're going back to the house. You kids ready to come?"

Evelyn said, "I would have forgotten them, and you remembered that of course they mustn't stay down here, alone."

"You're irresponsible," he said. "But it's all right if you forget everything else for me."

The kids came hurrying up from the shore in a line, Clay making heavy weather of the sloping bank; and Jeff went halfway down for him, swinging him up on his shoulder.

"Listen," Jeff said, addressing their solemn, sweating faces. "Your Aunt Evelyn and I have got a terrific secret. We're going to be married and go on a wonderful trip around the world, and when we've had the trip, we're coming back to see you and bring you all kinds of presents. Okay?"

"I'll say okay!" Andy said, and Maggie said, "Wull, all the people will be married, if it keeps on." But Mertis went silently over and slipped her hand into Evelyn's.

They walked together up the path, Maggie and Andy running on ahead, and presently Mertis squeezed Aunt Evelyn's hand hard, took her own hand away and ran up to join them. Clay wriggled to get down and pattered after, his legs pumping, and as he came up the path through the orchard, he came face to face with his enemy, the Rhode Island Red rooster. The rooster took a run at Clay, expecting him to give ground; but Clay was going too fast to stop easily. He tripped on the rooster and fell down; and the rooster, taking advantage, gave him a sound peck on the leg.

Jeff shouted, "Hey, shoo out of that!" and started to run, waving his arms.

But Clay had never tripped over the rooster before; the rooster had never got close enough to peck him. The shock, the surprise and pain suddenly crystallized into a wave of rage. He grabbed up a rock that was lying to his hand and let the rooster have it, amidships; the rooster went into the air with a squawk of astonishment; he fled, squawking, up the path. Clay picked himself up, his mouth a round O of surprise; then he walked on, strutting. He went out of sight around a turn of the path.

Smiling, Jeff turned to Evelyn.

"You see?" he asked. "Even Clay's growing up. So it's all right, Evelyn."

She nodded, and went into the house for her things.

In the kitchen, Jeff called a taxi. He turned around from the phone to see Myrabel standing behind him, arms akimbo. She said, "What you want a taxi for—you leaving so soon, Mr. Raymond?"

He nodded. On impulse, he leaned forward and kissed her, a good one, right on the mouth.

"Myrabel," he said, "God bless you. I'll see you again someday. I'm taking Evelyn with me."

Myrabel had brought up short. She had her hand pulled back to let him have a good slap for taking liberties with her, when she realized what he had said. A broad grin spread over her face. "Well," she said. "You're a one, you are. I always said so."

"Good luck," he said. "Good luck with Amos."

Myrabel sniffed. "Amos!" she said. "I can have good luck with him any time I want it."

In her room, Evelyn took her brush and comb off the top of the bureau. She looked around the room, holding them in her hand. After a moment, she slipped the thin silver chain from her neck, took the key over to the massive black wardrobe and put it in the lock. She left the key there without turning it, stood for a second in the middle of the room. What else was there?

Candace said from the door, "I've had this letter from Lynnie. She's not going to bother to come home. I must say, I'm not surprised, but it was the least she could do."

Evelyn slipped the brush and comb into her sweater pocket.

She said, "I'm sorry, Candy," and went past Candy, along the hall to the front door and out of the house.

Candace glanced sharply after her. She looked around the room. Her whole face seemed to thin out, as she saw, for once and at last, the key in the door of Gramp Malcolm's wardrobe. She went swiftly across the floor, turned the key and swung back the door.

The wardrobe was empty. The dust on its shelves was untouched, an eighth of an inch thick. It had been empty for years. Evelyn had never kept anything in it.

ON the evening after Labor Day, Jeb walked up the hill from Russ's house in town to say good-by to Aunt Candace. He was taking the late train from Bellport to Boston, and then to Providence, where, in a day or so, he would enter diesel school. He had put off for as long as possible going to see Aunt Candy; it did not seem to him he could bear to enter the house again, knowing Grampie would not be there. It had been different when his mother and the kids and Aunt Evelyn had been living in the house; then it had been home. Now it seemed like a ghost of a house, with big empty rooms peopled by silence and desertion; and only Aunt Candy left, of all the Ellises who, for years back in time, had been housed under its tremendous roof. It was hard to go there; it was hard to go any place where, suddenly, it would hit, like a blow in the chest with a hammer, that you wouldn't ever see Grampie again.

But Jen had persuaded him that he should at least call in and say good-by to Aunt Candace before he left; and he himself could see that it was the thing to do. Not that she cared whether she saw him or not; but if he left without seeing her she'd rankle over it for months.

He went doggedly up onto the back porch, not glancing at the wicker chair where Grampie had sat so much; and the back door opened in his face before he could put out his hand for the knob.

Aunt Candy was as usual.

She said, "Oh, it's you, Jeb. Well, I thought you'd probably be up to see me before you left. If you're looking for a tip, you ought to know I can't afford tips."

Jeb said, "No, Aunt Candy. I just came in to say good-by."

Don't look over her head at the kitchen, just as it always was, with the rocking chair by the table; and no grizzled old head nodding behind the newspaper there, now. Just say good-by and get away.

She said, "I suppose you think you ought to have some of your grandfather's things. Well, there isn't anything I want lugged out of the house."

"He left me his books and town records," Jeb said steadily. "And his navigation instruments, Aunt Candace. I'll want them someday. But if you don't want me to, I won't take anything now."

"H'm, I thought you'd come for something. Well, of course, your grandfather left the house mortgaged. Anything of his that I can realize on, I'll have to use."

"His life insurance paid the rest of the mortgage," Jeb said. "You know that, Aunt Candy."

He was in a fever, now, to get away. It was no use trying in any way to talk to her.

"H'm," she said again. "Well, good-by, Jeb. Study hard and don't fool your time away. Personally, I think it's a waste of Russ's money. You might just as well finish high school here, where you can get your education free."

He said, "Good-by, Aunt Candy," and went back down the hill toward the town.

She hadn't even asked him in; and when he'd turned to go, he couldn't but see how relieved she'd looked, closing the door, glad he was going without asking to come in.

At the fork in the road which led to the beach, he hesitated, then walked along to the fishhouse. He had a couple of hours before the train left; he didn't feel much like going home and talking to people just yet. He'd go to his own place. Russ's place was fine; he was glad his mother and the kids were with Russ and that she was Mrs. Russ Allen. But his own place, for a while now, was the place for him.

He found the key in his pocket, unlocked the padlock, went in and closed the door. He sat down in the darkness, in the old chair by the window. He put his head down on his hands and let the tears run through the big, rope-roughened fingers; he could feel the hard texture of his fingers against his face.

It was the first time he had cried; maybe going away was what had brought it out. It was good to have it out. He didn't feel, now, as though he was carrying it around inside his chest, a weight too heavy to bear.

The way Grampie went was as good a way as there was for a man to go, right in the middle of his work, at the top of his skill and nothing lost, knowing he had just done, and still could do, a good job.

It was time, not to forget him, but to look ahead; not to put out of your mind the men of the old times, they would always be there like anchors to windward, but to see now what was best to do with the time to come.

He got up, lit the lantern and found his fountainpen, fumbling for it in the pocket of his shirt.

On the cottony-textured, worn old chart hanging on the wall, he found the place and wrote in *"Jebron died,"* inking in the date with a steady hand.